THE STATE AND INSTABILITY IN THE SOUTH

The State and Instability in the South

Edited by

Caroline Thomas
Lecturer in Politics
University of Southampton

and

Paikiasothy Saravanamuttu
Lecturer in Politics
University of Southampton

St. Martin's Press   New York

First published in the United States of America in 1989

Printed in the People's Republic of China

ISBN 0-312-02447-9

Library of Congress Cataloging-in-Publication Data
The State and instability in the South/edited by Caroline Thomas and
Paikiasothy Saravanamuttu.
p. cm.
Includes index.
ISBN 0-312-02447-9
1. Political stability—Developing countries. I. Thomas,
Caroline. II. Saravanamuttu, Paikiasothy, 1958–
JF60.S695 1989
320.9172′4—dc19   88 – 28312
                                                              CIP

Contents

Notes on the Contributors

Richard Boyd is a Lecturer in the Department of Politics and Economics at SOAS, London University. He has a special interest in Japan.

Charles Gurdon is a doctoral candidate in the Department of Geography at SOAS, London University, and a freelance writer on the Sudan.

Fred Halliday is a Professor of International Relations at the LSE, London University, and has written widely on Third World revolutionary states.

George Joffé is a writer and broadcaster on Middle Eastern and North African affairs and is Consultant Editor at the Economist Intelligence Unit.

Chintamani Mahapatra was a Commonwealth Postdoctoral Fellow at SOAS, London University, 1986–7, and currently works at the Institute of Defence Studies and Analysis, New Delhi.

Nicos Mouzelis is a Reader in the Department of Sociology at the LSE, London University. He has a special interest in the Parliamentary Semi-Periphery.

Paikiasothy Saravanamuttu is a Lecturer in Politics at Southampton University and has a particular interest in the problem of ethnicity and state building in South Asia.

Caroline Thomas is a Lecturer in Politics at Southampton University, specialising in the non-military aspects of Third World security.

Tony Thorndike is Professor of International Relations at North Staffordshire Polytechnic. The Caribbean is his area of special interest.

Tom Young is a Lecturer in the Department of Politics and Economics at SOAS, London University, and researches on Southern Africa.

Notes on the Contributors

Acknowledgements

This volume is the product of an inter-disciplinary study group on The State and Instability in the South held in London during Autumn and Spring 1986–7. It was conducted under the auspices of the Ford Foundation-sponsored project on North/South Security Relations organised by members of the Politics Department of Southampton University, 1984–8. The editors gratefully acknowledge the help of Liz Schlamm in organising the study group, and Jo and Liz in the preparation of the typescript.

CAROLINE THOMAS
PAIKIASOTHY SARAVANAMUTTU

1 Introduction to the Problem of the State and Instability in the South

Paikiasothy Saravanamuttu

The concept of the state has been under-researched in international relations, despite the dominance of state-centric realism as the conventional orthodoxy. Together with the attendant notion of sovereignty, the state, defined in terms of an abstraction and employed as a heuristic device, has been posited as the starting point of enquiry. Consequently, as international events rendered this practice increasingly untenable, the basic assumptions of the discipline were opened to criticism from without and self-reflection from within. However, whilst theories of interdependence and transnationalism abounded and the concerns of foreign policy analysis and political economy attained respectability within the discipline, the need for an extensive explication of the concept of the state became more pronounced.

The international events that had prompted this revaluation, namely, the rise of the multinationals and the collapse of the Bretton Woods liberal international economic order, portended not so much the demise of the state *per se*, as the hitherto prevalent conception of it in the discipline. The expansion of international capitalism and the pressures generated by this process highlighted the inadequacies inherent in the assumptions of the latter. The formulation of the state as a socio-political unit invested with the sovereign will of the people who inhabited a clearly demarcated territory, and therefore the supreme authority within that territory, seemed unconvincing in the face of technological and capitalist advance. Equally unconvincing was the argument that the state was obsolete; after all, as the overthrow of Allende was to attest, states and multinationals could act in concert, with the actions of one being a necessary condition for the success of the other. Moreover, the increased assertiveness of the developing world in both the military and economic spheres of security, exemplified in the Yom Kippur War, the Organisation of Petroleum Exporting Countries (OPEC), continued support for national self-determination and the call for a New International Economic Order (NIEO), augmented the view

1

that although the state could no longer be seen as the *exclusive* actor in international relations it was the *primary* one.

It cannot be denied that the idea retains vitality in the empirical reality of international relations, despite its conceptual shortcomings in the academic discipline. Furthermore, the disjunction on this point between the theory and practice of international relations is at its most acute with respect to the developing world. Here the historical features underpinning the conventional orthodoxy's notion of the state do not obtain, nor can they be clearly discerned in their post-colonial experience. This point is brought into sharper relief when one considers the term 'nation-state' and the phrase 'the sovereign equality of states'.

The first is intended to denote the actual/ideal legitimate composition of the basic and primary unit of analysis in the discipline. The second is considered to be the formal attribute of the collectivity of such units and the indispensable convention that protects it from degenerating into anarchy, seen in this sense as chaos. Accordingly, anarchy, in the sense of an absence of government or a central authority to adjudicate in disputes between the units, is preserved, allowing for the dispersal of authority and power to produce order through self-regulation.

Nation-state, culled from European political evolution, assumes homogeneity; that the cultural and politico-territorial units are congruent and divisions within the unit of minor significance for international relations. Given the ideological bias of the Cold War, class was deemed an irrelevance until the events of the 1970s led to the co-option of political economy concerns and structuralist ideas under the collective umbrella of the discipline. A few notable exceptions apart, nationalism was mainly investigated in its European frame of reference, and ethnicity was largely the province of anthropologists and sociologists. Consequently, the application of nation-state, with its inbuilt Eurocentric bias, to the developing world was inappropriate and glossed over the tensions and divisions that bedevil the participation of Southern states in international relations.

In the bulk of the South, nation and state do not coincide. The territorially delimited units inherited by the successor regimes owe their boundaries to the fortunes of colonial rivalry and as such encompass a multiplicity of groups claiming the attributes of national identity and the right to independent statehood. This is expressed in secession and irredentism and attracts external intervention. The primacy of national sovereignty asserted in the former is threatened by the manifestation of the latter. Nation-building as the primary form of inculcating social cohesion is therefore the basic task for the South. Paradoxically, if it is the colonial legacy that has bequeathed successor regimes this problem, it is another aspect of this legacy that is utilised as the principal instrument in its resolution. This is the post-colonial state, defined not in terms of the conventional international relations usage, but as a set of bureaucratic and coercive institutions and processes that can be identified separately from the national context in which it is located.

Southern regimes invariably draw upon the coercive or non-coercive resources of the state to quell, pre-empt or deflect centrifugal pressures. The imposition of a single language through the state apparatus, with its attendant consequences for education and employment, is often used as a method of forging social cohesion, and the distribution of government revenue for economic development is employed as a means of dissipating these tensions. The application of military force on the grounds that the monopoly over the legitimate use of violence is an indispensable attribute of the state or on the grounds of national security, which effectively in these circumstances means the security of the state, invariably follows once less coercive means of incorporation or integration have failed.

The task of nation-building in the South, essentially that of state-nations attempting to become nation-states, contrasts with the European experience and is compounded by the contemporary international environment. The nation-state building process in Europe was spread over centuries, relatively uninterrupted by colonial conquest and external intervention. Its more sordid features were not held up to public scrutiny or subject to censure by an international community of states in the manner that Southern regimes are today. Moreover, apart from the mass democratic ethos and rights consciousness that pervades international relations, Southern regimes have also to contend with the globalisation of capitalism, which belies attempts to create self-contained units which are economically and politically viable. For if the claim of the state, to the nations within its boundaries, is that it possesses the means to provide for material prosperity, the existence of non-state actors with the demonstrable capability to satisfy this in part or frustrate the state's chosen path for doing so is deeply subversive of its authority. This challenge is represented not just by multi-nationals in the South but by a gamut of structural inequalities in the international system that are also illustrated in the actions of the international governmental and non-governmental financial institutions.

Similar difficulties arise in the application of the phrase 'sovereign equality of states' to the South. Whilst it may serve as a formal legal principle denoting status and attest to the continuity of the operational assumptions of international relations dating from the Treaty of Westphalia (1648), in practice it camouflages the real inequalities among the members of the international system. As noted above, the expansion of international capitalism and the incorporation of the South within it, in most cases before political independence, has institutionalised economic dependence and illustrated the argument that the dispersal of power and authority in international relations, amounts to its uneven distribution. Consequently, although the numerical superiority of the South in the United Nations and other international organizations may enable those states to set the agenda of international relations in terms of developmental priorities such as the New International Economic Order and non-intervention regimes, real disparities in capability militate against its realisation; likewise with external military intervention, overt and covert. The context within which nation-building has to be conducted and the distribution of power within it is such that it ceases to be a purely internal matter for the political community directly concerned. External intervention blurs the domestic/international boundary beloved by coventional international relations theorists and engrafts extraneous concerns upon the nation-building process. As a consequence the political evolution of a particular Southern state, in contemporary international relations, can be transformed into a test case for the stability of the prevailing international order.

Accordingly, the term 'stability' too, derived as it is from these post-Westphalian assumptions and shaped in turn by the contours of intra-European rivalry, has dissonant ramifications in its application to the South. 'Stability' and its ancillary conception 'order' are inextricably linked to the term 'nation-state' and the phrase 'sovereign equality of states'. The latter are the bedrock of the former. What have come to be accepted as the institutions of international relations – diplomacy, international law and organisations, war and the balance of power – are based on this formulation. The implication of this, given the problems highlighted above, is that these terms do not adequately describe the empirical reality of the South and that their constant usage obscures its very real tensions. Since they serve as a goal to be aspired to or form the criteria for judgement, they more often than not also exacerbate tensions. International stability therefore becomes the responsibility of those units upon whose historial and political experience the term has been defined. The South as a result is relegated to the position of a victim or bystander and deemed not mature or responsible enough to partake on an equal footing in the management of its destiny. The problem with these notions of stability and order is that they only acquire meaning outside the Southern experience and the mechanisms for their sustenance require a competence that is incidental to the immediate and pressing problems faced by these regimes. The point of contention is not the concept of stability or order *per se*, but the *particular* conceptions thereof that are adopted.

The foregoing has attempted to highlight the problems associated with the application of the conventional orthodoxy of the international relations discipline to the contemporary world and to point out that the resulting disjunction is particularly acute with respect to the South. Our understanding of the latter would be greatly enhanced if the discipline were to take a fresh look at the concept of the state in the spirit of critical theory.

The experience of the South confirms that avenues for fruitful enquiry can be found in the investigation of types of state formation, in the relations between states and other societal units, in the varying capacities of states to induce or enforce obedience and their relationship to the international context in which they are located. Such a pursuit requires an inter-disciplinary approach, especially a recognition of the valuable contribution of the historical and comparative sociologists in this field.

Hence this volume contains contributions from sociologists, international relations scholars, area specialists and historians. Forming part of the work undertaken in Southampton University's research programme entitled 'Into the 1990s: An Agenda For North-South Security Relations', the funds for which were obtained in the Ford Foundation's 1983 Institutional Competition in International Security and Arms Control, these chapters were first presented at a series of study groups in autumn 1986 and spring 1987. They were inspired by a sense of dissatisfaction in having to employ the categories of conventional international relations discourse in the analysis of Southern security problems and an awareness that any meaningful projections into the future required a reassessment of the terms of debate. As the title of the research programme indicates, the objective was to outline an agenda. Accordingly, this volume is presented primarily to sustain and stimulate debate.

The chapters are divided into two sections – the domestic and international contexts, the two broadly defined sites on which the dilemmas of nation-state building and international instability are to be found. Furthermore, each chapter is devoted to a single country, region or type of state in order to capture the diversity of the problem of nation-state building in the developing world and facilitate a coherent elaboration of the problem through the examination of historical and contemporary examples.

Chapter 2, by Nicos Mouzelis, focuses on 'The State and Politics in the Parliamentary Semi-Periphery', identified here as a comparison between Greece and the southern-cone countries of Latin America – Argentina and Chile. They have been chosen because politically and economically, as late-industrialising capitalist societies with early and persisting quasi-parliamentary polities, they more closely approximate the western European parliamentary democracies than the other states of the South.

Mouzelis's concern is to investigate the relationship between the development of politics and the state with the timing and type of industrial capitalist expansion in these societies. He points out that the western European experience of the demise of oligarchic politics was not duplicated here, but that the process was reversed; in the parliamentary semi-periphery, oligarchic politics declined before full-scale industrial-isation, but was abetted by what he terms 'precocious "modernisation" without industrialisation', as a result of integration into the world market in the last century. As a consequence of this 'more restricted and uneven' capitalist development, Mouzelis argues, populism and cliental-ism characterised the transition from oligarchic to mass politics in the parliamentary semi-periphery and have led to the use of 'incorporative', rather than 'integrative', mechanisms in this process. This in turn breeds the 'basic political contradiction of these societies' – high levels of participation which accentuate the shortcomings of the existing mechan-isms. Accordingly, Mouzelis's principal argument is that as the masses become politicised, none of the prevailing mechanisms of political inclusion can establish unequivocal and permanent dominance. The military's intervention in politics, as well as their inability to accomplish an indefinite consolidation of their rule, can be traced to this. Therefore he concludes that, given the 'structural tendencies' of political and economic development in the parliamentary semi-periphery, the form of state there will oscillate between quasi-parliamentary democracy and military dictatorship, with the chances for the institutionalisation of western European-style parliamentary democracy or alternatively, revolutionary transformation, in all probability, negligible.

Chapter 3, by Tony Thorndike, entitled 'Representational Democracy in the South: The Case of the Commonwealth Caribbean', is devoted to the relationship between the Westminster model of liberal democracy and nation-building. Thorndike begins with a discussion of the Westminster model, noting its inherent imprecision as regards necessary and sufficient features, but avers that it 'rests upon vague and *ad hoc* but firmly liberal bourgeois presumptions and assumptions'. Moreover, it 'assumes a political elite, a class, sharing conventions of political behaviour'. He goes on to argue that the model was 'demanded in its entirety', in the West Indies, substantiating this through a discussion of the region's history and political culture. Thorndike identifies a number of mitigating factors in the nation-building process, but contends that they cannot be attributed to the Westminster model. Instead, he states his belief in the durability of the model and its capacity to alleviate such tensions, given the degree of stability it has afforded the region and the extent to which its 'mores are so deeply embedded in the popular psyche'. Nonetheless, in conclusion, he points to the growing influence of the US, leaving open the question of whether this could lead to institutional changes in the West Indian polities.

Chapter 4 on 'Instability and the State: Sudan', by Charles Gurdon, is an analysis of the dilemmas incurred when the state is used as the principal instrument of nation-building. Gurdon maintains, through an essentially historical analysis, that 'while a Sudanese state has been created a Sudanese nation has not.' Drawing upon features unique to Africa and to Sudan, in particular, his analysis leads to the question of type of state formation and its suitability to the inculcation of national cohesion. Gurdon ends with a brief discussion of federalism, but notes that problems of organisation and implementation could bedevil such an exercise.

Chapter 5 on 'The Mutual Formation and Information of the State and International Order: The Case of Japan', by Richard Boyd, concludes the section on the domestic context. Although his chapter deals with an earlier period of state-building in a country not usually incorporated under the rubric of the South, Boyd emphasises its relevance to the themes of this volume. In particular, he points to the enduring validity of Japan to the South, as the 'first non-white, non Judaeo-Christian society to complete the arduous journey to full industrialisation' and as a society that has 'faced the challenge of orchestrating a cogent and politically coherent response to the impact of the West.' Furthermore, he augments his case by reference to the continuing Japanese experience of the simultaneous and dual pull of state-building and participation in international relations.

Boyd's primary concern is to investigate the argument about the congruence between Japanese traditions and the requirements of modernisation in the context of the institution of the native religion,

Shinto, as the basis of the modern state. His thesis is that tradition was less of a given and more 'a resource to be managed. . . .' It was, he contends a set of 'beliefs, attitudes and behaviours' which through 'management and manipulation' by a political elite, were presented as 'tradition'.

Chapter 6, 'States and Revolution in the South' by Fred Halliday, is the first in the section addressing the international dimensions of the state and instability in the South. Halliday notes that revolutionary upheavals in the South have led to and exacerbated East–West conflicts. Moreover, they have spawned states with specific sets of foreign policy goals and a distinctive impact on regional neighbours and other states in the South. His focus on this foreign policy dimension of revolutionary states and the concept of state underpinning it is that employed in recent historical sociology – 'the specific administrative and coercive apparatuses that control a particular society'. This facilitates Halliday's analysis of the dual internal/external orientation of revolutionary states' foreign policies in terms of internal socio-economic transformation, the promotion of revolution abroad and the search for new allies and socio-economic models. Halliday argues that revolutions are not 'aberrations or interruptions' in international relations, but important stages in the development of states. Furthermore, their repercussions 'reflect deeper international tensions . . ., ones that must be seen as a result of what are substantial transformations of the societies in question and the inter-national results of such transformations.' He also points to a dialectical relationship between the revolutionary state's pursuit of its foreign policy goals and the constraining pressures of the international system. In conclusion, he suggests that since revolution will remain a feature of international relations, it would be 'advisable', in the long run, to make the world safer *for* them, as opposed to the preoccupation of many current practitioners of international relations – saving the world *from* revolution.

Chapter 7, by Tom Young, on 'The State and Instability in Southern Africa', proceeds from an elucidation of the term 'instability', examined on three different sites, namely, the political community, the regime and the government – to the analysis of the nation-building strategies pursued by ruling elites and states. Young stresses that the 'constraints' and 'opportunities' that form part of this process are not defined in 'objective' terms, but are 'largely a function of policy assumption' by the latter. His principal theme is that instability and conflict in the region, can in large measure be attributed to particular nation-building strategies and types of state formations, attempted by the political leadership. Addressing the relationship between the apartheid regime in Pretoria and its neighbours, Young draws upon Barry Buzan's notion of 'structural political threats', whereby the bases of state formation are fundamentally opposed in a setting in which the states involved cannot ignore each other and as a consequence engage in zero-sum interaction. For Young, the interconnectedness of local and regional dynamics is such that in conclusion he identifies the resolution of the 'central question of the South African socio-political order' as the necessary condition for stability and 'good government'.

Chintamani Mahapatra's chapter, 'The US Response to Instability in South Korea', concentrates on the impact of external intervention in the nation-state building process, in a climate of domestic upheaval and regional socio-economic change. Employing a historical mode of analysis, Mahapatra illustrates the incorporation of South Korea into the US strategy of global containment and given the imperatives of the latter, charts the process by which internal political and economic development in South Korea has been thereby affected. Mahapatra emphasises that the US goal is to manage the outer limits of political development, in order to ensure that its over-arching containment objectives are not jeopardised. He points out that in the wake of Marcos's overthrow in the Philippines, this has entailed a greater sensitivity on the part of the US to the pressures within South Korea for reform. Nevertheless, in conclusion, he suggests that the US obsession with 'stability' may turn out to be an insufficient framework within which the indigenous forces agitating for greater democracy can be integrated. Mahapatra stresses the risks inherent in this exercise, and warns that, given its proclivities and the emergent dynamism of dissent in South Korea, Washington could well misjudge the unfolding process of political evolution.

The final chapter in this section, by George Joffé, considers 'International Law, Conflict and Stability in the Gulf and the Mediterranean'. Through an analysis of two conflicts, the Shatt al-Arab dispute, and the Gulf of Sirt, Joffé addresses the relationship between international law – a key institution of Eurocentric international relations – and nation-building in three Southern states with distinctive socio-economic formations – Iran, Iraq and Libya. Joffé illustrates how 'international legal principles are both manipulated for the sake of domestic stability and, at the same time are used to formulate relations between states. . . .' While noting the double standards that sometimes characterise the application of international law, Joffé emphasises its 'continuing vitality' in adapting to the circumstances of the South and its potential utility as an instrument in the 'creation of stable and coherent regimes of domestic order for modern states'.

In the Conclusion, entitled 'Southern Instability, Security and Western Concepts: On an Unhappy Marriage and the Need for a Divorce', Caroline Thomas makes the case for a reformulation of the terms of debate that eschews ideological and ethnocentric bias. By stressing the diversity in, and dilemmas of, the South, she points to the inadequacies of the lexicon of the international relations orthodoxy, especially its security concern, when applied to the South: nation-state, national security, strong/weak states and sovereign equality. Thomas favours Michael Mann's sociological schema for the state, which facilitates analysis of different state capacities with its distinction between the arbitrary power of rulers and infrastructural state development. She contends that this allows for the transcendence of liberal democratic bias, evinced in the strong/weak state and power debate in the international relations literature. She provides a critique of the prevailing notion of stability, challenging the sincerity and intellectual conviction with which the belief in plurality, central to the 'anarchic society' of nation-states, is held. She ends with a reiteration of the central themes of the volume, in particular the pressing need for a more self-critical awareness of diversity as an indispensable condition for the theory and practice of international relations.

Part I
The Domestic Dimension

2 State and Politics in the Parliamentary Semi-Periphery

Nicos Mouzelis

While it may be acceptable to say that there are systematic and qualitative differences between Western European capitalist development and the development or underdevelopment of all those countries which tried to catch up with the West a century or more later, the complexity and enormous variety of political systems to be found in the capitalist periphery are such that any attempt at an undifferentiated discussion of the nature and structure of the State in these social formations is bound to fail. It is necessary, therefore, to go beyond the 'Third World' blanket label and to build up sub-types for different capitalist trajectories. From this perspective the present analysis confines itself to a small number of societies which:

(a) managed, despite their late start and their failure to industrialise fully in the last century, to develop an important economic infrastructure (roads, railways, etc) during the second half of the nineteenth century, and then achieved a notable degree of industrialisation during the inter-war and post-war periods;

(b) being part of huge patrimonial empires, acquired their political independence as early as the beginning of the nineteenth century and already in that century adopted parliamentary, pluralistic forms of political rule;

(c) despite the constant malfunctioning of their representative institutions, their early urbanisation and creation of large urban middle classes provided a context within which bourgeois parliamentarism took strong roots and showed remarkable resilience; it survived more or less intermittently from the nineteenth century until the rise of military, bureaucratic-authoritarian regimes in the 1960s and 1970s – and, as I will argue below, the latter regimes do not necessarily imply the irreversible decline of parliamentary politics.

Following the above criteria, this chapter concerns itself with Greece and the southern-cone countries of Latin America (Argentina, Chile and

13

to a lesser extent Brazil[1]). A comparison of these four countries is of considerable theoretical interest, not only because they come closer *economically and politically* to the advanced, western parliamentary democracies than most so-called Third World countries, but also because this comparison of a Balkan society with Latin American ones is an attempt to construct a sub-type of late-industrialising capitalist societies based on more than common cultural/historical background or geographical proximity. An accurate label for such societies would be *late-industrialising capitalist societies with early and persisting quasi-parliamentary polities.* Since this is rather too cumbersome, I shall for the sake of convenience use the term *parliamentary semi-periphery*, or simply *semi-periphery*, with the proviso that this does not imply acceptance of Gunder Frank's or E. Wallerstein's views on the centre-periphery problematic.

Within this framework, my main concern will be to examine the ways in which the development of politics and the state is linked with the timing and mode of expansion of industrial capitalism in these formations. Three main arguments will be presented involving the timing and structure of capitalist industrialisation, the political structures of the parliamentary semi-periphery and the post-war rise of bureaucratic-authoritarian military regimes in the semi-periphery.

1   ON THE TIMING AND STRUCTURE OF CAPITALIST INDUSTRIALISATION

A.   The early demise of oligarchic parliamentarism

If in Western Europe the demise of oligarchic politics and the passage from 'clubs of notables' to political mass organisations has been closely linked with the development of industrial capitalism, in the countries of interest here the two processes were reversed: the decline of oligarchic parliamentarism[2] occurred before the economies concerned experienced full-scale industrialisation. Although the closer integration of nine-teenth-century Latin American and Balkan societies into the world market did not industrialise these economies, it did generate processes of commercialisation, urbanisation and state expansion which were much more accentuated than similar processes in pre-industrial or even early industrial Europe. For instance, in the UK in 1815 – i.e. at a time when industrialisation was quite advanced – only 10.2 per cent of the population lived in cities of 50 000 or more. In Germany in the 1860s, the

figure for cities with populations of 20 000 and over was 10.1 per cent
and goes down to 3.4 per cent for cities of 100 000 and more.[3] In
Argentina, on the other hand, around 1920 – i.e. at a time when the
country's industrialisation was relatively weak – the percentage of the
population in all cities of 50 000 inhabitants and over was 39.7, and in
cities of 100 000 it was 27.1. In Chile for the same period the figures are
32.7 per cent for all cities of 20 000 and 27.1 per cent for cities of 100 000
or more. In Greece in 1920 the equivalent figures were 17.6 per cent
(cities of 20 000) and 12.6 per cent (cities of 100 000).[4]

The differences are equally striking in terms of the growth of the state
in the centre and the semi-periphery. A comparison, for instance, of the
respective proportions of the labour force employed in public administration just before or around World War I shows that, despite extremely
low levels of industrialisation, the state apparatus in the semi-periphery
had reached or surpassed in size the public bureaucracies of the already
industrialised Western societies. Thus in the UK (1911) civil servants
made up 1.1 per cent of the total labour force, in Germany (1907) 1.4 per
cent and in France (1911) also 1.4 per cent. In Argentina (1914), on the
other hand, the figure was 3.3 per cent, in Chile (1920) 1.8 per cent and in
the Balkan countries between the two world wars around 1.1 per cent.[5]

Such relatively precocious processes of city and state expansion, even
if they did not *automatically* bring about the demise of oligarchic
politics, do tend to undermine it, especially when they operate in a
political context of parliamentary, multi-party systems of rule. Insofar
as oligarchic parliamentarism is predominantly based on the tight
control exercised over the lower rural classes by local potentates who are
relatively free from centralised state interference, city, market and state
expansion do weaken their local power base and, *in a context of party
competition*, provide a favourable framework for the broadening of
political participation.

Because of this precocious 'modernisation' without industrialisation,
it is not surprising that the transition from oligarchic to mass politics in
the parliamentary semi-periphery should have been characterised, not
by the crucial role played by trades unions and working-class parties, but
by the development of populist movements, or by the transformation/
broadening of the type of clientelistic parties existing in the oligarchic
period.

So in the Latin American semi-periphery, where urbanisation was
more highly developed and where the landowning classes were
politically and economically more powerful, it was predominantly in the
towns that populism flourished in the inter-war period – the rural

populations being firmly controlled by clientelistic or more coercive means. It was not through populism, however, that the transitional turning point was achieved. The actual breaking-up of the oligarchic system was effectuated by army interventions, with populist mobilisation coming *after* the initial break-through, i.e. after the 'new men', with the army's decisive help, had broken the oligarchy's political monopoly. From this point of view populism can be seen as a means of irreversibly establishing the broadening of the political system which had already taken place. In the face of the post-oligarchic persistence of the economic and (to a lesser extent) political power of the landowning classes, populism, in the form of political mobilisation of the urban lower strata from above, can be seen as an instrument by which these new men strove to safeguard and consolidate their gains against attempts at oligarchic restoration.[6]

By way of comparison it is worth mentioning here that in the northern part of the Balkan peninsula the pattern of populist mobilisation was very different from the Latin American one. Not only were the landowning classes much weaker there, and had been so ever since independence and the withdrawal of the Turkish landlords, but in the nineteenth and early twentieth centuries these societies also experienced much lower levels of urbanisation than either Greece or the southern-cone countries of Latin America.[7] This meant that in comparison with the societies we are concerned with here, their urban middle classes were numerically small and politically weak. The fact that neither the urban nor the rural economically dominant classes could exercise any strong control over the large number of small-holding peasants – at a time when the latter were fully exposed to the vagaries of national and international market forces – explains why agrarian populism could spread so widely in the northern Balkans; and why, in some cases, this type of mobilisation from below was strongly orientated against both the cities and industrial capitalism.[8]

Greece followed a different pattern in her transition to post-oligarchic politics, one which involved neither rural nor urban populism. If during the nineteenth century and up to World War II Greece's agrarian structures were quite similar to those of the other Balkan societies (i.e. relatively weak landowning classes, agrarian reforms during the inter-war years, prevalence of small landholdings), in terms of city, market and state expansion it rather resembled such countries as Chile and Argentina. Greece experienced the growth of a sizeable middle class which quite early on (1909) managed, with the help of army intervention, to break the restrictive system of oligarchic parliamentarism and, given the relative weakness of the landowning classes, to consolidate its power position within the post-oligarchic system without mobilising the lower classes in populist fashion in either the countryside or the cities.

In Greece, therefore, it was the expansion and 'modernisation' of already existing patron–client networks that marks the transition from the coteries-of-notables type of party, which had characterised the oligarchic era, to the more centralised and broad-based clientelistic parties of the post-1909 period. It was through this type of political inclusion that the peasantry and the urban lower classes were brought into the post-oligarchic political arena.[9]

What Greece and Latin America's southern-cone countries have in common, therefore, notwithstanding profound variations in the various patterns of transition discussed above, is that during their early changeover to post-oligarchic politics the numerically weak and state-dependent industrial classes played a less decisive role in shaping post-oligarchic political institutions. In the absence of strong trades unions and working-class parties, it is not surprising that the army (already professionalised and highly conscious of its corporate interests) was unavoidably drawn into the centre of the political stage. This involvement is perfectly obvious in that it was the military which played the key role in breaking up oligarchic parliamentarism.

In Greece, Brazil and Chile, although the processes which sapped the strength of oligarchic parliamentarism were very long drawn out, the actual opening-up of the political system was the direct result of military intervention.[10] Even in Argentina, where the Saenz Pena electoral reform law of 1912 (which led to the temporary decline of oligarchic rule) did not come as a result of open military intervention, it was partly fear of such intervention that forced the political oligarchy to accept the famous electoral reform.[11] Therefore after the initial breakthrough – and whether or not the dominant factions within the army persisted in their anti-oligarchic rule – in the course of the fairly long period of transition from oligarchic to mass politics the military emerged as the major political force, the major arbitrator/regulator of the political game. However, as will be argued below, despite the central position of the army in post-oligarchic politics, its dominance has been tempered by the importance of the middle classes in these societies.

B. The mode of expansion of industrial capitalism: restricted and uneven development

It is not only the timing of the emergence of industrial capitalism which explains the specific features of politics in the semi-periphery; another crucial element is the specific course taken by that capitalism. As already mentioned, all semi-peripheral societies experienced a considerable development of social overhead capital during the nineteenth century – a development linked, of course, with a considerable growth of their export sectors. It was in part due to their relatively developed infrastructure that they were able to react quite effectively to the 1929 world crisis and could reorient their economies towards import-substitution industrialisation. In the post-war period, finally, all of the semi-peripheral societies managed to extend their industrialisation further with the help of multinational capital. Today, as a result of these developments, all four of the societies under consideration here are clearly industrialised: in all of them the labour force employed in agriculture is less than a quarter of the total labour force, their industry contributes more to the GNP than their primary sector, and there has been a marked export shift from raw materials and agricultural produce to industrial goods.[12] Moreover, these very impressive developments have been accompanied by an even more impressive urbanisation process, so that at present the majority of the population in all four societies is urban.[13]

What needs stressing, however, is that the type of capitalist industrialisation experienced in these countries was radically different from that of the centre, and that it is these differences which are crucial for understanding the structure of these countries' politics. Since capital accumulation in the semi-periphery was not as indigenous a process as in the West, and in view of the timing of capitalist penetration, it is not surprising that capitalist development there took on a more restricted and uneven character: *restricted* in the sense that, despite dominance of the capitalist mode of production in industry, wage labourers working in capitalist enterprises proper constitute only a small fraction of the industrial labour force;[14] and *uneven* in the sense that there is marked organisational heterogeneity both within the industrial sector as a whole and between sectors[15] – a heterogeneity resulting in huge productivity differentials and imbalances/disruptions on a scale never experienced in the capitalist centre.

This becomes quite clear if, adopting a historical–comparative perspective, one examines for instance the strikingly different ways in which labour, becoming redundant in agriculture, has been employed in the centre and the semi-periphery respectively. Around the turn of the century, industrial employment in the UK constituted slightly more than half of all urban employment. This percentage, despite various fluctuations, was still practically the same fifty years later (51.9 per cent in 1951). In France the pattern was similar: industrial employment was 51.4 per cent of all urban employment in 1881, and 51.3 per cent in 1954.

In the Latin American semi-periphery, on the other hand, the highest ratio of industrial to overall urban employment was not only much lower than it had been in the West, but in the long term it appears to be shrinking further. So in Chile in 1925, the share of industrial employment in all non-agricultural employment was approximately 35 per cent, and by 1968 it was down to 22 per cent. In Brazil during the same 35-year span it dropped from 37 per cent to 27 per cent, and in Argentina from 30 per cent to 26 per cent.[16]

Given such imbalances and the marked heterogeneity of production structures, it is not surprising that income inequalities in the semi-periphery are much greater than in the centre. In the post-war period, for instance, definite progress in terms of reducing absolute levels of poverty (as some crumbs of the wealth generated by high rates of growth trickled down the social pyramid)[17] went hand in hand with huge inequalities between the bottom and top of the income scale. So in the 1960s and early 1970s, the top 20 per cent of the population in the semi-periphery received 50 per cent or more of the national income, whereas in the capitalist centre their average was well below the half-way mark.[18] Such discrepancies become even more significant in view of the fact that, according to the available time-series data, inequalities in the semi-periphery have not yet reached a plateau but continue growing.[19]

Needless to say this type of unequal distribution – characterised by the partial elimination of starvation levels of poverty and, at the same time, by an excessively high concentration of wealth at the top – creates very favourable conditions for the rapid radicalisation of the under-privileged, *especially when it takes place in a context of mass politics*. In the West, the 'hump' period of industrialisation (typified by huge disruptions and rapidly widening inequalities) occurred at a time when the majority of the population remained outside the political arena (late eighteenth and early nineteenth centuries). By the time popular demands for broader political participation became imperative, economic inequalities had reached a plateau, thus greatly facilitating the problem of the distribution of political power.[20] In the parliamentary semi-periphery, by contrast, the early and pre-industrial demise of oligarchic politics meant that the growing inequalities associated with rapid industrialisation occurred in a context where large sections of the populations were already in the political arena. Such a situation where growing inequalities are both more visible and less acceptable leads to high levels of mass radicalisation, and vastly accentuates the economic and political contradictions of the system. This brings us to a more systematic consideration of the relationship between economic and political structures in the semi-periphery.

2. ON THE POLITICAL STRUCTURES OF THE PARLIAMENTARY SEMI-PERIPHERY

Having briefly discussed the timing of capitalist industrialisation and its relatively restricted and unequal character, let us now see what structural limits are set by this type of capitalist trajectory on the political level.

A   The limiting framework

To begin with, both the restricted character of capitalist development and the marked organisational and technological heterogeneity between sectors present obstacles to a strong collective organisation of the working classes. Peripheral capitalist expansion being so restricted means that the proletariat is numerically weak, and that the overwhelming majority of the labour force operates in work contexts which are not conducive to the development of strong trades union organisations.[21] Also, the greater heterogeneity of productive structures, the large productivity differentials and ensuing income inequalities, as well as the marked differences in work conditions between technologically advanced and backward sectors, all tend to create severe cleavages within the working class. Of course such structural cleavages exist in the capitalist centre too, but in the semi-periphery they are more accentuated, and to that extent it becomes much more difficult to mobilise and organise the workers in such a way that long-term, broader common interests override the more narrowly defined interests which divide them.

If additionally one takes into account what has already been said about the expansion of the state before industrialisation, and its incorporative/paternalistic orientation vis-à-vis weak working-class organisations, it becomes obvious why a Western-style inclusion of the lower classes in politics – which, for lack of a better term, I shall call *integrative* – is highly unlikely in the parliamentary semi-periphery.

However, although the late and restricted character of capitalist industrialisation is no favourable ground for the development of integrative modes of inclusion, it *does* provide the conditions for rapid political mobilisation and radicalisation of the lower classes. The semi-periphery's early integration into the world market and the resulting rapid urbanisation, its early adoption of parliamentary institutions, as well as its recent industrialisation, have inevitably generated processes of large-scale political mobilisation as the self-containment of traditional rural communities was being eroded and the majority of the population drawn into national politics. Since, as we have seen, this drawing-in process occurred in a context of growing economic and social/political inequalities, it has been highly conducive to the rapid radicalisation of the masses. Nevertheless, this radicalisation does not lead to a revolutionary type of mobilisation threatening the bourgeois order, and that is a point which deserves some discussion.

Given the high concentration of the population in a few urban centres and the enormous repressive capacities of the modern state, the present chances of a revolutionary overthrow of the capitalist state in the parliamentary semi-periphery are rather low. Not only is the type of state collapse found in classical revolutionary situations (e.g. those of Bourbon France or Tsarist Russia)[22] not very likely, but the semi-periphery also lacks those isolated but at the same time highly populated regions which, lying beyond the easy reach of centralised State control, can become the breeding ground for effective guerrilla/revolutionary activities against the political centre.[23]

Moreover, the exceptionally high urbanisation rates in the semi-periphery are reducing the revolutionary potential of these formations in several other ways. First of all, a large-scale rural exodus to the cities often operates as a strong safety valve reducing revolutionary propensities in the countryside. Despite the huge dislocations created by rapid urbanisation (especially if accompanied by capital-intensive industrialisation), massive peasant migration can be a substitute for rural revolt or revolution. At the same time, of course, the early and impressive urbanisation of the semi-periphery has meant the growth of the urban middle classes which, as they become more numerous and differentiated and were accommodated in the post-oligarchic political arena, rapidly turned into the main pillars of the political and economic establishment. In fact, the chances of revolutionary upheaval are considerably higher when the radical, anti-oligarchic phase of the rising urban middle classes coincides with the radical mobilisation of the peasantry. However, as pointed out above, neither Greece nor the Latin American southern-cone countries experiences such an anti-oligarchic rural-urban alliance. In Greece, the relative weakness of the landowning classes meant that the break-up of the restrictive oligarchic political system was achieved without any populist mobilisation in either the towns or the countryside. In southern Latin America, the urban middle classes managed to accommodate themselves and to consolidate their power position in the post-oligarchic political framework by mobilising only the urban masses – leaving the peasantry under the control of its traditional masters.

When the peasants, at a much later stage, began to mobilise radically, the middle classes had long ceased to be political outsiders and became the main bulwark against any popular threat from below.

This post-oligarchic conservative role of the middle classes in the semi-periphery has been and is being performed quite effectively due to the relative strength of their political organisations. Even if the urban middle classes in the country we are concerned with cannot, in terms of political organisation, be compared with their Western European counterparts, they are much stronger than those in less urbanised and industrialised peripheral formations. The relatively early demise in the semi-periphery of arbitrary military rule and its replacement by constitutional government, as well as the subsequent establishment of a restrictive parliamentary system, has led to a situation where political parties, despite their clientelistic vertical character, have taken strong roots. Even in Brazil, a country with a weaker party system than Chile, Argentina or even Greece, the establishment of long monarchical rule (1822–89) led to the early demise of *coronelismo*; and Brazilian parties, already active under the empire, were playing a much more important role in the political system of the Old Republic than parties in countries like Nicaragua, Guatemala, etc.[24]

Another related factor which considerably diminishes the chances of an anti-capitalist revolution in the semi-periphery is the fact that the indigenous dominant classes were not controlled by foreign interests to the same degree as, for instance, in pre-revolutionary Cuba and several meso-American 'banana republics'. In the latter, the very high degree of foreign penetration and control of both the polity and the economy made it very much easier for the indigenous ruling classes to be identified with foreign domination – and therefore to bring about the mobilisation of the rural and urban masses for nationalist/revolutionary ends. The dominant classes in the semi-periphery, on the other hand, were not simple puppets manipulated by foreign interests – despite the importance of foreign interests in their export sectors, and despite the foreign-led character of their post-war industrialisation.[25]

The greater strength of the indigenous dominant classes in the semi-periphery, therefore, the early and rapid development of urbanisation and later of industrialisation, and the establishment of parliamentary party systems as early as the nineteenth century has resulted in the creation of a numerically large and relatively well-organised middle class with political formations which operated as effective buffers against the revolutionary potential of the lower classes.

The same set of circumstances explains why not only a revolution from below, but also a revolution from above is highly unlikely in the parliamentary semi-periphery. While the dominance of the military within the post-oligarchic power bloc is real enough, it is not an overwhelming one. Relatively strong civilian forces (compared to more peripheral formations) curb the army's proclivity for institutionalising military rule in an irreversible manner, or for acquiring the type of autonomy vis-à-vis civil society seen in Peru (1968–75) or in Kemalist Turkey.[26]

For the same reason it is difficult – perhaps impossible – to achieve the type of political solution which obtained in post-revolutionary Mexico, at a time when her middle classes were not yet strongly constituted on the level of collective action/organisation: a solution within which the holders of the means of domination managed to establish a political monopoly and permanent political dominance over the holders of the means of production within the power bloc. In other words, even if the political representatives of the civilian forces in the post-oligarchic semi-periphery did not manage to keep the armed forces and the State bureaucrats under the kind of hegemony that has prevailed in western parliamentary democracies, they have been strong enough to prevent a situation in which military or State bureaucrats can establish an overwhelming dominance within the power bloc. In fact, the lack of civilian hegemony – in a context where civilian forces are strong enough to prevent both the holders of the means of coercion and of the administration from establishing their own hegemony within the power bloc – constitutes a characteristic of the parliamentary semi-periphery democracies and the type of peripheral polities characterised by permanent military or one-party rule.

In conclusion, an analysis of the timing and structure of capitalist industrialisation in the semi-periphery suggests that, at least in the foreseeable future, the chances of a revolution, whether from below or above, are as low as those of achieving a 'western-type' integrative mode of political inclusion of the masses in the political arena. It these two unlikely prospects form the outer political limits in the parliamentary semi-periphery, what can be said about the political arrangements and structures typical within this limiting framework? What, on the level of political organisations, are the most typical forms of political inclusion of the lower classes in semi-peripheral politics?

B. Typical modes of political inclusion

Oversimplifying somewhat, one could name two other modes which play a very prominent role in semi-peripheral politics: clientelism and populism. It appears worthwhile at this point to present these two modes of political inclusion (which, of course, are not to be found in the parliamentary semi-periphery only), in a highly abstract manner, keeping in mind that in concrete political systems they never occur in their 'pure' form.

Clientelism – a distinct and, from the point of view of the maintenance of the status quo, rather 'safe' solution to the problems created by political mobilisation and enlarged political participation is the use of vertical networks of patron-client relationships for bringing the dominated classes into national politics. Indeed, clientelist networks were a typical form of organisation in oligarchic politics.

However, contrary to the belief of neo-evolutionist political scientists, 'modernisation' does not eliminate clientelism; patronage networks tend to persist in a modified, less traditional form even after the dominance of industrial capitalism and after the decline of oligarchic politics. As many empirical studies have demonstrated, the entrance of the lower classes into politics is perfectly compatible with the continuation of vertical/ clientelistic forms of organisation in peripheral and semi-peripheral capitalist formations.[27] Of course, capitalist penetration and the advent of mass politics considerably change the traditional forms of patronage which characterise pre-industrial formations. Industrialisation, State expansion, the emergence and political activation of new social strata eager to break the oligarchy's political control – all these are instrumental in weakening the exclusive patronage monopoly exercised over the rural populations by local potentates; they contribute to the multiplication and diversification of patrons at the local level, the centralisation of clientelistic parties, and the more direct involvement of clients with party and state bureaucrats at all administrative levels. In other words, they bring about a shift from oligarchic/traditional to more centralised forms of patronage.[28]

Populism is the other mode of political integration prevalent in semi-peripheral capitalist formations. Given the huge disruptions generated by the process of capital accumulation and the relatively abrupt[29] entrance of the masses into politics, clientelistic networks often fail to find room in their vertical structures for the new political participants. In the absence of strongly institutionalised horizontal organisations of the western type, populism can provide another framework for bringing in the lower classes. The populist mode – whether in the form of distinct organisations like parties, or in the more diffuse form of movements generated from above or below – always involves a specific type of political mobilisation of the masses and their involvement in politics: a type of mobilisation/inclusion which is *analytically* distinct from the clientelistic mode.

As far as the transition from oligarchic to mass politics in semi-peripheral quasi-parliamentary regimes is concerned, the passage from 'traditional' to 'modern' forms of clientelism and the rise of populist movements can, as already mentioned, be seen as two different ways of undermining oligarchic politics and of bringing about or consolidating less restrictive forms of political participation. In both cases the end result is the break-up of the political monopoly of a small number of powerful families, the entrance of new men into the power game, and the transition from the political clubs or coteries of notables to broadly organised parties. But despite such similarities, there are fundamental differences between clientelistic transformation and populist mobilisation as 'pure' modes of political inclusion. In the populist case, the new men achieve their entrance into the corridors of power through a type of mobilisation which, both in ideological and in structural/organisational terms, makes a more radical break with *ancien régime* oligarchic politics. One obvious difference is the fact that the ideological themes of the populist discourse focus predominantly on the antagonism between the 'people' and the 'establishment', the poor versus the rich, etc. – themes which, as a rule, play only a very minor role in clientelistic ideologies.[30]

On the organisational level, given the mobilisation-from-above element and the masses' relatively abrupt entrance into politics, it is the *plebiscitarian* leadership rather than intricate patronage networks which provides the basic framework for political incorporation. As a rule, populist leaders are hostile to strongly institutionalised *intermediary* levels, whether of clientelistic or the more bureaucratic type found in West European political parties or trades unions. The emphasis on the leader's charisma, on the necessity for direct, non-mediated rapport between the leader and 'his people', as well as the relative abruptness of the process of political incorporation, all lead to organisational forms of a fluid character. Even in cases of populist movements with strong grassroots organisations, in so far as the rank and file's allegiance is centred on the person of the leader, local or intermediary cadres are left without a structural basis for establishing some degree of political autonomy vis-à-vis the leader: all the power and legitimation they have is derived directly from his personal charisma.[31]

In actual, concrete situations the distinction between clientelistic and populist modes of inclusion is not, of course, as clear-cut as outlined above. For instance, concrete populist organisations or movements do not only have clientelistic elements but, given the fluid character of their organisational structure, 'clientelisation processes' can frequently be so strong as to lead to an eventual metamorphosis of a populist organisation into a clientelistic one, i.e. to a situation where clientelistic features overshadow populist ones. However, such cases do not invalidate attempts at differentiating as clearly as possible between the basic structures and 'logic' of the clientelist and populist modes of political inclusion, provided it is remembered that any clear-cut typologies established in the process will refer simply to structural tendencies – tendencies which are subject to greater or lesser accentuation in concrete situations.

The purpose of the above attempt to outline highly abstract models of clientelist and populist modes of political inclusion has been to highlight the contrast between the ways in which the lower classes were drawn into politics in the capitalist centre and the semi-periphery respectively. If the western mode of lower-class inclusion can be called *integrative*, it can be argued that clientelist and populist modes of political inclusion, especially when combined with weak and/or dependent trades union organisations, lead to the *incorporation* rather than *integration* of the lower classes in politics. In fact, what clientelist and populist modes have in common is that in both of them the lower classes are brought into politics in a more vertical, more heteronomous manner – i.e. in ways which facilitate State control and regimentation, and therefore lead to an over-developed State and a weak civil society.

One last point to be made about types of political control in the semi-periphery is that incorporative mechanisms of regulation are often supplemented by exclusionist ones, especially when the former are not by themselves capable of keeping political developments in check. For instance, all semi-peripheral politics have at certain periods of their parliamentary development introduced laws excluding specific parties from parliamentary representation.

Of course, there can be a great deal of variation within the semi-periphery as to the state–civil society relationship. At one extreme there are instances where the incorporative character of the State is very strong, and both trades unions and political parties are weak and precarious (e.g. Brazil). At the other extreme there is a stronger civil society where weak trades unions coexist with *relatively* strong political parties (e.g. pre-dictatorial Chile), or *relatively* strong trades unions with weak political organisations (e.g. Argentina). However, even in the latter instances there is a qualitative difference with the West: none of the above cases exemplifies the type of strong civil society which has for its backbone both strong trades unions *and* strong political parties – trades unions and political parties which, although closely linked, are relatively independent of both the state and each other.[32]

On the other hand, one must always keep in mind that, compared to peripheral capitalist formations, the societies under discussion here all have a relatively strong civil society. In that sense they are *semi-peripheral* in not only economic terms but also in *political* terms (i.e. their civil society and their parliamentary institutions are closer to those of the West than to other Third World societies).

C. The basic political contradiction

Having analysed the incorporative ways in which the lower classes were brought into the political arena in the semi-periphery, we can now formulate the basic political contradiction of our post-oligarchic semi-peripheral societies: the contradiction between, on the one hand, high levels of political participation/mobilisation and, on the other, the prevailing incorporative modes of political inclusion which are incapable of coping in any stable manner with either the successive waves of new entrants into politics, or the higher levels of activation/radicalisation of those already inside the political arena.

It is, of course, only the integrative mode of inclusion which, *other things being equal*, can on a long-term irreversible basis accommodate the massive entrance of new participants into the political game without reinforcing any tendencies for a breakdown of the parliamentary institutions and the intermittent imposition of dictatorial solutions. It is only within an integrative context that the new entrants, given the horizontal/non-personalistic mechanisms of inclusion, will reinforce the strength and autonomy of existing collective organisations. It is only then that the distribution of political power between rulers and ruled can be solved in such a way that civil society is further strengthened – and this strengthening, as the Anglo-Saxon model of political development has shown, not only presents no threat to the bourgeois order but, on the contrary, further legitimises it by making it more hegemonic.

An overall incorporative context is, on the other hand, less capable of a similarly stable, long-term assimilation of the masses in active politics and, therefore, of any effective solution to the political distribution problem. The more accentuated the economic and political processes which lead to a state of mass politics, the greater the inequalities in the distribution of power, and the more inadequate the weakly institutionalised political mechanisms of inclusion for coping with the ensuing political mobilisation and unrest. For example, as the politicisation/radicalisation of the masses increases, clientelistic mechanisms of inclusion become more fragile and precarious – not only in the urban centres but even in the countryside.[33] If it is clear that restricted and uneven capitalist development does not irreversibly destroy but merely transforms clientelistic networks, it is just as clear that in the process clientelism not only changes its complexion, but also that it becomes more fragile and precarious. In the rapid development of urbanisation, commercialisation and industrialisation, patronage networks are constantly disrupted by the emergence of non-clientelistic organisations (whether populist or not) which are equally unstable and precarious.[34]

My major argument, therefore, is that as the masses in the parliamentary semi-periphery tend to become fully politicised, none of the major political mechanisms of inclusion discussed above is capable of establishing a clear and irreversible dominance. Although horizontal/non-clientelistic forms of inclusion emerge which, in combination with other processes, weaken vertical organisational forms, for reasons noted above, they do not manage to achieve dominance and so cannot contribute to a strong civil society and to the permanent subjugation of the military and of State bureaucrats by civilian forces. Even when in some exceptional cases (e.g. Chile) they do assume some importance, they coexist, without becoming hegemonic, with clientelistic and populist modes of inclusion which are equally incapable of providing long-term political solutions.

Looking at this situation now from a more dynamic standpoint, we see that the increasing contradiction between high levels of political participation and persisting incorporative control mechanisms results in the prevailing relations of domination being challenged from below by organisations and movements trying to establish a degree of autonomy incompatible with the incorporative mode. Such a challenge to the incorporative character of the relation of domination means, of course, a challenge to the military as the effective monitor of the incorporative/exclusionist system of controls; it means, in other words, a challenge to the power position of the armed forces within the State.

Finally, it should be stressed here that the contradiction between high political activation and incorporative modes of control, which is basically a question of the distribution of political rights, is becoming ever greater in a context where economic distribution problems too (i.e. stabilisation of inequalities, development of welfare) are becoming extremely acute. Unlike western Europe, where the problems of economic and political distribution were tackled *consecutively*, i.e. the distribution of political rights came *after* the 'hump' period of industrialisation), in the parliamentary semi-periphery the problems of economic and political distribution achieved acuity *simultaneously*.

If this same centre–semi-periphery difference is regarded in terms of collective actors, one can argue that the development of inequalities and contradictions in the West (and especially in the Anglo-Saxon West) clearly came about in such a way that the economically and politically dominant groups were faced, on the one hand, with more manageable contradictions or dilemmas and, on the other, with a strongly organised working class which ensured that the solution to those dilemmas took its collective interests into account. This meant that the western dominant groups could pursue a more 'enlightened', conciliatory policy — both because it was systemically easier (i.e. in terms of the nature and sequence of systemic contradictions), and because a head-on conflict with a numerically strong and organised working class would have been a highly costly and risky enterprise.

In the parliamentary semi-periphery, however, the dominant groups have in the post-way period been faced with much more unmanageable contradictions, as well as with a poorly organised working class whose demands (even when non-revolutionary) cannot be met as easily as had been possible in the West. In the semi-periphery, therefore, the trend towards the redistribution of economic rewards and political rights is undermined by the existence of more severe contradictions *and* by the weakness of the working-class movement. Together, these two factors make the option of dictatorial exclusion that much more attractive to those who control the State's highly sophisticated political and military mechanisms of repression.

To put it even more simply: from the point of view of those who economically and politically dominate a social formation, it is easier to apply less repressive means of political inclusion when popular demands are 'reasonable' (i.e. can be met without seriously jeopardising the existing relations of production and domination), and when those who articulate such demands are organisationally strong. If popular demands are difficult or downright impossible to meet within the prevailing system of exploitation and domination, and if those who formulate them are weakly organised, then there will be a very strong tendency to impose dictatorial 'solutions'.

3. ON THE POST-WAR RISE OF BUREAUCRATIC-AUTHORITARIAN MILITARY REGIMES IN THE SEMI-PERIPHERY

It is in the light of the above considerations that the rise of dictatorial military regimes in all semi-peripheral societies during the 1960s and 1970s should be examined.

A.   On the establishment of military dictatorships

In every one of these societies, significant levels of capitalist industrial-isation have aggravated economic and political inequalities and have led to the rapid politicisation and radicalisation of the popular masses. Such an unprecedented wave of political mobilisation – whether predominan-tly linked with economic or with political contradictions – has posed a serious threat to the political and/or economic status quo, a threat which existing incorporative mechanisms of control were hardly able to deal with. The form this politicisation has taken has varied, or course, from one case to the next in accordance with the always unique political conjuncture. Nevertheless, it is possible to distinguish in broad terms two different types of 'threat' to the status quo resulting from the high level of political activation:

(a) *A strictly political* threat, in that is was the *relations of domination* which were seriously challenged. In that case the incorporative controls which the politically dominant groups exercised over civil society via the State apparatus were endangered by the development of organisations or movements (political parties, trades unions) endeavouring to reject specific forms of State tutelage, or the prevailing overall distribution of political power between rulers and ruled. (This was clearly the case with the 1967 Greek coup.)

(b) A broader, all-encompassing challenge to *not only the relations of domination but also to the dominant relations of production.* In that case, the lower classes could no longer be contained or safely incorporated within the overall bourgeois order, in that strong left-wing organisations or movements posed a serious threat to the process of capitalist accumulation. Such a threat need not take the form of an explicitly revolutionary movement challenging capitalist relations of production in direct, frontal manner; it can just as well, and usually does, take a more indirect form – as for instance the articulation of demands for redistribution which, when implemen-ted, lead to investment strikes or to such high rates of inflation that the whole fabric of bourgeois society is disrupted (i.e. the pre-coup situation in Chile).

What it is important to emphasise here is that the threat from below, whether strictly political or more general, relates directly to the subsequent military intervention and the imposition of long-term military rule: a popular threat from below, even when it focuses only on the relations of domination, is a direct threat to the military's power position within the overall system of domination. If, as the Greek case indicates, such a threat does not always affect the bourgeoisie directly, it does invariably endanger the type of army dominance which is typical in the post-oligarchic semi-peripheral State; not countered in time, it does mean the development of a strong lower-class movement or party drastically challenging the incorporative and exclusionist controls and, therefore, the army's power position within the State.

In other words, if the army intervenes to stem the growing threat from below, it does so not merely to safeguard capitalist interests, or because the military officers are of middle-class origin; it intervenes also in order to safeguard its own corporate interests – which are to be understood not simply as a concern over pay or military expenditures, but primarily as *power interests*, threatened in a variety of ways through high levels of popular mobilisation. Not only can such mobilisation endanger the position of the armed forces' top personnel but, more importantly, it can also challenge the tutelary functions of the military institution *per se*. (For instance, in Greece the rising forces of George Papandreou's liberal party directly challenged the highly interventionist role played by the monarchy and the army in Greek politics, and that challenge was related in a straight line to the 1967 coup.)

More seriously still, popular mobilisation/radicalisation can even go as far as to undermine the power position of the armed forces from within, by challenging the very hierarchical unity on which the military's organisation is based. (Before the 1964 Brazilian coup, for example, severe political splits started developing between low and high-ranking officers as well as within the rank and file.) As such threats to the army's power position are, at the post-war stage of political participation, linked to structural rather than merely conjunctural developments, brief military interventions are no longer effective. It is only by establishing more permanent dictatorial controls that at least some factions within the army can hope to hold on to the type of privileged power positions they had acquired in the immediate post-oligarchic period.

B. Structural sources of instability of military dictatorships

If quasi-parliamentary forms of politics are inherently unstable in semi-peripheral societies, the dictatorial-military forms of political rule are too – at least at the present stage of mass politics. This becomes obvious if one considers what has been said about the semi-periphery's relatively strong civil society and the inability of the military, despite their relative dominance within the power bloc, to consolidate their position irreversibly.

In fact, other things being equal, the long-term institutionalisation of military dictatorial regimes is fairly easy in societies which have not yet reached high levels of political participation/mobilisation, and/or where civil society is very weak (as for instance in several African societies). At the stage of mass politics, on the other hand, and in a context of a relatively strong civil society, the long-term institutionalisation of military rule, even when supported by large factions of the bourgeoisie, is a much more difficult enterprise. Such a long-term consolidation of the army's dominance over civilian forces would require going beyond the type of control that the mere use of repressive State apparatuses can give. It would require *either* the creation of some sort of organic/corporatistic representation within which various institutional interests are allowed some very limited existence under strict State 'guidance', a type of control which excludes active popular mobilisation; the building up of a mass party through which the people are mobilised and brought into politics in a fascist or quasi-fascist manner.[35]

However, neither way of going beyond the typical military-bureaucratic authoritarianism has much chance of success in the semi-periphery at its present stage of capital accumulation and mass involvement. The external obstacles to such solutions are related to the fact that, after the defeat of the Axis forces, fascist and organic/corporatistic models have been discredited as an alternative to free party representation; and to the fact that the present-day heavy reliance by semi-peripheral capitalist formations on foreign capital makes it much more difficult to drum up popular support and legitimation by means of xenophobic, chauvinistic nationalism or by adopting isolationist policies of capitalist growth.[36] Moreover, internally the necessity of controlling inflation and keeping down wages does not make it any easier to gain the support of large sections of the rural and urban working classes; nor are the huge inequalities and the systematic exclusion of a sizeable part of the labour force from the productive process conducive to building up mass organisations capable of providing widespread grassroots support for authoritarian rule. Yet without such mass organisations the military cannot consolidate their dominance vis-à-vis recalcitrant civilian forces (trades unions, left-wing parties, those political representatives of the economically dominant classes who resent their displacement by the military and their loss of political power, etc.). The only way to shatter such forces is through a mass party – which, however, the military seem unable and/or unwilling to build up.

In addition to these considerations, the relatively long parliamentary/democratic traditions and their strong ideological roots among large sections of the population in semi-peripheral politics oblige the military to legitimise their intervention as an attempt at redressing democracy and establishing a strong and 'healthy' parliamentary system. The more they prolong their dictatorial rule, therefore, the more they are subjected to pressures, internally as well as from the international community, for adhering to their initial proclamations and withdrawing from the direct exercise of governmental power. As pressures from below and abroad keep growing, cleavages develop within the ruling military groups, between those who favour a withdrawal or a limited liberalisation as a means of safeguarding army unity and prestige, and those who want to maintain or reinforce dictatorial controls. As such intra-junta rifts widen, those political groups which had been linked with parliamentary institutions and which were displaced by the junta will try to accentuate the split further and do their best to mobilise the population in an effort to win back their previous dominant positions.

What gives this type of structurally generated process a more dramatic and acute form is the occurrence of a crisis (whether economic, a question of 'succession', a defeat in war etc.). Such a crisis invariably exacerbates faction divisions and strengthens popular pressures for democratic change.

Certain military bureaucratic regimes are, of course, less unsuccessful than others in establishing some sort of organisational base. If the military intervention – like the Greek one was – is in reaction to power struggles and rearrangements within the State, i.e. when the relations of production are in no serious danger and economically dominant classes do not, therefore, give their *active* support to the new dictatorial order, then it is difficult for a dictatorship to rest on any organisational foundation. But when the dominant classes not merely acquiesce in dictatorial rule but are actively involved in bringing it about, then consolidation is easier to obtain. Still, even in such cases the long-term institutionalisation of a military dictatorial regime is extremely problematic. Short of a process of full-scale and successful right-wing mobilisation, dictatorial regimes in semi-peripheral capitalist formations at the present stage of economic and political development are brittle and precarious, whatever the means of coercion.

The permanent consolidation of dictatorial rule in the semi-periphery has, therefore, proved as difficult as that of parliamentary democracy – hence the regular opening up and closing of the political system, and the alternation of quasi-parliamentary and dictatorial forms of control as the dominant classes try to cope more or less haphazardly with the huge disruptions and inequalities generated by peripheral capitalism. Moreover, it is possible to see the very pendulation between dictatorial and parliamentary regime forming by itself a mechanism helping to safeguard the bourgeois order. For in times or open quasi-parliamentary politics, the dominant classes can always explain social disruptions as the consequences of repression and mismanagement in the preceding dictatorial period; and during the dictatorship, all difficulties can be ascribed to the corruption and demagogy of professional politicians. In this way the fact that neither dictatorial nor parliamentary regimes can solve the basic economic and political dilemmas of semi-peripheral capitalism can be systematically concealed.

Having stressed in very general outline the pendulating tendencies of the semi-peripheral State, it is now necessary to add some clarifications and qualifications.

First, the fact that there are pendular regime changes in the semi-periphery does not, of course, mean that all open or closed solutions are similar, regardless of the stage of accumulation reached, or of the extent of mass participation in politics. For instance, military interventions and the imposition of dictatorial controls during an earlier period of accumulation (the import-substitution phase) were qualitatively different from the post-war bureaucratic-authoritarian type of military dictatorship.

Secondly, the pendulating movement does not have to swing symmetrically with respect to the duration of each alternating phase. It goes without saying that long periods of dictatorship are not necessarily followed by long periods of parliamentary rule, or *vice versa*.

Thirdly, and most important, the closing or opening-up of the political system can occur without a complete regime change. If in some instances the opening-up phase involves a full-scale transition from dictatorial to multi-party democratic rule (e.g. in Greece after the fall of the junta in 1974, or in Argentina after Peron's return in 1973), in others it can be limited to a process of *liberalisation without democratisation* – i.e. to a situation where there is a loosening up of dictatorial controls in the sphere of press freedom or in the handling of political prisoners for instance, without at the same time the institutionalisation of a genuine pluralistic parliamentary regime (e.g. post-1974 Brazil).

The same consideration holds for the closing-down phase. In some instances the closure might involve the imposition of a full-scale military dictatorship (e.g. Chile since 1973); in others the closure might be effected by means of indirect or covert military supervision, through the army drastically extending the already considerable control it usually exercises over the political process – for example by the imposition of detailed demands with which the politicians must faithfully comply (e.g. Argentina 1959–62).

The important thing to note here are the qualitative differences between the modes of functioning of the respective parliamentary institutions in the centre and the semi-periphery. In the latter case, both full-scale and more limited pendulations involve fundamental change in the distribution of civil and political rights, i.e. they bring a drastic alteration of fundamental constitutional rules. In that sense the political process differs sharply from the functioning of stable parliamentary regimes, particularly of the Anglo-Saxon type. There, the constitutional rules referring to basic civil and political rights, although not immutable, undergo change so slowly (e.g. the gradual ascendancy of executive over legislative power) that there is a definite qualitative difference between this type of gradual change and the frequent alternation between granting and abrogating basic civil/political rights which is so typical of semi-peripheral politics.

Another way of putting this is to say that in the more established parliamentary western democracies, economic and political contradictions can be handled effectively through an alternation of political parties and policies, without any brusque change in the basic constitutional rules of the parliamentary game. For example, insofar as there is a growth-*vs*-distribution dilemma in the economic field, it tends to be dealt with by the alternation of predominantly pro-growth with pro-distribution parties in power. In the semi-periphery, given the greater depth of political and economic contradictions and the type of linkages between the States and civil society, the growth-*vs*-distribution dilemma, especially in the post-war period, tends to be dealt with not by party, but by either half-baked or full-scale regime alternation.

Fourthly, it should be stressed that the pendulating movement, even when it does not involve a full-scale regime closure and opening, quite *genuinely reflects the uneasy and vacillating* balance of power between civilian and military forces in a political context of long democratic/parliamentary traditions. In that sense the pendulations of the semi-peripheral State must be clearly differentiated from cases where army (or one-party) dominance is permanent, and where political change consists of 'palace coups' (which merely bring a change of personnel at the top), or from pseudo-democratic openings which are simply public-relations exercises and do not in the least diminish the military dominance over civilian forces.

It goes without saying that the above rather pessimistic generalisations on the oscillating character of semi-peripheral politics are not intended as 'iron laws' but as *structural tendencies* which may be neutralised or reversed by a host of conjunctural events,[37] as well as by growing political awareness of their existence and the formulation of conscious strategies for overcoming them.

In conclusion, my major argument has been that the limits within which state forms vary in the post-war parliamentary semi-periphery are defined *on the one hand* by the low chances of a long-term irreversible institutionalisation of parliamentary structures as these operate in the western democracies; and *on the other hand* by the equally low chances of an overall revolutionary transformation of these polities from either above or below.

Within these limits, the regime forms typical in the post-war semi-periphery are either quasi-parliamentary democracies, characterised by incorporative mechanisms of inclusion (or a mixture of incorporative and exclusionary ones); or military dictatorships of the bureaucratic-authoritarian type. Given the weak institutionalisation of both regime forms, there is a clear tendency for the change from one to the other and back again as the economically and politically dominant groups try to cope with the growing contradictions of semi-peripheral capitalism.

Notes

1. Although *southern* Brazil is very similar to Chile and Argentina in terms of levels of urbanisation, the importance of urban middle classes etc., Brazil as a whole – given her huge size and her more heterogeneous social structure – portrays characteristics which place her at the margin of our parliamentary semi-periphery concept. For instance, contrary to the rest of the sample, during the classical period of oligarchic parliamentarism (1891–1930) one does not witness in Brazil the emergence of significant parties on the *national level*; parties of an oligarchic nature were only important on the level of individual states – national politics being predominantly shaped by dealings between governors of key states and the government at the national centre. However despite such differences, given the dominant economic and political role that the southern states played in twentieth-century Brazil, overall political developments are quite comparable with those of the other southern cone countries. For instance Brazil, just like Chile and Argentina, developed a very important urban/modern sector, with similar effects in respect of political mobilisation and the demise of oligarchic politics. See on this point G. O'Donnell, *Modernisation and bureaucratic-authoritarianism* (Berkeley: University of California Pre II, 1973).

2. By *oligarchic parliamentarism* I mean a system of rule where active politics is the concern of a small number of privileged families which, on the one hand, manage to maintain a pluralistic system of power based on free

speech, free association, etc., but on the other succeed, by means of a variety of mechanisms, in keeping the majority of the population outside the political arena. Such means of popular exclusion can either be legal (e.g. voting rights being conditional on property or educational qualifications), or they may result from the fact that a few families of notables control lower-class votes automatically, often through fraud or coercion. Oligarchic parliamentarism functioned relatively stably in Greece from 1864 to 1909, in Brazil from 1891 to 1930, in Argentina from 1853 to 1916, and in Chile from 1891 to 1924 – where relative stability of oligarchic rule in these periods refers to *regime*, not governmental stability.

3. cf. A. S. Banks, *Cross-polity time series data* (Cambridge, Mass: The MIT Press, 1971) pp. 48 and 69.

4. *ibid.*, pp. 59, 62, 72. In Brazil, urbanisation levels were lower: 11.2 per cent (cities of 50 000 plus) and 9.5 per cent (cities of 100 000). However, given that Brazil has a much more heterogeneous social structure than either Chile or Argentina, comparisons with data on the national/aggregate level are misleading. Southern Brazil has similar patterns of urbanisation as her southern neighbours; and inter-war Brazil, just like Chile and Argentina, developed a very important urban/modern sector, with similar effects in respect of political mobilisation and the demise of oligarchic politics. cf. G. O'Donnell, *op. cit.*

5. cf. League of Nations, *Statistical yearbook 1927* (Geneva, 1928) Table VII.

6. For a view of populism as a means for breaking up the oligarchy's monopoly of power cf. J. Malloy (ed.), *Authoritarianism and corporatism in Latin America* (University of Pittsburgh Press, 1977) pp. 8ff.

7. For instance, as late as 1948 Yugoslavia still had 77.8 per cent of her labour force in agriculture, and Bulgaria (1946) 75.5 per cent. cf. T. Deldycke *et al.*, *The working population and its structure* (Brussels, Institut de Sociologie, 1968) pt. I.

8. For an analysis of Balkan peasant movements and ideologies cf B Peseltz, *Peasant movements in south-eastern Europe* (PhD thesis, Washington DC: Georgetown University, 1950).

9. cf. N. Mouzelis, *Modern Greece* (London: Macmillan, 1978 chs 1, 5, 6.

10. In Greece in 1909, Chile in 1924, and Brazil in 1930.

11. cf. A. Rouquié, *Pouvoir militarise et société politique au République Argentine* (Paris, 1978) pp. 700ff.

12. For instance, in 1978 the contribution of the agricultural sector to the GNP was only 10 per cent in Chile, 13 per cent in Argentina, 11 per cent in Brazil, and 17 per cent in Greece. In the same year industry's contribution was 29 per cent in Chile, 45 per cent in Argentina, 37 per cent in Brazil, and 31 per cent in Greece (cf. World Bank, *World Development Report* (Oxford University Press, 1980) table e, p. 115). For figures concerning the shifts in exports from the southern-cone countries cf. B. Kadar, *Problems of economic growth in Latin America* (New York: St Martin's Press, 1980) p. 81, and on exports from Greece, see N. Mouzelis, *op. cit.*

13. cf. World Bank, *op. cit.*, table 20.

14. This is true even for Chile and Argentina which, in terms of proletarinisation, are more advanced than Greece or Brazil. In 1952, industrial wage earners in Chile numbered approx 229 000 out of a total labour force of

2 187 000 (a roughly 1:9 ratio), and adding those employed in the mining industry (85 000 in 1952) to the industrial work force does not change this ratio significantly. Even in Argentina, a country with economic structures which most nearly resemble those of the West, there were only 900 000 industrial wage earners in 1947 out of a total labour force of 7.5 million (a roughly 1:7 ratio). The contrast with Western Europe is considerable. Belgium, for instance, in 1961 had approx 1 million industrial wage earners in a total labour force of 3.5 million (roughly 1:3.5); in the UK (1951) the ratio was 1:3.2. (Information for both the centre and the semi-periphery is drawn from *ILO Yearbook* (Geneva, ILO, 1964), Table 5. Unfortunately, later ILO Yearbooks stopped providing this type of information.)

15.   As far as the industrial sector is concerned there are, on the one hand, a few very large capitalist enterprises which employ a considerable section of the wage earners and contribute by far the largest share of total industrial output; on the other hand there is a plethora of small, family-oriented artisanal units with very low productivity and with loose and/or precarious linkages to the dynamic capitalist sector. In fact, one of the most striking characteristics of semi-peripheral industry is the persistence and even proliferation (especially in the more traditional industrial branches), of small inefficient units existing side by side with huge firms (usually State or foreign-controlled) which exercise a quasi-monopolistic market control. For instance, in the middle of the 1960s, out of a total statistical population consisting of industrial establishments with five or more workers, those employing more than 100 accounted for 65 per cent of the total sample in Chile, 7 per cent in Brazil, and 10 per cent in Argentina. These relatively large units employed 58 per cent of the industrial labour force in Chile, 61 per cent in Brazil, and 58 per cent in Argentina. In all three countries they also contributed more than 65 per cent of the total industrial value-added. Small industrial establishments (5–19 workers) on the other hand, accounted for 58 per cent of the sample in Argentina, 72 per cent in Brazil, and 68 per cent in Chile. The contribution of these units to the total industrial value-added was 13 per cent in Brazil and 10 per cent in Chile (cf. D. C. Lambert and J. M. Martin, *L'Amerique Latine* (Paris: Armand Colin, 1971) p. 325. For similar data concerning Greece, see H. Ellis *et al.*, *Industrial capital in the development of Greek industry* (Athens: Center of Economic Research, 1965) pp. 197–204.

16.   cf. Economic Commission for Latin America *The process of industrial development in Latin America* (New York: United Nations, 1966) pp. 36ff. In Greece, with a similar capital-intensive pattern of industrialisation, the labour-absorption capacity of the industrial sector is equally low. However, unemployment in the 1960s and 1970s was less severe than in Latin America because of massive Greek labour migration to Western Europe. For further comparative data on labour employment in early industrial Europe and present Third World countries, cf. p. Bairoch, *Le tiers monde dans l'impasse* (Paris: Gallimard, 1971).

17.   With the partial exception of Brazil, most researchers agree that the increase in inequality is not so steep as to completely offset the growth of per-capita income levels of the poorest strata. cf. M. S. Ahluwalia *et al.*,

'Growth and poverty in developing countries', *Journal of Development Economics* (September 1979).

18. It is 40.5 per cent for the UK (1968); 45.6 per cent for West Germany (1970); 45.6 per cent for Canada (1965); and 40.2 per cent for the USA (1970). cf. M. S. Ahluwalia, 'Inequality, poverty and development', *Journal of Development Studies* (3 December 1976) p. 340, table 8.

19. cf. for instance I. B. Kravis, 'A world of unequal incomes', *Annals of the American Academy of Political and Social Sciences*, **409** (1973) pp. 61–80; M. S. Ahluwalia *et al*, 'Growth and poverty . . .', *op. cit.*; and C. Zuvekas Jr, *Income distribution in Latin America: a survey of recent research* (Centre for Latin America, Milwaukee: University of Wisconsin, 1976) pp. 17ff.

20. cf. on this point K. Schweinitz, *Industrialisation and democracy* (London: Collier-Macmillan, 1914). On the long-term pattern of inequalities in Western Europe cf. also the classic article by S. Kuznets, 'Economic growth and income inequality', *American Economic Review*, **49** (March 1955).

21. From this point of view, Argentina's relatively strong trades-union movement constitutes an exception, partly explained by the fact that among all semi-peripheral societies, Argentina's industrial capitalism is the least restricted. Even in Argentina, however, trades unions were not only quite feeble before Peron, but their growing strength during the first Peronist period was due to the massive unionisation of workers newly arrived in industry from the rural areas. These newly-formed unions were, however, merely a personalistic organisational weapon created and used by Peron to consolidate his power position – not only against the oligarchy, but also against the older, more established and autonomous socialist and communist-controlled unions.

22. cf. Theda Skocpol, *States and social revolution: a comparative analysis of France, Russia and China* (Cambridge University Press, 1979) pp. 51–66 and 81–98.

23. Urban guerrilla activities have, of course, developed extensively both in Argentina in Uruguay, but these activities have never, despite their disruptive effects, posed a really serious threat to the bourgeois state.

24. cf. R. H. McDonald, *Party systems and elections in Latin America* (Chicago: Markham, 1971).

25. cf. on this point F. H. Cardoso and E. Faletto, *Dependency and development in Latin America* (Berkeley: University of California Press, 1979).

26. cf. E. K. Trimberger, *Revolution from above* (New Jersey: Transaction Books, 1978).

27. E. Gellner and J. Waterbury (eds) *Patrons and clients in Mediterranean societies* (London: Duckworth, 1977).

28. cf. A. Weingrod, 'Patrons, patronage and parties', *Comparative Studies in Society and History*, **x** (1968) pp. 377–400.

29. For the link between populism and relatively abrupt entrance of the masses into politics, cf. di Tella, 'Populism and reform in Latin America', in C. Veliz (ed) *Obstacles to change in Latin America* (Oxford University Press, 1965).

30. On the antagonistic character of populist ideologies see E. Laclau,

Politics and ideology in Marxist theory (London: New Left Books, 1977).

31. In contrast, the power position and autonomy of local patrons vis-à-vis their superiors in clientelistic political organisations can be considerable. One need think only of the well-documented cases of 'captive voters', cases where local clients owe personal allegiance to the local patron rather than to the national party leadership – to such an extent that the patron can even change parties without losing his political clientele. Although, given the particularistic ties between clients and local patrons, this type of extreme localism is generally more prevalent at the stage of oligarchic politics, such patrons do retain some power and autonomy even in modern, more centralised clientelistic parties.

32. Furthermore, neither Chile's parties nor Argentina's trade unions can, in terms of internal organisation and their relation to the State, be seriously compared with equivalent organisations in western Europe. On Chile's party system and its pervasive clientelistic elements at the grass-roots level cf. A. and J. S. Valenzuela (Eds) *Chile: politics and society* (New Jersey: Transaction Books, 1976) pp. 13ff.

33. For example, the considerable development of rural organisation and the mobilisation/radicalisation of the peasantry in Chile and Brazil during the past decades clearly indicates the weakening of the landlords' clientelistic controls over the peasants. cf. e.g. J. Petras, *Politics and social forces in Chilean development* (Berkeley: University of California Press, 1969); R. Kaufman, *The politics of land reform in Chile* (Cambridge Mass., Harvard University Press, 1972); and P. Flynn, *Brazil: a political analysis* (London: Westview Press, 1978). A similar weakening of clientelistic controls has occurred in the Greek countryside during the last two decades. cf. M. Comninos, *The development of the patronage system in Aitolo-Akharnania and Kavala* (unfinished PhD thesis, London School of Economics).

34. For a development of this point cf. N. Mouzelis, 'Class and clientelist politics: the case of Greece', *Sociological Review*, November 1978.

35. On this cf. J. J. Lintz, 'Totalitarian and authoritarian regimes', in F. Greenspine and N. Polsey (eds) *Handbook of political science* (Reading, Mass: Addison-Wesley, 1975) **III**, pp. 300ff.

36. As Cardoso has rightly pointed out,

> Economic expansion requires technicians, competence and a certain cultural sophistication. When this is found in the context of a dependent economy, the society is necessarily open because a current of information, people and attitudes accompanies the flow of merchandise. There are pressures which are uncontrollable because of this fact.

F. H. Cardoso, *On the characteristics of authoritarian regimes in Latin America* (Centre of Latin American Studies, University of Cambridge Working Papers, **30**)

37. For instance, Greece's entrance into the EEC and her participation in the institutions of the Community will restrict (without eliminating) the options of those forces that aim at reimposing dictatorial rule.

3 Representational Democracy in the South: The Case of the Commonwealth Caribbean

Tony Thorndike

From the time of the attainment of formal independence by Common-wealth Caribbean states to mid-1987, there have been 34 general elections. Of those, 11 resulted in constitutional changes in government, twice in the cases of Barbados, Jamaica and St Lucia. To these elections should be added those which took place in the smaller Eastern Caribbean islands during the period of Associated Statehood status. By restricting British reserve powers to defence and foreign affairs this status effectively granted independence in internal matters to the six territories concerned. From the time it was inaugurated under the provisions of the West Indies Act in 1967 to when independence was granted – between 1974 (Grenada) and 1983 (St Kitts-Nevis) – there were 15 general elections involving six changes of government, giving an overall total of 49 and 17 respectively (for details, see Appendix).

Of the total number of elections, only the four in Guyana (1968, 1973, 1980, 1986) were clearly fraudulent through official rigging and intimidation, although that of 1976 in Grenada was subject to wide-spread corrupt practices. Only one, the 1984 Grenadian poll, was accompanied by overt foreign political and financial pressures, most notably by a US military presence and substantial financial aid by the US Republican party and conservative pressure groups. That of 1980 in Jamaica was also influenced by US pressures – both official and private – but more indirectly. All the other elections recorded were relatively free of intimidation and overt exogenous political influence. Furthermore, the Commonwealth Caribbean – or to use its older and in some cases more well-known term, the West Indies, a useful label that clearly distinguishes the black-creole-English–French-speaking social and political complex from that of the Hispanic-mestizo-white of the Spanish-speaking Caribbean, has experienced only one coup. That was the dramatic takeover of state power by the New Jewel Movement

41

(NJM) in Grenada on 13 March 1979, although the event could more accurately be described as an insurrection.[1]

If it is accepted that essentially free general elections indicate at least a broad acceptance of the general principles of parliamentarty democracy, particularly on the lines of the Westminster model, then the Commonwealth Caribbean stands in stark contrast to continental post-independence Commonwealth Africa. There, only one general election has resulted in a peaceful and constitutional change of government, that in the tiny Gambia in 1966, all other changes having followed military coups, insurrections and, in the case of Uganda in 1979, invasion.

Such a record prompts questions. Has the liberal democratic political system of the Westminster variant shaped, contributed to or hindered the nation-building process, particularly after independence? Related to that is a second, namely has it been an aid or an obstacle to economic development? There is no doubt that the Grenadian NJM revolutionaries, and others in the region similarly persuaded by Marxist-Leninist ideology infused by Black Power philosophy, saw the Westminster model as a hindrance to both political and economic development for all the people. But this is denied equally vehemently by the great majority of West Indians, to whom the Westminister model is critical and absolutely central to West Indian political culture. Before analysing the why and wherefore of this phenomenon, what is understood by the Westminster model?

THE WESTMINSTER MODEL

Given its citation in the literature and by political and bureaucratic elites generally, it is surprising that no definition exists and that there exists no agreement as to its extent. Constitutions, especially when dealing with division of powers, have to be as legally precise as practicality permits. However, this is not a predominant feature of the Westminster model.

The broad basis of the model is a system of parliamentary government held responsible to the people through the electoral system of the simple 'first past the post' type. The model appears to incorporate five assumptions, each less clear than the other. First is a cabinet, ensuring a strong executive but one also responsible to parliament. Second is the organisation and articulation of interest through competing parties; more particularly through two parties in an adversarial legislative framework, critical to the working of which is the concept and practice of loyal opposition. Third is a non-partisan and corruption-free bureaucracy and military. Fourth are freedoms of expression, press and assembly, backed up by the concept of the rule of law. This we can take to mean a situation where law ultimately reflects and depends on the society's shared values; normatively controls the forms of both economic and political action; guarantees a fair trial for those accused, free from political consideration; and ensures all citizens are subject to the law and are made aware of their duties and rights, including rights to redress. The rule of law also implicitly demands the privacy of constitutionalism and an independent judiciary over the power, especially discretionary power, assumed or exercised by the government of the day.[2] Bound up with this is the fifth assumption, the notion of equality, at least of opportunity. While capitalism and the capitalist ethos is on the whole accepted with varying degrees of reservation, wide variants in income and landed property are not conducive to the model's ideal working. In short, the whole rests upon vague and *ad hoc* but firmly liberal bourgeois presumptions and assumptions: no wonder it is an easy target for authoritarians, whether of the left, right or of the bureaucratic-military variant. It is a target for another reason: it assumes a political elite, a class, sharing conventions of political behaviour.[3] A former Colonial Secretary of State, Oliver Lyttleton, all but admitted this in expressing his conviction that 'no political institutions can be founded without a political class, and no political class can be established without political institutions in which to practice the arts of democratic government.'[4]

Reflecting its vagueness is mystery as to its emergence. It might be argued that the *Durham Report* of 1839 was the first manifestation of sorts, propounding as it did a division of responsibility between the Imperial and domestic governments through a process of constitutional assimilation within a bare statutory framework. Self-government was not enough: it had to be *responsible* and the absence of responsibility meant demagogy. 'The colonial demagogue', Lord Durham thundered, 'bids out for popularity without the fear of future exposure. Hopelessly excluded from power, he expresses the wildest opinions, and appeals to the most mischievous passions of the people, without any apprehension of having his sincerity or prudence thereafter tested by being placed in a position to carry his views into effect'. Compounding this was the British practice of directing Governors 'by instructions, sometimes very precise, as to the course of which he is to pursue in every important particular of his administration', so that it became inevitably his policy 'to endeavour to throw responsibility, as much as possible, on the Home Government'. The irresponsibility of the demagogue was therefore joined by that of the Governor and 'the real vigour of the Executive has been essentially impaired'. Once responsible government is established, all have to live with their actions. 'If the colonists make bad laws and select improper persons to conduct their affairs,' he advised, 'they will generally be the only, always the greatest sufferers and like the people of other countries, they must bear the ills which they bring upon themselves until they choose to apply the remedy.'[5]

However, the grant of responsible government was to be restricted to territories with a sizeable British settlement, where it went as 'accompanied baggage'.[6] For the tropical colonies, administration was what was required until London was forced to give consideration to the 'export' of the Westminster model. To Lord Lloyd, Governor of Egypt (1925 to 1929),

> good administration is the Egyptians only desire and concern – and it is because we have allowed administration to be obscured by political issues that we have brought such heavy troubles on the shoulders of all concerned. In these contries the real problem has been administrative and we have chosen to regard it as political.[7]

The clash between 'administration' and 'politics' was but one colonial dilemma. Another was *what* was to be eventually exported. Reference to the 'British model' began to appear in the 1920s, for instance in the 1928 Donoughmore Report on the constitution of Ceylon, but interestingly there was no attempt to impose it on the Grade A Mandated Territories in the Middle East, Egypt and Iraq, when they assumed independence in 1935.[8] The first mention of the 'Westminister model' appears to have been at the Commonwealth Parliamentary Conference in 1947 (the first so named), where there was a strong emphasis upon the party system as the only path to eventual responsibility.[9] That prompted the encouragement of political parties by the Colonial Office often, as in Africa, on a narrow tribal or a pro-settler/merchant class basis. Although that did little for the development of national unity, a difficulty later met by the post-independence assertion of one-party regimes, these creations helped to serve another purpose, that of neutralising as far as possible emergent homespun nationalist movements and an uncontrollable political elite. Colonial Office officials had to be even more imaginative and create institutions denied to the home of the model, such as public service commissions, Bills of Rights and the like; and the requirement in some areas, such as Ceylon and Malaya, to make allowance for the very un-Westminster problems of communal and minority representation. As to *how* the model would be exported was an even more difficult problem. The creation of a bureaucracy answerable only to the Governor created considerable difficulties of adjustment when ministerial forms were introduced. The notion of compartmentalism, namely the separation of bureaucratic decisions from local political considerations, flew in the face of political reality. The fond belief that public decision-making could proceed on a merely incremental process by a depoliticised public service was dashed against the rocks of increasingly popular nationalist feeling. It is no wonder that the 'preparatory process' was so late in formulation and even later in implementation, in some cases in Africa only one to three years before independence, particularly if forms of indirect rule were involved.[10]

All this, and more, is familiar ground to the student of African decolonisation and its aftermath. Autochthonous constitutions, in whole or part, were rare, in accordance with the idea that development must actually be the more or less satisfactory working out of exported Westminster models[11] which, after independence, became less and less apparent. But the same cannot be said for the West Indies. The model and its underlying assumptions was demanded in its entirety, no matter the incoherence. Not only that, but local political institutions as they developed, trade unions for instance, were amended to suit. There was no need to encourage political parties; on the contrary, they proliferated. After independence, deviations from the basic institutional assumptions of the model are clear exceptions from the rule and a focus for widespread adverse comment, deep suspicion and political discontent. The example of Guyana, a parody of socialism, let alone parliamentary democracy and human rights, comes immediately to mind. The reason for 'this enthusiasm for parliamentary democracy is simply historical.

THE WEST INDIAN HISTORICAL EXPERIENCE

All societies are products of their past and nowhere else in the Third World is this more apparent than in the West Indies. Virtually all its peoples are descendants of those displaced from their original homelands either by slavery, as in the case of the Africans, or indentured labour, as with the Indians (locally called East Indians), and who experienced in some cases over three hundred years of colonial rule. Indigenous cultures, especially those from Africa, were all but lost in the brutal transplantation process: not surprisingly, the language and societal institutions are that of the former master. The result is a deeply ingrained psychological dependency, whereby political, social and legal assumptions derived from the European – and latterly North American – experience have been adopted virtually without question.

To this must be added a structural dependency of unparallel proportions. Export agriculture based upon the sugar trade was the original *raison d'être* of the West Indian colonies, the maximisation of which necessitated considerable food imports. Trade in the scale practised meant extraordinarily open economies where metropolitan market interests were, and remain, of central importance. Even Jamaica, arguably the most developed economy in the contemporary Common-wealth Caribbean, relies on trade for some 40 per cent of its GDP.[12] Trade did not bind the West Indian colonies only to Britain; on the contrary, while their agricultural exports mainly crossed the Atlantic, much of their foodstuffs and other imports originated from Canada and the United States. Exports to the latter increased dramatically with the harnessing of Trinidad's oil riches for the war effort from 1940–1. North American trade was later augmented by bauxite in Jamaica and the then British Guiana, the development of which was entirely by US and Canadian capital. The warships-for-bases deal struck between Britain and the USA in 1940 permitted the construction of US air force bases on several territories from the Bahamas to British Guiana, and firmly established the US strategic interest in the West Indies. The Americans were welcomed for not only were their political values derived from the European and their social manners informal and more in tune with those of the West Indian but, more importantly, they held the promise of economic recovery. The British had neglected their oldest colonies once sugar ceased to be king and even Lloyd George took time off in 1917 from considering the slaughter in Flanders to label them as 'the slums of Empire'.[13] The largely US-dominated tourist trade developed after World War II, exploiting the ex-USAF bases as airline gateways, thus reinforcing US involvement. Economic hopes became consumerist demands by the demonstration effect of the trade, and of the US military before it, and were subsequently fed by migration to Britain, Canada and the USA, as well as to oil-rich Trinidad and the US Virgin Islands. The American capitalist ethos was embraced and foreign capitalist penetration found few opponents except when its operations trespassed beyond the broad consensus of what was politically acceptable. Geo-politics had effectively joined history. But however much West Indians thought of themselves as *of* the First World, they found they were not *in* it.

The persistence of psychological dependency is understandable in such circumstances. To Major C. F. L. Wood, it was a clear asset to be exploited. As Under-Secretary of State for the Colonies, he had been despatched to the area in response to demands for constitutional advancement by the growing middle-class, largely mulatto-centred Representational Associations. Clearly struck by the attachment of West Indians to the Crown, 'the feature of our tour . . . which I recall with the greatest satisfaction', he reported to the Westminster Parliament that although they were African in descent, they were British in language, customs and traditions and wanted to participate in the political institutions that they had been taught to admire.

> The whole history of the African population of the West Indies inevitably drives them towards representational institutions fashioned after the British model. Transplanted by the slave trade or other circumstances to foreign soil, losing in the process their social system, language and traditions and, with the exception of some relics of obeah, whatever religion they may have had, they owe everything that they have now, and all that they are, to the British race that first enslaved them, and subsequently to its honour restored to them their freedom. Small wonder if they look for political growth to the only course and pattern that they know, and aspire to share in what has been the particularly British gift of representational institutions.

But specifically he went on to introduce the racial element so important to the British official classes in their administration of the colonial empire.

> Further, it must be borne in mind that in the West Indies there is a considerable population of mixed stock who while coloured in appearance, possess a large infusion of European blood. Those of mixed race throw up not a few individuals of somewhat exceptional capacity and intelligence. . . . We shall be wise if . . . we take steps to build upon the foundation of the remarkable loyalty to the Throne by which these people are inspired, and avoid the mistake of endeavouring to withhold a concession ultimately inevitable until it has been robbed by delay of most of its usefulness and of its grace.[14]

Despite favourable comments, there was in his judgement insufficient of the mulatto middle class, their pigmentation the result of degrees of miscegenation in the search for higher social status, to provide what he termed 'a class of leisured citizens' able to participate in active political life with 'that detachment of outlook necessary for the effective conduct of services controlled by Government'. Therefore, steps towards representational government were to be limited; those towards responsible government not to be trodden at all.

Wood's meetings were almost entirely with the middle stratum who had supplanted the feudalistic and reactionary planter class during the years from the emancipation of the slaves in 1834. which saw a gradual decline in sugar prices. The West Indian possessions were from 1865 one by one stripped of their white planter governments by Britain and Crown Colony status instituted. The old 'Representative System' had become an anachronism, exclusively for large property owners who argued that they represented all those on their estates. The largely unwritten constitutional conventions rendered successive Governors powerless if the Assemblies disagreed, as they invariably did with reform and expenditure proposals, but the Assembly could do nothing without his agreement. By the mid-1860s total apathy towards political matters and a supreme indifference pervaded the West Indian atmosphere. The climax came in Jamaica with the Morant Bay rebellion in 1865. It was savagely repressed and hundreds of blacks killed. A shocked British Parliament could move only one way to neutralise the violent passions, the bitter animosities and the complete absence of toleration that the bloody rebellion and its aftermath represented. Only Barbados and the Bahamas escaped, their respective Assemblies surviving because they were willing to permit reform to accommodate the growing middle classes and their interests.

Although Crown Colony rule firmly established the British administrative credo, there was limited scope for political participation by the middle classes especially after Wood's recommendations were accepted, although major passions seemed to have been centred upon the social invitation lists of successive Governors. There was, however, no scope for the black masses. Wood had assumed that their loyalty to the Crown and to British institutions was as that of their social and economic superiors. He was broadly right, but London and the local bourgeousie was shaken at the extent of working-class discontent with the atrocious conditions and wages which exploded in a series of strikes and demonstrations between 1935 and 1939 in the majority of the territories. But although mass politicisation was established through violence and strife, it was to fit readily into the imperial groove. The British government despatched a Commission of Inquiry under Lord Moyne to the area to investigate the disturbances; central to the subsequent Moyne Report was the recommendation that trade unions be legalised.[15]

Organised on the British pattern, they spawned political parties as the suffrage was gradually extended. They appealed readily to the peasantry who had become established where land was available, such as on former estates, to the growing urban black working class which had abandoned ill-paid estate work and to the remaining estate workers. The unions and their parties firmly regarded themselves as democratic socialists, but their ideology was better described as 'labourism' or the improvement of labour within existing society.[16] No socialist reorganisation was envisaged: rather, strategies such as state capitalism and 'industrialisation by invitation' were promoted. The enemy was the remnants of the plantocracy; anti-colonialism was limited to the promotion of self-government rather than independence, to ensure the proper representation of working-class interests as and when necessary.

As important as the eclipse of the plantocracy and the development of a peasantry – where permissible – and a black urban working class was to mass politicisation, was the impact of democratic and liberal social forces from Europe in general and Britain in particular. Trade unionism was joined by the acceptance and expectation of social welfare and public policies geared to the needs of ordinary people. Just as the middle class became socialised heavily into Western European liberal political values, so eventually did the working classes. Also the long drawn-out process of decolonisation prolonged the period of British political impact just when these liberal forces came to their zenith. Furthermore, this long process

> provided long periods of grappling for power through competitive elections in which the European colonizer controlled the police and the armed forces. This limited the opportunity for emergent political leadership to manipulate these groups and to drag them into political power struggles. Further it enabled a political climate for the development of traditions of power competition that was made free from access to, or control over, the means of state violence[17].

As Prime Minister Eric Williams of Trinidad and Tobago told his party faithful in 1980, 'if the Westminster model has helped Trinidad and Tobago in not producing our own barbarities and ministers, then we need not be too perturbed about the non-uprooting of our colonial structure.'[80]

However, given the deep impression that the Westminster model and its operating practices had already made, the long time-scale was not critical. Nevertheless, the varying reasons for the delay are worth reviewing. A major reason, at least for the larger islands, was the diversion of energies throughout the 1950s to the byzantine complexities of the federal experiment: after 11 years of negotiation, the federation of the West Indies emerged in 1958 only to collapse formally in 1962. However, the immediate subsequent accession to independence of Jamaica and Trinidad and Tobago was due as much to the demonstration effect of the independence of what were considered relatively less developed countries in Africa and Asia as the attraction of full international personality as such; likewise with the Barbados in 1965. Guyana had to wait until 1966 while Britain, in association with the USA, consolidated the People's National Congress government of Forbes Burnham against a pro-Soviet opposition. Burnham's victory in 1964 was only made possible by the introduction of proportional representation, a marked deviation from the Westminster norm, in a racially-divided society. For Belize, independence finally came in 1981 after an unprecedented 17 years of internal self-government because of the Guatemalan claim to most of the territory. As for the small islands, the less developed, independence was on the whole reluctantly sought; it was primarily in response to the pressing need to expand the aid base to that available to sovereign states, in order to combat the problem of 'viability' given their size but also to meet relatively high development and consumerist expectations.[19] As Grenada's notorious first Prime Minister, Sir Eric Gairy, announced, 'Independence will support Grenada, the people of Grenada do not have to support independence.'[20]

THE WEST INDIAN RECORD

Although the Westminster model has been thoroughly embraced, its application in the region has inevitably been affected by local political conditions. There were in mid-1987 two one-party governments, in Antigua and Barbuda and in Jamaica respectively. While the former is due to a dividend non-parliamentary opposition, Jamaica's case arose out of the refusal of Michael Manley's People's National Party (PNP) not to contest the December 1983 election, on the public ground that an agreement reached in 1980 between him and Prime Minister Edward Seaga and leader of the ruling Jamaica Labour Party (JLP) that only updated voter lists would be used was not fulfilled by Seaga. Although the JLP's economic record since 1980 was prominent in the July 1986 local government elections, the Jamaican public also expressed anger and disquiet at what the PNP styled as the 'bogus' parliament. The 58 per cent vote for the PNP and the 42 per cent for the JLP, in what was widely regarded as a national referendum, almost exactly reversed the 1980 verdict. There are one-party dominant states, notably Guyana where a small number of opposition seats are allocated by the ruling People's National Congress. But in all the other cases of one-party dominance, in Belize, Barbados, St Kitts-Nevis, St Vincent and Trinidad and Tobago, the ruling party won state power in election victories of landslide proportions, displacing parties which had equally been dominant. Only St Lucia and Dominica have significant opposition representation. In St Lucia's case it was sufficiently strong for Prime Minister John Compton in 1987 to call two elections, one after the other, in order to gain a greater majority to avoid any of his party taking advantage of a 9–8 margin ' to hold me to ransom'. He knew full well that individualism and idiosyncratic behaviour by West Indian politicians are not unusual. Perhaps the power of auto-suggestion worked in Compton's favour, as within days of the 9–8 verdict of the first election being confirmed by the second, a prominent opposition member crossed the floor to be rewarded with the External Affairs portfolio.[21] Such fragility of party loyalty was laid bare more dramatically in Grenada. Dissatisfaction with Prime Minister Herbert Blaize's leadership and the direction of the New National Party, which was contrived and constructed out of several other for the post-US invasion poll in December 1984, led progressively to 6 of its original 14 parliamentary members (out of a 15-seat House of Assembly) to cross the floor to form a disunited opposition.

Virtually all the present Commonwealth Caribbean territories have at least two parties, most more. St Vincent and its 136 000 population have five. Except in Guyana, none are notably identified with ethnic interest. The ruling United Democratic Party of Belize and the once dominant People's National Movement in Trinidad and Tobago, which crashed to defeat in 1986 after thirty years of uninterrupted rule, tend to attract Afro-West Indian voters in their respective multi-ethnic countries, but they have had to be nationally based to be successful. Some parties have broad class connotations, as would be expected, but in most cases this is not politically significant, as witness the right-wing and pro-business JLP's success in attracting the support of substantial numbers of the Jamaican working class.

Several territories have Marxist-Leninist parties, for the most part tiny, most of which contest elections. Two, the Antigua Caribbean Liberation Movement (ACLM) and the Worker's Revolutionary Party of Barbados, stand aloof from the electoral process: the ACLM because it does not wish to run the risk, however small, of having to compromise its principles should it gain state power, the latter out of a refusal to participate in what it regards as a bourgeois charade. In sharp contrast, the October 1986 congress of the Worker's Party of Jamaica decided to modify its vanguard structure and to assume the characteristics of a mass party more in line with Jamaican political reality and West Indian political culture generally.[22] There is but one coalition government, that in St Kitts-Nevis, and that for a highly specific reason, namely to contain the secessionist tendencies of Nevis. To ensure unity, an inter-island alliance was forged in 1980 against the former dominant St Kitts Labour Party. In the smaller, mostly still dependent, territories, Independents are common and sometimes hold the balance of power, as in the British Virgin Islands until 1986. The extreme is the Cayman Islands where no parties exist at all, together with an abject refusal to consider independence.

Apart from Guyana, the 'first past the post' system has never been seriously questioned. Rather, it has been effectively used to centralise power when there exists a splintered opposition. This was acknowledged in the 1974 report of the Constitutional Commission of Trindad and Tobago, established by Williams to consider new changes in, *inter alia*, the voting system. 'In reality,' it argued, 'the Westminster political system has a propensity to become transformed into dictatorship when transplanted into societies without political cultures which support its operative conventions'.[23] It concluded in favour of a limited form of proportional representation alongside existing practices, and so incurred Williams' anger as the inherited electoral system was to his advantage and that of his Peoples National Movement. His riposte, however, was couched in terms of national unity.

> In a period when Trinidad and Tobago is at the mercy of all sorts of unpredictable international influences which require immediate and firm action . . . a Government of Trinidad and Tobago could not hope to survive if it is in the hands of an unstable coalition of proportional representation parties and individuals where a crucial issue might depend upon the placation on the vote of some one or other of them . . .[24]

In short, it is the argument used by successive British governments.

Although the record of political activity through parties and elections is enviable in the Third World context, even more deeply embedded in the West Indies are the legal attributes of the Westminster model. Rule of law principles are broadly respected and public discontent is apparent when they are not, as in Guyana. When they were suspended by the People's Revolutionary Government (PRG) in Grenada, most Grenadians thought this justified as a temporary expediency. But when the withdrawal of *habeas corpus* and the introduction of 'preventive detention', press censorship and an end to free speech became permanent, the issue of human rights not only constituted a grave internal weakness which was readily exploited by the PRG's enemies but also tended to obscure the very real social and economic gains of the revolution. As in Guyana, socialism became equated with authoritairanism. It was indeed ironic that the PRG seized power, in the cause of human rights, from the corrupt rule of Sir Eric Gairy. The courts in the region do effectively challenge the exercise of state power by governments. An example was the rejection by the East Caribbean Court of Appeal on constitutional grounds of public order charges brought by the Antiguan government against the ACLM in 1985. Another was the inadmissibility by many courts of proposed legislation aimed at the press in several islands in the 1970s and 1980s. As any visitor to the West Indies will confirm, the press is libellously free and for the most part highly partisan, and political meetings long, emotional and exciting.

But the courts can do little against the susceptibility of leaderships and elites in the ministates[25] in particular to creative entrepreneurs and assorted carpet-baggers attracted to the region. This arises as much out of an astonishing degree of naivety as greed, although the impact of the drug trade is a factor. Since the end of the Vietnam War in 1975, the Caribbean generally has become a huge transit area, placed as it is between the South American suppliers and North American consumers. It is also encouraged by the widespread establishment of offshore banking facilities through which illicit profits can be processed. Several of the mini-states, including some of the British dependent territories, have joined the Bahamas in encouraging offshore financial centres in response to their extremely limited opportunities for economic development. Size, however, has one advantage in that military forces are of necessity small or virtually non-existent. More to the point, all West Indian military and para-military forces respect political control. On the one occasion that an army assumed power, in Grenada following the massacre of over sixty civilians and the killing of the PRG Prime Minister Maurice Bishop and several of his cabinet supporters on 19 October 1983, the People's Revolutionary Army tried desperately to establish a form of civilian government before being overwhelmed by US forces six days later. Only in Guyana has there been a risk of a takeover as more unusually found in Africa, but that would be dependent upon the four distinct branches of the armed forces working together and so surmounting the deliberate divide and rule policy of the government.

What then are the problems facing the adoption of the Westminster model in the Commonwealth Caribbean? They are highly region-specific: ideological and environmental. The ideological is represented by two sets of authoritarianism: the state socialism of Guyana and the former People's Revolutionary Government in Grenada, both classified by one commentator as 'populist-statist' political regimes.[26] The environmental is the impact of physical and demographic smallness on political systems.

Guyana's variation from the Westminister model, both before independence in May 1966 but more especially afterwards, stemmed from its multi-ethnic society composed of the Afro-Guyanese and the East Indians. Their differences were fanned and exploited by internal and external forces. The first Premier, Cheddi Jagan, headed what was then a national-based People's Progressive Party (PPP), which won the first universal franchise election of 1953. But he was a Marxist leading a distinctly left-wing administration. The shock to the colonial system was immense: within 133 days the constitution was suspended and Colonial Office interim rule established. Jagan's deputy, Forbes Burnham, attempted to become leader. He failed and left to form the People's National Congress (PNC), appealing specifically to the mainly urban Afro minority. When elections were held under a modified constitution in 1957, the PPP again won. The same happened in 1961. There followed a well-documented series of manoeuvres involving the PNC, the US and British governments and the CIA, to create internal unrest and to install proportionate representation.[27] As Afro-Guyanese were more likely to register and vote than the more rural Indians, the PNC won the 1964 elections. This cynical manipulation of the constitution helped lay the foundations for the future authoritarian state where neither rulers nor ruled in Guyana have functioned within a legal framework containing the exercise of state power. A hegemonic class grew and became consolidated through the progressive nationalisation of multinational-owned assets in the sugar and bauxite sectors in particular. By the late 1970s, the state sector comprised 85 per cent of the economy. As if to reinforce the point, the PNC declared itself 'paramount' in 1973, with all state and para-statal bodies and instruments having henceforth to be regarded as extensions of the party. That the process paralleled gross economic mismanagement and corruption is not entirely coincidental.

The Grenada case involved far less economic upheaval but aroused much more controversy. At least elections were held in Guyana, however rigged. The PRG denied them absolutely, arguing that economic reconstruction was more important and that a new socialist constitution would eventually be agreed on which new forms of elections would be based, presumably in the context of a one-party democratic-centralist state. The 89 000 Grenadians looked forward to the restoration of their traditional rights after the abuses of Gairysim. Although village-based institutions of 'popular-democracy' were established, they were ineffective in practice and were under firm vanguard party control; they and progressive and extensive social development were certainly no substitute in the popular mind for lost civil liberties. When the revolution bloodily imploded and an incompetent military government was hastily installed, it is not surprising that Grenadians turned out *en masse* to welcome the US forces as heroes.

The environmental factors are less dramatic but no less problematical. The small size of many West Indian territories, dependent and independent, encourages the development of personalist rule, with the most minor of incidents having the propensity to become political crises of the first order in what are in effect 'goldfish bowl' societies. Factionalism is never far from the surface; political feelings become intense, neutrality is difficult and the powers of governmental or, more particularly, Prime Ministerial, patronage become critical. It cannot be otherwise in small economies where public administration can and does constitute up to 30 per cent of middle-class employment and 20 per cent of total employment, leaving aside the labour forces of nationalised and para-statal bodies such as utilities and marketing boards. Whereas in established West Indian tradition unions are linked to political parties, the potential for strife is clear. Not that this is unique to mini-states, as the many examples of politicised industrial disputes in Jamaica and Trinidad bear ample witness.

POLITICAL AND ECONOMIC DEVELOPMENT

The Westminister model's application in the Commonwealth Caribbean has undoubtedly contributed to the general political stability which the region enjoys. Indeed, instability appears to occur in inverse proportion to variations to the model, as suggested in Guyana, Grenada and Jamaica at various times. This is not surprising as West Indians know no other system and, for the time being at least, will permit no alternative. But there are problems of nation-building. The casual observer might focus upon the divisiveness of the party system, which is at its most extreme in Jamaica. There, inter-party violence is fanned by party-financed armed gangs and partially sustained by illicit funds from the 'ganja barons", those who buy and sell locally grown marijuana. The gangs are for the most part drawn from and operate in the worst slum areas of the West Indies, in West Kingston. Here, political partisanship is at its most expressive and the lumpen proletariat are the main victims. Over a thousand deaths in the last true general election, that of 1980, is no advertisement for the Westminster model.

Although it is at the extreme, the Jamaican party experience shows that, in reality, the problem is not the party system as such. It is rather unemployment and relative deprivation in a country – and region – with very wide income ranges. State power means patronage, nepotism, favours and jobs. Ideology is less important than these basic bread-and-butter issues in what are Third World economies. To this must be added the phenomenon of personalist leadership, generally but by no means exclusively associated with size.

As for economic development, although political partisanship can distort planning, the problem of size – population, land, resources – is far more important a factor. The smaller territories of the Eastern Caribbean depend virtually exclusively upon the protectionist Lomé Convention for the export of their agricultural products to Europe. The production cost of their bananas, for example, is substantially higher than that of those produced in the huge US multinational corporation-owned plantations in Central America and Ecuador.[28] Even the larger ones have few chances of operating economies of scale, particularly as the regional trading organisation, the Caribbean Community (CARICOM), has suffered a decline in opportunity and activity since the mid-1970s. Tourism is for many the answer, but that often serves only to increase further material expectations through the demonstration effect of the far richer visitors and to exacerbate the propensity to import and hence the balance of payments.

CONCLUSION

The problems of political and economic development in the Commonwealth Caribbean do not derive from the Westminster model but from size, expectations, dependency and history. Whether the working of

Westminster model can, or will, alleviate these largely structural
difficulties through giving the region a degree of stability and predic-
tability on a larger scale than that found in other Third World areas is
open to debate. It probably will as its mores are so deeply embedded in
the popular psyche. Even Guyana moved towards a recognition of
traditional constitutional norms once Forbes Burnham died in 1985.
The question must therefore be: where to now? The Westminster model
cannot be static and, given the constantly strengthening political
influence of the United States on the West Indies, will we see changes in
structures and operations of government, perhaps later confirmed
constitutionally, as new sets of imported values come to challenge the
old? Will it then be the case of the West Indies influencing Britain's
constitutional forms and behaviour? If so, it will be the ultimate case of
the Empire striking back.

Notes

1. It was popularly acclaimed and involved little bloodshed: see Tony
   Thorndike, *Grenada: politics, economics and society* London: Frances
   Pinter, 1985) p. 55.
2. This is partially derived from A. V. Dicey's formulation of 1885 as
   discussed in P. Harris, *The sociology of law: an introduction* (London:
   Butterworth, 1984) pp. 168–71.
3. J. M. Lee, *Colonial development and good government* (Oxford: Clarendon
   Press, 1967) p. 196.
4. Lord Chandos, *Memoirs* (London: Macmillan, 1962) p. 389.
5. Lord Durham, *Report on the state of Canada*, 1839, quoted in H. E.
   Egerton, *A short history of British colonial policy*, 6th edn (London:
   Methuen, 1920) p. 259.
6. Lee, *op. cit.*, p. 1.
7. Lord Lloyd, *Egypt since Cromer* (2 vols, London: Macmillan, 1933) vol. 2
   pp. 4–5.
8. Royal Institute of International Affairs, *The colonial problem* (Oxford
   University Press, 1937) pp. 249–55.
9. Commonwealth Parliamentary Association, *Report of the 1947 conference* (London: CPA, 1948) p. 106.
10. B. B. Schaffer, 'The concept of preparation: some questions about the
    transfer of systems of government', *World Politics*, XVIII (1965) 1, 42–67.
11. Kenneth Robinson, 'Autochthomy and the transfer of power' in K.
    Robinson and F. Madden (eds) *Essays in imperial government* (Oxford:
    Basil Blackwell, 1963) pp. 251–3.
12. *Economic and social survey Jamaica 1985* (Kingston: Planning Institute of
    Jamaica, 1986) p. 13.
13. Eric Williams, *From Columbus to Castro: a history of the Caribbean,
    1492–1969* (London: André Deutsch, 1970) p. 473.

58   *Representational Democracy in the South*

14.   *Report of the Hon E. F. L. Wood, M.P., on his visit to the West Indies and British Guiana*, 1922 (London: HMSO, Cmnd. 1679/1922). Extracts reproduced in Ann Spackman, *Constitutional development of the West Indies 1922–1968: a selection from the major documents* (Barbados: Caribbean Universities Press, 1975) pp. 76, 77.
15.   *West India Royal Commission Report, June 1945* (London: HMSO, Cmnd. 6607/1945), pp. 198–206.
16.   P. Henry, 'Decolonization and the Authoritarian Context of Democracy in Antigua', in P. Henry and C. Stone (eds) *The newer Caribbean* (Philadelphia: Institute for the Study of Human Issues, 1983) p. 297.
17.   C. Stone, *Power in the Caribbean basin* (Philadelphia: Institute for the Study of Human Issues, 1986) p. 21.
18.   Dr Eric Williams, *Forged from the line of liberty: selected speeches of Dr Eric Williams*, compiled by Paul Sutton (Trinidad: Longman Caribbean, 1981) p. 425.
19.   Tony Thorndike, 'The political economy of independence of the former associated states of the Commonwealth Caribbean', in P. Sutton (ed.) *Dual legacies of the contemporary Caribbean: continuing aspects of British and French domination* (London: Frank Cass, 1986) p. 166.
20.   *Trinidad Guardian*, 1 November 1972.
21.   *Caribbean Contact*, June 1987.
22.   Dr Trevor Munroe, *Has the Workers Party of Jamaica (WPJ) a future in the national politics of Jamaica?* (Kingston: University of the West Indies Symposium on Electoral Reform, mimeo., 1 November 1986).
23.   Trinidad and Tobago, *Report of the Constitution commission* (22 January 1974) para. 27.
24.   Dr Eric Williams, 'Proportional representation in Trinidad and Tobago: the case against', *The Round Table*, 250 (April 1973) p. 245.
25.   Ministates (or 'microstates') are generally defined as states with less than 100 000 population. Although population is the preferred criterion, physical size is also important. All the independent Commonwealth Caribbean states with under 100 000 population are under 750 square kilometres in size. For a discussion of ministate criteria, see Elmer Plischke, *Microstates in world affairs* (Washington DC: American Enterprise Institute for Public Policy Research, 1977) pp. i–iii.
26.   Stone, *op. cit.*, p. 37.
27.   Colin Henfrey, 'Foreign influence in Guyana: the struggle for independence", in E. de Kadt (ed.) *Patterns of foreign influence in the Caribbean* (Oxford University Press, 1972) pp. 71–9.
28.   World Bank, *The Commonwealth Caribbean: the integration experience* (Baltimore: Johns Hopkins University Press, 1977) pp. 142–3.

Appendix

1. *General elections in independent Commonwealth Caribbean states. Those involving changes of government are shown in italic.*

	Independence	*Elections*
Antigua & Barbuda	1981	1984
Bahamas	1973	1977
		1982
Barbados	1965	1966
		1971
		1976
		1981
		1986
Belize	1981	*1984*
Dominica	1979	*1980*
		1985
Grenada	1974	1976
		1984[a]
Guyana	1966	1968
		1973
		1980
		1986
Jamaica	1962	1967
		1972
		1976
		1980
		1983[b]
St Kitts-Nevis	1983	1984
St Lucia	1979	*1979*
		1982
		1987
		1987
St Vincent	1979	1979
		1984
Trinidad & Tobago	1962	1966
		1971
		1976
		1981
		1986

[a] No constitutional government had existed since March 1979.
[b] Not contested by opposition parties.

2. *General elections in Associated States, 1967–83. Those involving changes of government are shown in italic.*

	Elections
Antigua & Barbuda	*1971*
	1976
	1980
Dominica	1970
	1975
Grenada	*1967*
	1972
St Kitts-Nevis-Anguilla[c]	1971
	1975
	1980
St Lucia	1969
	1974
St Vincent	1967
	1972
	1974

[c] Anguilla was *de facto* separated from the three-island administrative union upon secession in 1969 and *de jure* separated in 1980 by Act of the British Parliament.

General elections in dependent territories are not included.

4 Instability and the State: Sudan

Charles Gurdon

Since Sudan became independent on 1 January 1956 it has experienced two civil wars. The only period in which there has been peace was between March 1972 and mid-1983. It therefore seems obvious that there must be factors which make the country inherently unstable. This chapter seeks to determine what these factors are and why they have had such a strong influence on Sudan's post-independence history.

The central theme of the chapter is that, although the area within its borders has been a single state since 1916, no government has succeeded in creating a Sudanese nation. Before outlining the creation of the Sudanese state it is necessary to define what is meant by 'state' and 'nation' in this chapter. A state refers to a political community which lives within defined territorial borders and which is administered by a central government. The Sudanese state lies within its defined borders and is ruled by the central government in Khartoum. A nation is a group of people who share the same cultural and racial heritage and usually, although not always, live in one area under a single government. In some cases, such as in the USA, a nation can be created when disparate groups come to believe that the unitary concept of the state is more important than their original heritage. Unfortunately as we shall see this has not occurred in Sudan and while a Sudanese state has been created a Sudanese nation has not.

THE CREATION OF THE SUDANESE STATE

When Sudan became independent it had only been a single unitary state for forty years, the independent sultanate of Darfur having been brought into the Anglo-Egyptian Condominium of Sudan in 1916.[1] Areas that had little or no common history were united in a single state. However, there had been a number of pre-colonial states which had, at different times, ruled various regions in northern Sudan. The riverain areas had been ruled by a succession of kingdoms and empires since the eleventh century BC, while there had had also been other states in central

61

and western Sudan. A brief outline of Sudan's pre-independence history is necessary to understand some reasons for the country's current instability.

The first major civilisation in the area now occupied by the state of Sudan was the Kushite kingdom, which was established along the River Nile near modern-day Karima during the eleventh century BC. Its character was very Egyptianised, largely because of the earlier Egyptian occupation of the region. The Kushites were eventually strong enough to conquer the whole of Egypt and the 25th Dynasty, which was founded in 725 BC, was ruled by the Kushite kings. Although they were forced out of Egypt in 656 BC they ruled the Kushite kingdom for a further thousand years until 350 AD. Their capital, which had been moved to nearby Merowe in 591 BC, was a major trading town which was well known by Greek and Roman writers.[2] The relationship between Sudan's northern region and Egypt is very old and their history has been interwoven for over 3000 years.

There was then a long and confusing period when there were a number of minor kingdoms in northern Sudan. Three of them converted to Christianity in the sixth century but, following the southwards spread of Islam, the last Christian kingdom eventually fell to Muslim Nubian tribes in 1504 AD.[3] This was followed by the large-scale immigration of Muslim Arab teachers, merchants and tribes into the area which is north of modern-day Khartoum. They mixed with the indigenous tribes through marriage and gradually spread Islam throughout the region.

Soon after they captured the last Christian capital at Soba in 1504 AD the Nubians were themselves defeated by the very powerful Funj sultanate.[4] From its capital at Sennar the Funj soon came to dominate the whole of riverain Sudan, north of the equatorial swamps, for the next three centuries. The Funj, who were definitely African and were originally non-Muslims, are believed to have originated from somewhere south-west of the Shilluk heartland in Upper Nile Region of Southern Sudan.[5]

As various ethnic and political groups were conquered they were incorporated into a confederation of semi-autonomous states which were ruled by the Funj. The sultanate was divided into at least six provinces whose people were classified by the Funj according to the hue of their skin as well as other physical characteristics. Calliaud reported that the most important group were known as 'El-Soudan-Azraq (or the Blues) – their colour is copper, they are the Funj'.[6] Each of the provinces were ruled over by a 'manjil' or king whose wives always came from the Funj royal clan.[7] By establishing and enforcing the very rigid relationship with vassel states, which was similar in many ways to the feudal system in medieval Europe, the Funj sultanate was able to rule an area larger than France.

At its height in the early eighteenth century the Funj capital at Sennar was a large, prosperous and very cosmopolitan city. The sultanate was also a major trading power with ships arriving at the port of Suakin from as far afield as south-east Asia.[8] Part of the sultan's power was derived from his control of both international and domestic trade.

The decline of the sultanate during the eighteenth century can be broadly attributed to the erosion of traditional Funj institutions and values under the combined pressure of Islam and commerce.[9] Although its rulers had first converted to Islam in the sixteenth century and Arabic had become more widespread, the Funj court retained much of its traditional characteristics and language. It was challenged by a new pious Muslim merchant class whose increasing economic power was based on the slave trade. The sultanate was forced to make numerous concessions to the merchants which sapped its own strength and which eventually led to a series of revolts. Consequently the Funj sultanate had largely disintegrated and was in no condition to resist the 1820 Turco-Egyptian invasion.[10]

The other major sultanate which the Egyptians encountered was the Keira Dynasty which had controlled most of Darfur, as well as parts of Kordofan, since the mid-seventeenth century. Although little is known about their predecessors this was the third dynasty in succession to rule the Fur people. The non-arab sultanate was gradually converted to Islam in the same way that had occurred in the Funj sultanate. Although it was more loosely structured than the latter, it employed a similar system of political and economic control. Its principal source of revenue was its control of the long distance trade caravan routes in general and of the famous *darb al-arba'in* (or 'Forty Days Road') to Egypt in particular.[11]

Like the Funj sultanate, the fall of the Darfur sultanate was precipitated by the growing strength of the Muslim merchants and slave raiders. In order to circumvent the Turco-Egyptian administration in riverain Sudan, which was trying to abolish slavery after 1877, the slave raiders moved westwards, thereby encroaching on Darfur territory.[12] In 1874 the sultanate was eventually overthrown by the private army of Al-Zubayr Rahma, who had created a vast slave-trading empire in southern Kordofan and Bahr El-Ghazel. Despite this the Fur continued to resist external control and after a series of revolts were only finally brought under the central government control in 1916.[13]

Turco-Egyptian forces invaded Sudan in 1820 in order to defeat the independent power of the renegade Mamelukes and to obtain exotic goods such as gold and ivory.[14] A more important aim, however, was to obtain slaves for the Egyptian army and agricultural estates. During the 1820s the Egyptian army lived off the land, imposed heavy taxes and conducted widespread slave raids along the White Nile. In 1822–3 alone an estimated 30 000 slaves were captured in southern Sudan.[15] Although Egyptian rule became less harsh after its initial conquest of Sudan, slavery continued.

The slave raiders first acted as middle men for the Turco-Egyptian administration and then established independent operations to capture slaves. The majority were from the Muslim merchant class in northern Sudan or they were other Arabs or renegade Europeans. As the areas closest to the White Nile were depopulated, the slave raiders moved into the more remote areas of southern Sudan. In most cases this was the first contact that these regions had with the northern Sudanese Muslim culture. Despite the efforts after 1877 to abolish slavery it was not completely eliminated until the 1920s and even today southerners are often nicknamed *abid* or slave.[16] It is therefore not surprising that suspicion, later fuelled by the missionaries, affected the attitude of the southern Sudanese to the northerners.

After its initial slave-raids the Turco-Egyptian administration was primarily involved in supressing first revolts in Darfur and Bahr El Ghazel and then slavery after 1877. This eventually led to the emergence in 1881 of the religious leader Mohamed Ahmed who presented himself as the Expected Mahdi.[17] He acted as a focus for Muslim Sudanese opposition to the Turco-Egyptian administration and its Christian administrators including General Gordon. After a series of victories his forces eventually captured Khartoum in January 1885.[18]

Although the Mahdi died of typhoid, in the same year his successor, the Khalifa Abdullahi, sought to expand the Mahdiyyah. While it succeeded in achieving control of most of northern Sudan and parts of modern-day Ethiopia, it also suffered 'from a continuing revolt in' Darfur as well as a series of devastating harvests, epidemics and famines.[19]

In 1898 the British army, under General Kitchener, eventually defeated the Mahdist forces at the Battle of Omdurman. The Anglo-Egyptian Condominium which replaced the Mahdiyyah ruled Sudan from 1899 until it achieved independence in 1956. While the Agreement recognised Egyptian rights in Sudan it reserved almost complete autonomy to the British governor-generals and their administrators. Initially they sought to pacify hostile tribes and to secure their authority within the borders which had been carved out at the Treaty of Berlin. In 1916 the independent sultanate of Darfur was invaded and then incorporated into Sudan after the sultan Ali Dinar, influenced by the pan-Islamic propoganda of the Turks and the Sanussi, had inadvisedly declared war on the British.[20] Therefore, although there continued to be revolts as late as 1928, the Sudanese state, as opposed to nation, was really created in 1916.

When considering the inherent instability of that state, a number of factors about the Anglo-Egyptian Condominium must be considered. These include the paucity of the education system that it installed in the South, its policy of separate development for southern Sudan and the concentration of economic development in the northern heartland around the Gezira.[21]

Each of the major missionary societies was allocated a specific area in the South where they largely retained responsibility for education. Unfortunately after 58 years of British rule the South entered independence having only five graduates, one secondary school, five junior administrative officers and no doctors, engineers, agriculturalists or technicians.[22]

In general the British sought to create a separate and distinctive administration in the South. In December 1917 the last garrison of northern soldiers left the region and the following year Sunday rather than Friday was made the day of rest.[23] Senior British officers also proposed that the South should be separated from the North and should be linked to British controlled territories in East Africa. The governors of the three southern provinces held annual meetings to coordinate policy in the South, but were excused from attending the annual meetings of provincial governors in Khartoum. The 1922 Closed Districts Order and the 1925 Permits to Trade Order effectively closed the South to most northern Sudanese.[24]

In January 1930 an official but confidential memorandum defined government policy in southern Sudan as being to: 'build up a series of self-contained racial or tribal units with structure and organisation based, to whatever extent the requirements of equity and good government permit, upon indigenous customs, traditional usage and beliefs'.[25]

Between 1930 and 1946 very stringent measures were taken to end all Arab influence in the South. These included the repatriation of northern merchants and officials, the banning of Arab clothes, the discouragement of mixed marriages, and the suppression of Arab names and the Arabic language.[26]

The Sudanese nationalist movement, which was largely influenced by the Egyptian nationalists, became increasingly vocal after the end of World War II. In 1946 the government therefore decided to reverse the separatist policy and became committed to integrating the South into a unitary state.[27] Despite the economic, educational and other disparities between the South and the rest of the country, less than a decade later Sudan achieved full independence. Given the Condominium government's schizophrenic southern policy it is little wonder that independent Sudan immediately experienced such profound problems and instability. While the British may have created a Sudanese state, their policies irrevocably hindered the chances of creating a Sudanese nation.

THE PROBLEMS OF MAINTAINING THE NATIONAL UNITY

Having examined the way in which the Sudanese state was created, we now turn to an analysis of some of the problems of maintaining its stability and unity. These can broadly be divided into five groups of factors – the geographical, demographic, historical, economic and political obstacles to national unity. Although they may seem relatively insignificant when considered in isolation, in combination they make Sudan more difficult to unite than any other country in the region. Furthermore they have frustrated all attempts to foster the spirit of national unity which is a precondition to the formation of a Sudanese nation.

Geographical Factors

One of the principal factors which makes it so difficult to foster Sudanese national unity is the geography of the country.[28] Sudan is the largest country in Africa and the ninth largest in the world, covering almost one million square miles. As such it is larger than all the countries of the European Community put together, or as large as the part of the USA which is east of the Mississippi River.

Besides being so large Sudan is both geographically very diverse and climatically very harsh. Although there are a few isolated large towns such as El Obeid, El Fasher and Nyala in western Sudan, it is only really the riverain areas that can sustain large sedentary populations in the desert and semi-desert of northern Sudan. Consequently, vast areas are inhabited only by nomadic tribes who have largely remained outside the control of central government.

In the more fertile southern Sudan it is the surfeit of water which has made communications and therefore national unity so difficult to foster.

The vast Sudd swamp, which covers an area of 4800 sq kms in the dry season and which takes it name from the Arabic for barrier, has indeed made links between northern and southern Sudan difficult to sustain.[29] Ewart Grogan, the first man to walk from Cairo to the Cape, described the physical hardships of the Sudd with only slight exaggeration. He wrote: 'For God-foresaken, dry-sucked, fly-blown wilderness, commend me to the upper Nile, a desolation of desolations, an infernal region, a howling waste of weeds, mosquitoes, flies and fever. I have passed through it and now have no fear of the hereafter.'[30]

Besides it size and harsh environment, the paucity of Sudan's infrastructure is another major geographical obstacle to its national unity. It has a single port on the Red Sea and goods can often take months to reach the southern and western peripheral regions of the country from Port Sudan.[31] Given that the Kenyan port of Mombassa is much closer than Port Sudan, it is not surprising that much of southern Sudan's trade is directed south rather than north. At the same time the dilapidated roads and railways, particularly in the South and West, make transport and communications very difficult. Many districts are cut off from central government control during the long rainy season and have very few if any links with the Sudanese government.

Demographic Factors

In large part Sudan's demographic complexity lies at the root of the country's instability. The issue is usually over-simplified so that it is seen in terms of an Arab Muslim North and an African Christian South. The reality is much more complex and divisive and Sudan is probably the most heterogeneous country in Africa, if not the world. It has a total population of about 22 million people from an estimated 597 different tribes who speak 115 distinct languages.[32]

Islam is the unifying element in northern Sudan and Arabic is spoken by the majority of the population. There are, however, major non-Arab groups in the region. The largest and most important of these are the Nuba in southern Kordofan, the Fur in Darfur and the Beja in the Red Sea Hills. It is estimated that there could also be as many as two million Sudanese of west African descent, generations of whom have settled in the country before reaching their pilgrimage destination of Mecca.[33] The demographic pattern is further clouded because of centuries of mixed marriages between different tribes so that no northern Sudanese is a pure Arab.

The South is broadly divided between the Nilotic, Nilo-Hamitic and Sudanic tribes. The former, which include the major Dinka, Nuer and

Shilluk tribes, mainly live in the Bahr El Ghazel and Upper Nile regions. The numerous but less populous Nilo-Hamotic and Sudanic tribes are mainly from Equatoria province in the far south of the country.[34] Tribal rivalries, which are principally focused on the Equatorian's fear of Dinka domination, have plagued southern politics for years.

The assumption that the Southern Region is predominantly Christian is incorrect.[35] Only about 15 per cent of southerners, or 4 per cent of Sudan's total population, are Christian.[36] As already noted, however, until independence the missionary societies were largely responsible for education in the southern provinces. Consequently the majority of educated southerners, who include most of their political leaders, are Christian. The vast majority of southerners have, however, retained their animist religions, although increasing numbers have become Muslims since independence.

Besides its very diverse ethnic, linguistic and religious makeup, Sudan's population is also very mobile with 15–20 per cent of the total being on the move at one time of the year or another.[37] Besides the approximate two million true nomads who are mainly in Darfur and Kordofan, there are also the Nilotic cattle owning tribes which practise transhumance, the half million season workers who migrate between the large-scale agricultural schemes, and the refugees.[38] Although the numbers vary from month to month, there are probably currently about 1.2 million refugees from Ethiopia, Chad and Uganda.[39] Naturally the mobility of such a large proportion of the population make the central government's tsk of creating a sense of a single Sudanese nation much more difficult to achieve.

Post-Independence Political Factors

We have already seen how the modern-day Sudanese state was only really created at the beginning of the twentieth century. While the country may officially have been a single unit since 1916, however, we also saw how the administration of the Southern Region was separated from the rest of the Sudan until as late as 1946. At independence, only a decade later, the relationship between the northern and southern Sudanese was still based on racism and mutual suspicion. The northern Muslims generally despised the less developed animist negroid southerners. The latter, who still had very vivid memories of slavery, were deeply suspicious of Arab domination. They resented the fact that the Sudanisation of the civil service, during the transitional period before independence, led to the replacement of the British administrators by northerners rather than southerners.[40] Therefore when these and other factors are taken into consideration it is not surprising that post-independence Sudan has remained such a very fragile state.

Sudan's post-independence politics have been dominated by the political parties of the two principal Islamic tariqahs or brotherhoods.[41] The Umma Party is the political arm of the Ansar tariqa which is led by the descendents of the Mahdi. His great-grandson, Sadiq El-Mahdi, has been the Prime Minister both in the mid-1960s and now in the late 1980s. The Mirghani family have been the traditional leaders of the Khatimiyya tariqa and its own political party. This began as the National Unionist Party (NUP) but, after a series of splits and coalitions, became the Democratic Unionist Party, (DUP). Unionist in this case refers to the NUP's original aim of unifying Sudan and Egypt, although the idea of actual political union has now been dropped. By contrast the Umma Party has traditionally been more nationalistic and has had strained relations with Egypt.[42]

Between 1956 and 1969 there were seven coalition governments, as well as a six-year military regime.[43] They were generally characterised by inter-party rivalry and instability in which the pursuit of power appeared more important than what was achieved once in power. At the same time a minor mutiny in the South was allowed to escalate into the bloody and tragic first civil war which lasted until 1972 and which, directly and indirectly, is believed to have been responsible for the death of over 500 000 people.

The only brief period when there was a degree of national unity was after the broad-based and popular October Revolution in 1964 when the Abboud military regime was overthrown. A Round Table Conference began to resolve the crisis in southern Sudan but the re-election of the two traditional parties put an end to peace efforts for a further seven years.[44]

Eventually the first civil war was ended in 1972 when the Addis Ababa Agreement gave the three southern provinces a large measure of regional autonomy in the newly created Southern Region.[45] Under the agreement a regional government and parliament has authority over all aspects of life in Southern Sudan except for national defence, external affairs, currency and coinage, foreign trade and national planning. In the euphoria after the peace settlement, the agreement was seen as a model for other unstable heterogeneous African countries. The heart of Sudan's foreign policy became the role that it carved out for itself as a bridgehead between the Middle East and Africa.[46] Furthermore, it seemed that the Sudanese were beginning to identify themselves much more with the concept of Sudan as a nation rather than as a collection of disparate tribes within the boundaries of an artifically created state.

During the mid-1970s it seemed as if Sudan was entering a phase of relative stability when it could concentrate on its considerable economic potential. Despite its many faults the Nimeiri regime was generally seen as a stabilising influence on the country. Unfortunately this was largely thrown away as President Nimeiri became increasingly autocratic and despotic, particularly after the two coup attempts in 1975 and 1976.[47]

In 1977 the official policy of National Reconciliation led to the return of leading northern opposition politicians including the Muslim Brotherhood. This, in turn, led to the increasing role of Islam in Sudanese politics which alarmed both southerners and other non-Muslims. Under the 1973 Permanent Constitution, Islamic Law and Custom is the main source of legislation, but under Article 9, the concerns of non-Muslims are governed by their personal laws. Article 16 safeguards complete freedom of religion for all, with equal protection for all monotheistic religions.[48]

Despite this, a form of Islamic sharia law was introduced in September 1983, which led its Muslim critics to call them the 'September Laws'. During post-independence Sudan's darkest hour there was a five-month State of Emergency betwen May and September 1984. During this period specially established 'courts of decisive justice' handed out draconian punishments to Muslims and non-Muslims alike. These included public floggings,[56] amputation of limbs and a number of executions.[49]

This was the final straw for the southerners and many joined the nascent Sudanese Peoples' Liberation Army (SPLA). The euphoria of the Addis Ababa Agreement had long since evaporated and there had been increasing mismanagement, corruption and inter-tribal rivalries in the new regional government. The smaller Equatorian tribes urged President Nimeiri to redivide the South into its three original provinces in order to end the perceived Dinka domination of the region. Despite accusations from the Dinkas and others that this would weaken the South in its relationships with Khartoum, the redivision was authorised in May 1983.[50]

At the same time there was increasing southern opposition to Khartoum's perceived theft of southern natural resources. The giant Jonglei Canal project, which was designed to reduce the water loss in the Sudd swamp and thereby transport more water to northern Sudan and to Egypt, was also opposed because of the environmental damage that it was expected to cause.[51] Meanwhile the proposed project to export crude oil from the newly discovered southern oil fields via a pipeline to Port Sudan was criticised by southern politicians as another example of the theft of southern natural resources.[52]

All these issues, as well as other factors, eventually led to a revolt by troops in three southern garrisons in January 1983. Together with other southerners from the army, police, prison and game warden services, the SPLA was formed under the leadership of Colonel John Garang. This small guerrilla army, which did not initially represent a threat to the government, received a major fillip as a result of the introduction of Islamic sharia law in September 1983.[53] From these very small beginnings the SPLA has become a large guerrilla army which has now plunged Sudan into a second major civil war. This threatens the political stability of the whole country and remains the most intractable problem facing the new civilian government.

Economic Factors

If all these political factors were not destabilising enough, the disparities in regional economic development have also been a destabilising influence. Both during the Anglo-Egyptian Condominium and after independence economic development projects were concentrated in the heartland of the country rather than in the peripheral provinces in western and southern Sudan. The vast Gezira cotton scheme, which was started by the British in the 1920s so that the Lancashire mills had a stable supply of cotton, has acted as a magnet for both people and projects.[54] Later the claylands around Gederef in the east became the focus of the new mechanised farming areas.[55] By contrast the vast regions to the west of the White Nile and to the south of the Gezira have undergone comparatively very little development. The result has been that the heartland of the country has become an island of relative prosperity in a sea of absolute poverty.[56]

In many ways this concentration of development projects in the heartland is logical. Population density is greatest in this area and its infrastructure is comparatively well developed. By contrast southern and western Sudan are vast sparsely populated regions where the logistical problems of developing any project are a nightmare. It is therefore obvious that investors will concentrate their efforts in the heartland where there is also the largest domestic market. The problem is that this has simply exacerbated the regional inequalities which have naturally led to increasing resentment in the peripheral regions. If these economic factors were not enough the political instability of the two civil

wars have also seriously reduced the prospects for any real economic
development in the Southern Region.

The disparities in regional economic development have been one of
the most destabilising factors behind the conflict in southern Sudan. In
1970 Joseph Garang, a leading Communist who was also the Minister
for Southern Affairs in the new Nimeiri regime, continued to emphasise
this fact. In a meeting at the British House of Commons he said that 'the
cause of the southern Problem is the inequality which exists between
North and South by reason of an uneven economic, social and cultural
development'.[57]

Fifteen years later the leader of the SPLA, Colonel John Garang (no
relation), is also emphasising the regional economic disparities as one of
the reasons for his rebellion. In order to try and win over other non-Arab
groups in the SPLA's fight against the so-called 'Khartoum clique' it has
also highlighted the lack of economic development in central and
western Sudan.[58]

As we have seen, the accusation that Khartoum was 'stealing'
Southern natural resources is also central to the SPLA's philosophy.
While the government should have been much more sensitive to
southern feelings and should have established a precise mechanism for
the region to benefit from the development of the oil-fields, the
establishment of a major oil refinery in Southern Sudan would have been
totally impractical. The demand for oil products in the region is minimal
and the financial and logistical problems of constructing a 100 000
barrel/day refinery in such an isolated region remain insuperable. It
would have been far more beneficial for the South to have received a
proportion of the royalties, possibly in a trust fund such as the Alberta
Heritage Fund (HEF), which could then be used for the economic and
social development of the region. The HEF is a very cash rich trust fund
which sets aside and invests a proportion of the oil royalties received by
the Alberta provincial government for the long-term benefit of province's population. Instead the resumption of the civil war has led to the
cancellation of the project and, although much will depend on both
peace and world oil prices, it is unlikely that oil will be extracted from
southern Sudan before the turn of the century.

The SPLA's actions have also postponed the completion of the
Jonglei Canal project. While it is true that northern Sudan and Egypt
would be the principal beneficiaries of the project, this does not mean
that the South would not have benefitted. Ancillary economic and social
development projects in the canal zone were planned and this would
have brought much-needed investment to the area.[59] Once again the
combination of central government insensitivity and southern suspicion

hindered a project which could and should have been beneficial to the whole country.

From this it can be seen that there are economic factors which have exacerbated the instability of the country. While they should not be over-emphasised, neither should they be ignored. All developing countries must face the problem of disparities in regional economic development. In the case of Sudan, however, demographic, logistical and political factors have made the economic development of the peripheral regions even more difficult. This, in turn, has been a major contributory factor in the inherent instability of the Sudanese state. Furthermore it has reduced the prospects of any government being able to foster the spirit of national unity which is necessary to create a Sudanese nation.

The Current Situation

Sudan is probably less stable than at any time since independence. President Nimeiri was overthrown in April 1985 in a broad-based revolution which was very similar to the 1964 October Revolution.[60] He was replaced by a one-year Transitional Military Council (TMC), which governed the country together with a civilian non-political cabinet until elections could be held in April 1986. Unfortunately, as in 1965, the civil war prevented the elections from taking place in most of southern Sudan. This led to the formation of a grand coalition government, under the leadership of Prime Minister Sadiq El-Mahdi, between the Umma Party and Democratic Unionist Party which between them won 162 of the 264 seats which were contested.[61]

By its very nature the coalition government has proved fragile and it collapsed twice between the April 1986 elections and August 1987. The instability of the country centres on three problems; the continuing civil war, the role of Islam in such a heterogeneous country, and the crippling debt crisis. At the time of writing the war shows no sign of ending and the government and SPLA seem further than ever from a political settlement. Besides the use of much more sophisticated and deadly weapons there is another major difference between the first civil war and the current conflict. Instead of the rebels demanding the secession of the South, the SPLA are seeking the overthrow of the government and an end to the perceived domination of the country by the Muslim Arab 'Khartoum clique' who are blamed for all of Sudan's ills.[62] Instead there is increasing, although unofficial, support in northern Sudan for the separation of the south from the rest of the country.

One of the SPLA's principal preconditions for a political settlement to the conflict is the complete abolition of Islamic sharia law and a return to a secular constitution and legal system. The problem for the government, however, is that the National Islamic Front (NIF) opposition party is very strong and well organised and will not countenance such a move. Furthermore Sadiq el Mahdi's position is complicated by his role as both Prime Minister and leader of the Ansar religious movement. Because of the fear of losing support amongst his traditional followers to the NIF, he cannot afford to be seen as the man who weakened the role of Islam in Sudan. Given the considerable support that the NIF enjoys within the army, any dilution of Islamic sharia law could not politically very dangerous for the government.

If these political problems were not enough, Sudan is bankrupt and has external debts of over $10 000 million which it has no hope of repaying. It will have to reach an agreement with its major creditors to reschedule its debt repayments. Such an agreement, however, is dependent upon the introduction of an major austerity programme which would include further currency devaluations, tax increases and the removal of food price subsidies. If such a programme were introduced there is every possibility that there could be riots, as in January 1982 and April 1985, which might eventually lead to the overthrow of the government. Its room for manoeuvre is therefore very limited and the political and economic stability of the country is consequently very fragile.

THE UNIQUE PROBLEMS OF CREATING A SUDANESE NATION

There are distinct differences between a state and a nation. While a Sudanese state has been created it has proved impossible for any government to engender a sufficient degree of national unity to create a Sudanese nation. While many of the reasons for this are common amongst other large heterogeneous developing countries, the case of Sudan is almost unique. It certainly does not fit easily into the same pattern as the other countries in the Middle East or Africa.

In most countries in the Middle East, although not in Francophone North Africa, the concept of nationalism arose because of unifying influence of the Arab culture and/or of Islam. The Nasserists and Baathist doctrines of pan-Arabism and socialism were very influential in some countries. At the same time, although there are important non-Muslim minorities in the Middle East, the unifying influence of Islam in the Arab world was also significant in the creation of nation states.

In Sub-Saharan Africa the nation state has generally developed in a different way. The African states, as opposed to nations, were largely the creation of the European colonial powers. Although there had been indigenous tribal city states, the twentieth century state as we know it today was really an alien concept which the European colonial powers super-imposed on designated regions with little regard to their heterogeneous nature. As Gellner observed, 'Black Africa has inherited from the colonial period a set of frontiers drawn up in total disregard (and generally without the slightest knowledge) of local culture or ethnic borders.'[63]

Despite this, attempts to adjust inter-state boundaries or to replace an alien European colonial language as the official language of government have largely been unsuccessful. There are a number of principle reasons for this, the most important of which is that once the legality of one border is brought into question no African frontier will be secure. Fear of the Balkanisation or break-up of such fragile nation states, with the inherent loss of power and influence, has therefore forced post-independence African governments to accept the sanctity of the continent's borders. Therefore the principle of *uti possidetis*, which provides that successor states accept international boundaries set by a predecessor regime, has been an important concept for the Organisation of African Unity (OAU). Together with the priority of colonial populations to self-determination over all other rights, including historical ones, the sanctity of the inherited frontiers was enshrined in the Article 3 (3) of the OAU's Charter and its 1964 Cairo Declaration.[64]

African nationalism was essentially a product of the struggle against colonialism, whether this was in Algeria, Ghana, Kenya, Zimbabwe, Angola, Mozambique or other countries. Although they usually surfaced after independence, the tribal rivalries in these hetero-geneous countries were temporarily set aside in the cause of freedom. In some countries this struggle fostered a nationalist spirit which has been strong enough to survive since independence, while in other countries it dissolved into fractious tribal battles. Regardless of this, however, in almost all African countries the post-independence government which replaced the colonial administration was also African.

In most of the OAU countries the language of the colonial rulers, whether it is French, English or Portuguese, was retained after independence. The maintenance of a European language which is a second language to the whole population ensures that one indigenous language, and therefore ethnic linguistic group, is not perceived as dominant. In addition such a '*lingua franca*' is often essential for communications in countries with numerous tribal languages.

In many ways the creation of the Sudanese nation state is much more difficult to catagorise and explain because of its multi-layered nature. In the pre-Islamic era this vast area was inhabited by a collection of independent ethnic groups and city-states which had few formal links with each other. The spread of Islam and the Arabic language began to unite large areas of northern Sudan, although it was not until the formation of the Mahdiyya in the 1880s that a large unified Islamic state was created.

Like most African countries, the borders of modern-day Sudan were largely the result of the European carve-up of the continent in the 1885 Treaty of Berlin. Therefore, when the Mahdiyya was overthrown in 1898, the Anglo-Egyptian Condominium largely inherited the modern frontiers. Once it had put down various revolts it was powerful enough to create a single Sudanese state and government. Despite this, however, heterogeneous Sudan remained a complex patchwork of ethnic, tribal, linguistic and religious groups. Therefore, although a state had been superimposed on a traditional Afro-Arab society, this was not a Sudanese nation.

In the 1920s a nationalist movement, which was modelled on that in Egypt, developed in northern Sudan. It was the students and urban intelligensia who were at the forefront of the nationalist movement. Despite this, however, it was the two major traditional Muslim religious brotherhoods and their respective political parties who inherited political power after independence.

Although tribalism remains a major problem in other Sub-Saharan African countries, their governments and the rest of the population are at least fellow Africans. By contrast in Sudan's important non-Muslim regions the European colonial administration was replaced at independence by the equally alien authority of the northern Sudanese Muslim-Arab government.

The Sudanese state is therefore composed of four or five elements. These were the original patchwork of tribes, the spread of Islam in the north, the European administration which was super-imposed on this base, the twentieth century secular Arab-influenced nationalist movement, and finally the dominance of the two largest Muslim religious brotherhoods in post-independence Sudan.

There is probably no other country in the Middle East or Africa which is more heterogeneous than Sudan and in which the obstacles to the creation of a nation state are more difficult. Consequently it must be asked whether the current state is the most suitable form of government for Sudan. Given the country's tragic post-independence history this has to be doubted. Whether there is a more viable solution, however, is open to debate.

THE OPTION OF A FEDERAL STRUCTURE

The question which has to be asked is what are the prospects for the country and are there any possible solutions to its instability. In the short term its prospects are very gloomy and the likelihood of a military coup within the next few years, if not sooner, cannot be ignored. Unless Sudan's major problems can be resolved it is likely that central government control will continue to disintegrate. The peripheral regions, where central authority has always been weak, are likely to become even more alienated. Unless there are solutions to these problems it is likely that, while the government will continue to function in Khartoum, it will be a national government in name only.

In the long run there might be a solution to Sudan's instability through the formation of a federal structured administration. In March 1979 ex-President Nimeiri asked the Central Committee of the ruling Sudanese Socialist Union (SSU), to consider a proposal to divide Sudan into four semi-autonomous regions.[65] Besides the existing Southern Region the rest of the country would be divided between Western, Eastern and Central or Northern Regions. Each would have a legislative council or parliament which would have similar powers to those of the defunct Southern Regional Assembly. The central government would retain responsibility for overall national and international issues, such as defence, foreign affairs, international trade and strategic planning.

A similar, if not necessarily identical, federal structure would give the peripheral regions increased powers and would reduce their perceptions of Khartoum's neglect of their economic development. There are, however, a number of obstacles which would have to be overcome before such a federal structure could be created. There is a danger that initially all it would do is create an expensive additional tier of government. The question of how the regional governments would be funded also remains problematic since the majority of the government's domestic revenue is raised through excise duties rather than income tax.

These are only two of the more important questions which would have to be answered before a federal structure could be created. Until then such a solution to Sudan's instability will have to remain on the drawing board. The need for such a solution is, however, essential because Sudan is currently sliding into longterm political and economic chaos. If Sudan is to survive as a single state it is vital that its inherent instability is arrested and that a more successful and equitable system of government is established.

Notes

1. R. S. O'Fahey and J. L. Spaulding, *Kingdoms of the Sudan* (London: Methuen, 1974) p. 186.
2. Sudanow, *Sudan yearbook* (Khartoum, 1983) p. 7.
3. ibid., p. 8.
4. J. Bruce, *Travels to discover the Source of the Nile in the Years 1768–1773* (Edinburgh: Gregg International, 1971) pp. 369–71.
5. O'Fahey, *op. cit.*, p. 24. Southern Sudan refers to the three provinces of Bahr El Ghazel, Equatoria and Upper Nile which became an autonomous region in 1972.
6. F. Cailliaud, *Voyage à Meroe, au Fleuvre Blanc* (Paris. 4 vols, 1823) p. 273.
7. O'Fahey, *op. cit.*, pp. 48–9.
8. J. Castro, *Roteiros* (Lisbon, 1939) pp. 80–4.
9. O'Fahey, *op. cit.*, p. 78.
10. ibid., pp. 184–6.
11. G. W. Browne, *Travels in Egypt, Syria and Africa* (London, 1799) pp. 180–215.
12. Sudanow, *op. cit.*, p. 8.
13. O'Fahey, *op. cit.*, p. 180.
14. Sudanow, *op. cit.*, p. 8.
15. Ministry of Foreign Affairs, *Peace and unity in Sudan: an African achievement* (Khartoum, 1973) p. 18.
16. C. G. Gurdon, *The geographical problems of national unity in Sudan* (unpublished M.Sc thesis, SOAS, University of London, 1981) pp. 39–41.
17. Sudanow, *op. cit.*, p. 9.
18. ibid., p. 9.
19. ibid., p. 9.
20. O'Fahey, *op. cit.*, p. 186.
21. Gezira (from the Arabic for island) is the area between the Blue and White Niles which extends south from Khartoum to a line between Sennar and Kosti.
22. J. Garang, 'An historical perspective', in *Horn of Africa* (Summit, New Jersey) vol. 8, no. 1, pp. 21–31.
23. M. O. Beshir, *The Southern Sudan: background to the conflict* (Khartoum University Press, 1968) p. 39.
24. ibid., p. 41.
25. ibid., pp. 115–18.
26. ibid., pp. 48–60.

27. ibid., pp. 61–9.
28. Sudan Ministry of Information and Culture, *Sudan Today* (University Press of Africa, Tavistock, p. 7. 1971)
29. Gurdon, *op. cit.*, p. 4.
30. Sudan Ministry of Culture and Information, *op. cit.*, p. 1.
31. The 'peripheral regions' refer to the three provinces in the Southern Region as well as Darfur and Kordofan in western Sudan.
32. Sudanow, *op. cit.*, p. 12.
33. Economist Intelligence Unit, *Country Report: Sudan* (London, 1987) no. 1, p. 11.
34. C. G. Gurdon, *Sudan at the crossroads* (Wisbech, Menas Press, 1984) p. 7.
35. The autonomous Southern Region was created in March 1972 as part of the Addis Ababa Agreement which ended the first civil war.
36. Gurdon, 1984, *op. cit.*, pp. 9–10.
37. ibid., p. 9.
38. ibid., p. 9.
39. Economist Intelligence Unit, *Country Report: Sudan* (London, 1987), no. 3, p. 16.
40. Beshir, *op. cit.*, pp. 70–9.
41. Sudanow, *op. cit.*, pp. 23–9.
42. Gurdon, 1984, *op. cit.*, p. 13–19.
43. T. Niblock, *Power and Class in Sudan* (London: Macmillan, 1987) pp. 204–32.
44. Beshir, *op. cit.*, pp. 88–97.
45. H. Assefa, *Mediation of civil wars: approaches and strategies – the Sudan conflict* (Boulder, Colo.; Westview Press, 1987).
46. Ministry of Foreign Affairs, *op. cit.*
47. Gurdon, 1984, *op. cit.*, pp. 23–59.
48. Sudanow, *op. cit.*, p. 23.
49. Economist Intelligence Unit, *Country Profile: Sudan 1986/87* (London, 1987) pp. 7–8.
50. ibid., pp. 5–7.
51. National Council for the Development of the Jonglei Canal Area, *Jonglei Canal: a development project in the Sudan* (Khartoum, 1980).
52. Gurdon, 1984, *op. cit.*, pp. 76–86.
53. ibid., pp. 87–110.
54. Niblock, *op. cit.*, pp. 13–19.
55. Sudanow, *op. cit.*, pp. 163–4.
56. The 'Heartland' of Sudan refers to the area around Khartoum, the Gezira and the major agricultural schemes where the majority of the population live and where the economic development has been focused.
57. Garang, *op. cit.*
58. Sudanese People's Liberation Movement Stated Position of the Rebels, in Horn of Africa, *op. cit.*, pp. 39–46.
59. National Council for the Development of the Jonglei Canal Area, *op. cit.*
60. R. Greenfield, 'Two months that shook Sudan', in *Horn of Africa, op. cit.*, pp. 5–21.
61. Economist Intelligence Unit, *Country Profile: Sudan 1986/87* (London, 1987) pp. 8–11.

62.   Sudanese People's Liberation Movement, 'Stated position of the rebels', in *Horn of Africa, op. cit.*, pp. 39–46.
63.   E. Gellner, *Nations and Nationalism* (Oxford: Basil Blackwell, 1983) p. 81.
64.   OAU Assembly AHG/Res 17 (1), Cairo Ordinary Session, 17–21 July 1964. Also see I. Brownlie, *African boundaries: a legal and diplomatic encyclopaedia* (London, Hurst, 1979) p. 11.
65.   B. Malwal, *People and power in Sudan: the struggle for national identity* (London: Ithaca Press, 1981) pp. 187–92.

5 The Mutal Formation and Information of the State and the International Order: The Case of Japan

Richard Boyd

It is legitimate to question the inclusion of Japan in a study of the state and instability in the Third World and, equally, it is instructive to consider the reasons why.

But first, a comment upon 'stability' since, by Third World standards, Japan is exceptionally stable. Its territorial integrity has withstood infrequent challenge for more than a thousand years. Prior to the end of the Pacific War and the arrival of General MacArthur and the US armed forces, occupation was unknown. The unitary state structure has an uninterrupted history of more than three hundred years and an interrupted history which is substantially longer.[1] The renewal and modernisation of these structures after 1868,[2] created an institutional framework for the conduct of politics and the pursuit of modernisation at home and parity with the Western powers abroad. The framework was at once flexible – the evolution of political forms led to the characterisation of the post 1918 regime as Taisho Democracy[3] – and resilient, due to its close fit with social and cultural practice.

Defeat in World War II, while leading to a further development of these institutions,[4] sharpened an already keen sense of the possibility of institutional remaking, which is itself a critical contribution to the long-run stability of the Japanese state and, perhaps, the single most important legacy of the Occupation period.

Moreover, it underlined in blood and ashes the lesson learnt in 1868, to wit that domestic stability was inextricably bound up with questions of international relations. Policies for post-war reconstruction (1950s), high growth (1960s) and post 'oil shock' structural adjustment (1973–) were legitimated by reference to earlier and current experience of Japan as an element in, dependent upon and constituted by the international system. For the Japanese state, policy is a single thing which has two aspects: one internal (*naimu*, loosely, 'domestic') and one external

81

(*gaimu* or 'foreign'). The relationship between these two aspects is complex and characterised by a high degree of mutual information; even so, one is tempted to say that they are not equally weighted and that, *grosso modo*, the external aspect is determinant.[5]

The immediate post-war period was, inevitably, a period of adjustment. The particularities of the external aspect of policy were governed by the relationship with the USA. However, the new political edifice, designed by SCAP (Supreme Command of the Allied Powers), had yet to settle on its domestic foundation. When it did – a point conveniently marked by the formation of the ruling Liberal Democratic Party (LDP) in 1955 – the almost exaggerated informality of much of organisational life in Japan (exaggerated by Western standards that is), meant that the gap between normative and pragmatic rules, between constitutional prescription and practical interpretation, was often wide.[6]

This has meant that although constitutional description is sometimes misleading, constitutional practice is congruent with social and cultural practice – something which is an important source of the stability of the post-war political order.

The political stability of Japan extends to each of the fundamental levels of political organisation, state, regime and government. The suzerainty of the state is beyond question. There is no serious challenge to the liberal democratic regime from either the Left or the Right. The residual transformational instincts of the Japan Socialist Party and the Japan Communist Party,[7] are attenuated by the fear that constitutional change would lead to a return to the pre-war militarist regime. Government has been the exclusive preserve of the Liberal Democratic Party since its inception. So ingrained is the habit of electoral victory that any result limited to an absolute majority is regarded as a catastrophic failure and is likely to lead to an apology and even the resignation of the LDP president and ex officio Prime Minister.[8]

There remains the problem of including Japan in a group of 'Third World' states. This is, of course, a notoriously broad and catholic church but even so, it is perhaps stretching things to include Japan, a country which has only known the colonial experience when it was itself a colonial power, in the first half of the twentieth century, moved by imperial ambitions and directly reflecting the model of the Western imperialist powers (Japan's political structures are borrowed from and bear comparison with those of the West. Moreover, she enjoys levels of economic well-being and has reached levels of literacy, scientific and technological achievement which are equalled only in the West.[9]

On the other hand, Japan is inextricably part of an Asiatic cultural whole and like any Islamic, Indian or Chinese culture experienced the threat of Western encroachment and of a forcible opening, and so faced the challenge of orchestrating a cogent and politically coherent response to the impact of the West. The terms in which the challenge was presented and even the resources and constraints which shaped the Japanese response stand comparison with, for example, the Chinese and the Korean (ROK) cases.

This and, above all, the fact that Japan surmounted the challenge to become the first non-white, non Judaeo-Christian society to complete the arduous journey to full industrialisation has given the Japanese case a particular relevance for the Third World within which it is even seen as a model to be emulated – such is the sense, for example of the Look East movement in Malaysia.

In short, although Japan fits readily into the category of advanced industrial nations and its stability is beyond question, its relevance as a model is conceded throughout the Third World. If we move from consideration of the general relevance of Japan to the particular theme of the present book, the case is stronger still. The recent history of Japan is an eloquent illustration of the dilemma faced by the Third World power which confronts simultaneously the two-way pull of state building and the threat and promise of participation in the international system. As has been noted, the imbrication of the foreign and the domestic persists to the present day in that country in an equally real, if less acute, form.

However, a note of caution is in order with respect to both the procedure and the interest of such an inquiry. First, there is the matter of time scale. Japan faced the challenge of state-building in an international order predicated upon the state one hundred years earlier than the 'new nations' which emerged at the end of the colonial period. Accordingly, whereas it is appropriate to consider state-building and stability in the new nations from the perspective of the post-war period, it is inappropriate so to consider Japan. There the critical period extends from the middle of the nineteenth century to the outbreak of World War I.

Moreover, whereas our understanding of the post-war political order and stability might well highlight the debstabilising effect of domestic fragility upon the international order (and, conversely, of the domestically destabilising effects of the international system), the Japanese case affords us a stark reminder that strong states which emerge in response to the challenge of the international order can subsequently threaten and finally overturn that order with disastrous human consequences.

THE ARGUMENT

It is a commonplace that the formation of the modern Japanese nation-state was triggered by the impact of the Western imperialist powers in the mid to late nineteenth century. Earlier Japan had benefited from an almost perfect absence of readily marketable raw materials, manufactures, markets, strategic significance and other desirables which, at that time, made a country prey to Western incursion. She was a small and unattractive prize and so was left free to pursue a policy of isolation, albeit relative, from the rest of the world. The arrival of Perry's warships in 1853 signalled the end of this freedom. A sense of the Western threat combined with an acute sense of the humiliation of China, defined the objectives of an indigenous elite, renewed rather than replaced in 1868, which were to construct a state apparatus on the model of, and able to contend on equal terms with, the modern Western nation states.[10]

Not only did Japan contrive to do this (albeit at enormous human cost), but, it is believed, she did so without any substantial erosion of those indigenous traditions which make Japan Japanese and more remarkably still, in some ways those native values lent themselves to the task of development to such an extent that it is possible to speak of a 'fit' between traditional Japan and what once was termed the 'requirements' of modernisation. The principal concern of this chapter will be to examine these views in the light of the establishment of the native religion, Shinto, as a foundation of the modern state.

In particular, it will argued that, in this instance, tradition appears much less as a given, an ineluctable force bearing down upon the present, and rather more as a resource to be managed, to be worked, even to be reconstructed and deployed. Indeed, it is more accurate to think in terms of the invention of the modern Japanese polity and within that process of invention, of the management and manipulation, by a political elite, of a set of beliefs, attitudes and behaviours which have come to be known as 'tradition'.[11]

The argument is of interest in itself. However, it will further be noted[12] that the foundations upon which the State was established, and the basis upon which domestic stability was secured, were to have great significance, not only for domestic stability, but also for the extent and terms of subsequent involvement of Japan in international politics, as well as for the way she construed her security in an international context.

The Meiji Restoration

The collapse of the *ancien réime*, the Tokugawa polity, was triggered by its patent inability to resist foreign encroachment. It was overthrown in a series of events known as the Meiji Restoration – which has been termed a conservative revolution from above. The major participants in the crucial period from 1853 to 1873 were confined to the elite, court and samurai strata – other classes were largely bystanders.

However, this was no mere palace coup. The Restoration widened the elite stratum and resulted in the abolition of feudalism and the expansion of education, economic opportunities and social mobility – the essential preconditions for the modernisation process that was to follow the consolidation of the Restoration leadership in 1881. It is that process of consolidation and above all its ideological aspects which is of immediate concern.

The Problem of Legitimacy

The Meiji elite was persuaded that Japan had to modernise militarily, politically and economically in order to withstand the West. This meant that the han or fief system would be dismantled. When this went the material supports of feudal loyalties, that is to say, the material foundation of that system of values and beliefs which sustained and glued together the feudal would collapse and would have to be renewed or replaced if the political order was to be preserved.

Inevitably, the creation of a new national army and the transfer from the domains to the central government, of the obligation to pay *samurai* (warrior) stipends, first weakened and finally ruptured the link between the *samurai* and the *daimyo* (feudal lord).

In the short term, then, the Meiji elite was constrained to find a new title to rule, and not only that but to guarantee its acceptance, in the first instance among the circle of erstwhile members of the feudal classes.

The Solution: Imperial Legitimacy

The solution was to make the Emperor the idological centre of the new state, to locate sovereignty in his person and later to make him the cornerstone of the first constitution of 1889. To understand the choice and its significance, we need to consider the traditional terms and symbols of legitimation as a repertoire upon which a cohesive and self-conscious elite can draw, instrumentally, for its own contemporary, political purposes.

A remarkable characteristic of the Tokugawa polity was the relation-ship between the Shogun (military chief) and the Emperor[13] – the power and influence of the latter was almost negligible. The Emperor and his court were relegated to the city of Kyoto, placed under restrictions imposed by the shogunate, policed by shogunal ministers and subject to the scrutiny of shogunal spies.

The power of the Shogun was seemingly absolute: he disposed of the feudal lords, decided the closing of the country to foreign travel, conducted negotiations with foreign powers, minted and taxed without so much as a nod in the direction of Kyoto. It might then reasonably be assumed that the independence of the one and the dependence of the other was also absolute. It was not. Indeed, the fact of the matter was that the Shogun subordinated himself to the Emperor. As John Whitney Hall noted twenty years ago, 'such submission was no less real, even though the emperor was powerless and the act of submission was voluntary.'[14]

Powerful as the Shogun might be, that final composure of power[15] signalled by the achievement of legitimacy eluded him. The title of Shogun carried with it no powers – and yet justified the exercise of any and every power the Shogun could personally command. The imperial monopoly of legitimacy was complete and particular. There was never any prospect of its transfer, and so, regardless of whether or not the Shogun had received a specific delegation of powers from the Emperor (and in 1603 the Emperor had no real powers to delegate), the Shogun was constrained to act, as if such a delegation had occurred.

A fact of central importance is that the imperial line has been unbroken since the seventh century. The continuity of the imperial institution, the continuity of the dynasty, is neither invention nor legend. It is an undeniable and remarkable fact of Japanese political life.[16] The particularity of the legitimacy which accrues to the Emperor upon his accession depends upon the relationship between the 'lineage-deity' (*uji-gami*) and the 'lineage-head' (*uji-no-kami*). Each successive head of the lineage (i.e. the Emperor) renews the tie between the sun-goddess Amaterasu (the lineage deity) and himself through ceremonies perfor-med in the presence of the earthly body of the sun goddess. The presence of the latter is secured by use of the sacred mirror of the sun-goddess.

Once the bond is established, the Emperor takes on the power of the deity and becomes a living god – a possibility that is available only to the head of lineage however powerless, and inaccessible to generals and Shoguns however powerful because succession is genealogical. Like 'divine right', legitimacy is finally the private concern of the sun goddess and the Emperor; unlike 'divine right', the Emperor is not sovereign by the grace of god. Once the bond is made and the sacred necklace which symbolises the identity of emperor and Amaterasu has been accepted, he is a god, a manifest god in whom sovereignty is vested as of his own right.

The legitimacy of the imperial institution was a key resource in the state-building exercise. No less an advantage was the powerlessness of the Emperor at the end of the Tokugawa period, since it meant he was not held responsible in any way for the failings of the *ancien régime*. So it seemed that feudal loyalties might readily be refocused upon him. At the same time, of course, that same powerlessness meant that it was little more than a convenient fiction to speak of the Restoration to the emperor of powers usurped by the Tokugawa Shogunate.

The Problem of Projecting the Imperial Presence beyond the Feudal Classes

The Imperial Sanction was a necessary, if insufficient, condition for securing the legitimacy of the new government within the confines of the old feudal classes, perhaps 450 000 or so of them. However, it was recognised from the first that the establishment of a modern nation-state would require popular involvement on an unprecedented scale.

The problem here was that Tokugawa society knew no generalised and pervasive loyalty. Loyalty was the preserve of the aristocracy; framed by aristocrats for other aristocrats – clearly this was an important resource which might be mobilised and refocused, however it did not touch those commoners who were soon to constitute the masses. Indeed, 'Commoner society was excluded from the network of feudal loyalties – for the commoner the closest counterpart was an ethic of obedience, of blind submission to law and order – an ethic in no sense compatible with the new national task.'[17]

The problem of hearts and minds was real and exacerbated by the question of constitutionalism. This was in part an imperative of real politik. Unequal treaties had been imposed upon Japan by the Powers – before these might be revised, Japan had to demonstrate that she had become a citizen, a fitting member of the international community. The marks of citizenship were many and varied and to be divined by Japan. As one of the Meiji oligarchs put it,

in order to attain an equal footing with the Powers, it was necessary to change the national institutions, learning and education. Hence the replacement of clans by prefectures took place as well as coinage reform, enforcement of the conscription law, revisions of various other laws and promulgation of new ones, establishment of local assemblies and the granting of local self-government, a step that led at length to the promulgation of the constitution.[18]

But this was not all there was to the question of constitutionalism – anticipating by more than a hundred years the West's obsession with how Japan does it, Japanese leaders, in the last third of the nineteenth century, were anxious to know the West's secret. For the government leaders who toured the West under Prince Iwakura between 1871 and 1873 the West was a cultural complex, the strengths of which were conceded, but within which railroads, guns, bibles and constitutions were interrelated and all but impossible to isolate and weight.

Very serious consideration was given to the possibility that the secret was the harnessing of national energies, by giving the commoners a sense of participation in the life of the state by means of a constitution. Kido Koin of Choshu put the possibility powerfully; much impressed by the fate of Poland, he was moved to argue that 'laws and constitutions which prevent arbitrary action by governments in the pursuit of selfish ends are the only guarantee of national survival'.[19]

So perhaps a constitution was a good thing in itself, and certainly to satisfy the Powers one had to be adopted. However, theories of natural rights were highly problematic in themselves[20] and incompatible with national unity, at a time when this was more important than ever – given the challenge of the West. Notions of popular sovereignty were unfamiliar and unattractive in their implicit challenge to oligarchic rule, and all but incomprehensible in virtue of the *tradition*, which located sovereignty in the person of the Emperor, by virtue of the performance of Shinto rites and the *practice* of a separation of power and authority which stripped the Japanese concept of sovereignty of any notion of 'rule over'.

Popular Ignorance of the Emperor

The existence of a problem was recognised by leading figures in the post-Restoration period: samurai such as Okubo Toshimichi and Kido Koin and court nobles such as Iwakura Tomomi and Sanjo Sanetomi were sensitive from the first, to the fact that 'in Tokugawa times only the shogunate was known to the realm and people were unaware that the imperial house existed. . . . Even now that the realm is at last secured, the imperial will is as yet unknown in the remote and distant parts'.[21]

Accordingly, the Emperor was sent on the first of his 102 imperial excursions to the remote and distant parts of Japan.[22] In much the same way the removal of the capital from Kyoto to Tokyo was used to dramatise the goal of 'conducting all state affairs by imperial decision', and 'to provide the domains and villages along the way with palpable and impressive evidence of the new imperial presence'.[23] It was an enormous and dramatic procession of 3300 princes, nobles and attendants that would require a Kurosawa to do it justice.

But these were no more than temporary expedients – to contain constitutionalism and to generalise the new title to rule rather more was needed. The challenge, as percieved by the Oligarchs, was to extend the code of imperial loyalism to all and to embrace those who had hitherto been untouched by notions of public life or even society. The task was entrusted to the religious and educational apparatus of the Meiji state. Their instrument was to be Shinto.

Shinto on the Eve of the Meiji Restoration

At first sight Shinto might not have seemed a suitable vehicle for the projection and generalisation of a nationwide cult of the emperor: Fukuzawa Yukichi, one of the most influential thinkers of the Meiji era, regarded Shinto as 'derivative, ephemeral and self serving, a puppet of Buddhism'.[24] In fact, before the Meiji Restoration there were very few centres devoted exclusively to Shinto worship. The great majority of shrines were small and poorly staffed. Typically, and with the exception of a few very large and powerful shrines, they were located on the same site as a temple and indeed existed as one component within a single entity which comprised both shrine and temple. Generally, the whole complex was managed by the Buddhist clergy.

They were merged not only geographically but doctrinally and doctrine explicated the dependence of Shinto upon Buddhism. The doctrine in question was known as *honji suijaku*. The doctrine taught that the Shinto deitites or Kami are the protectors and phenomenal manifestation (*suijaku*) of a higher order of Buddhist divinities which are pure, undifferentiated and original form (*honji*). Implicit was the idea that Kami are beings of lower spiritual attainments than the buddhas, second-class gods, perhaps.

Religious practice mirrored doctrine, even in the great Shinto centres such as Ise. Although there was a nominal ban on Buddhism, it was ignored. In 1868 there were nearly 300 temples (n.b. not shrines) at Ise;

the recital of Buddhist sutras before the alters of the kami was common and many Buddhist priests would make pilgrimages to Ise.[25]

The Political Utility of Shinto

What Shintoism lacked in organisational and doctrinal specificity, it more than made up in terms of scale and social penetration. It is claimed that, 'Probably no single Edo-period religious practice rivalled in scale and extent of influence the Ise pilgrimages, which, by the end of the Edo period served a network of confraternities which extended right across the nation.[26]

Something between 80 per cent and 90 per cent of the nation were linked to Ise, the principal Shinto shrine, by a network of *o-shi* or parish priests. Hardacre tells us that the more powerful *o-shi* might have as many as 4000 to 10 000 households under their control. They travelled all over Japan. They developed currency exchange facilities and even their own pseudo-currency. Popular attachment had a quasi-religious foundation; the people viewed the Ise deities as harvest gods or gods who could protect the faithful and they visited shrines to pray for abundant crops and personal well-being.[26]

The Shinto message was of no political significance in itself. Shinto priests preached very much the same message as their Kokugaku, Shingaku, Hotoku and Buddhist counterparts. The political utility of Shinto derived from its religious centres which were hugely popular – by the end of the Edo period it was generally held that one 'ought' to make a pilgrimage at least once and, above all, they were connected to the emperor. The greatest Shinto shrines dedicated to the Throne were the shrine to the sun-goddess at Ise and the Iwashimazu Shrine between Kyoto and Osaka. Ise was the home of the sacred mirror, one of the imperial regalia and the ultimate symbol of legitimacy. Kyoto, the seat of the Imperial Court in the Tokugawa period, had never been a place of popular worship but, by reinforcing the link between the Shinto shrines and the emperor, the elite could hope for that projection and generalisation of imperial loyalty upon which they might found the state.

The Role of the State in the Creation of State Shinto

These were the materials with which the Meiji elite chose to work so as to secure its own position and to secure the affective foundations of the state. The Meiji policy for Shinto was simple and comprehensive: whereas in the Tokugawa period Shinto practice had been voluntary and had affected only part of the population, it was to become, under Meiji, compulsory and universal. Where Shinto had been amorphous, heterogeneous, local and diffuse, it was to become systematic, institutionalised, national and statist. Rival cosmologies were to be inhibited, marginalised and worse.

A number of measures were enacted to give effect to this policy: State Shinto (Kokka Shinto) or Shrine Shinto (Jinja Shinto) was to be distinguished from independent, Sectarian Shinto (Shuha Shinto). The latter was left dependent upon the parishioners for support while the former received public assistance. All shrines were brought under the umbrella of the Ise Grand Shrines. Rites were standardised by reference to Ise practice, a requirement which was to apply to the smallest of local shrines – 86 000 of which were eliminated by 1940. The concern here was to overcome local superstition and heterogeneity in the interest of ceremonies that fostered the community of imperial worship and national solidarity. Not only the forms of worship but the gods themselves were affected by the process of standardisation – as the Meiji era closed and the Taisho era opened the state favoured shrines which honoured either Amaterasu or the Emperor Meiji and discouraged the adoption of other deities.

By the early 1880s, regulations had been issued whereby recognised institutions were to reserve to themselves the title *jinja*, whilst non-official ones were deemed *kyokai* or churches and accorded the same subordinate legal status as Christianity and Buddhism.[27]

Further to cement the identity of religious rite and government, every important event in the life of the nation – the beginning of war, success in arms, the conclusion of peace, births in the royal family, changes in the government and anything else of significance in domestic or foreign affairs – was duly announced before the Shinto gods, in a form of address known as a *saibun* in which their favours were acknowledged and their blessings invoked.

Major public pronouncements, imperial rescripts, edicts and precepts and the preamble to the 1889 Constitution[28] insisted upon a Shinto – sanctioned identity of government and religion and a simultaneous identity of the Meiji polity and that of the ancestors (Shinto is often referred to as 'ancestor worship).

Not all of these initiatives met with unqualified success – far from it. In 1871 the oligarchs instituted the practice of universal shrine registration – in place of the former and popular Buddhist temple registration scheme. Shrine registration was intended to transfer from Buddhism to Shinto the census-keeping functions formerly performed by the temples.

The proviso, that every citizen was to receive a shrine talisman at birth, was, it has been suggested, an attempt to unify the nation in the worship of Ise deities. Neither measure was particularly successful.[29]

The message preached in official documents was carried to every corner of Japan by *the Great Promulgation Campaign*, which was announced in 1870. When this came to an end, the task of inculcating the ideology was taken up through the national education system and by means of conscription to the national army. The process persisted, without interruption, until 1945.

The Imperial Legacy and the Perception of the International Order

This chapter has been concerned with one aspect of the process of state-building in response to pressures which emanated from the international environment. By way of conclusion, it can be noted that the process was not exclusively one way. State-building in Japan, stimulated by the West, was later to rebound on the West.

Whereas the process of establishing the state on Shintoist foundations presents tradition as a resource to be managed, in the case of elite perceptions of international relations, the element of instrumentality seems to have been absent; indeed, elite perceptions were very closely conditioned by tradition. The international order was assimilated to familiar, indigenous meanings without any great transformation or qualification of those meanings. Two aspects of this process of assimilation are of particular interest.

As to the first, there is some evidence that pre-1900 elites understood international politics by analogy with inter-*han* politics and the simple expedient of substituting state for fief. It would be wrong to claim that Japan's frontiers were hermetically sealed in the Tokugawa period – for example, there was regular contact with Korea who sent missions and emissaries to Japan – however, the closed country policy was sufficiently effective to preclude the need for conceiving of Japan as one actor in an international play. When the need arose, the word for 'country' favoured by the elite was *kuni* – which hitherto had been used to refer to my fief, or my *han*. Britain, America, France and the rest were barbarous to be sure but for all that, they were KUNI. The accuracy or at least the utility of the analogy is perhaps a factor in explaining the relative ease and rapidity with which Japan came to understand the international game, its dangers and the possibilities it afforded her.

At the same time, however, the analogy was dangerous, and likely to destabilise the international order because it was inherently revisionist in the sense that Michael Howard uses the term.[30] If the notion of competing *kuni* or feudal fiefdoms was the explanatory predicate of power relations in the international context, then authority, in the international context, was to be understood in terms of the Japanese imperial institution. As has been noted, no person could substitute for the Emperor in the authoritative bonding of emperor and sun goddess. There was no superior priesthood in Japan or anywhere else. Accordingly there could only ever be one foundation for a settled international order – the authority of the Imperial Household.

The argument is graphically illustrated in Aizawa Seishisai's *Shinron* or *New Proposals*;[31] a work written in 1825 and which, before World War II, was acclaimed as one of the classic essays of loyalty and patriotism.

Our Divine Land is where the sun rises and where the primordial energy originates. The heirs of the Great Sun have occupied the Imperial Throne from generation to generation without change from time immemorial. Japan's position at the vertex of the earth makes it the standard for the nations of the world. Indeed, it casts its light over the world, and the distance which the resplendent imperial influence reaches knows no limit. Today, the alien barbarians of the West, the lowly organs of the legs and feet of the world, are dashing about across the seas, trampling other countries underfoot, and daring, with their squinting eyes and limping feet, to override the noble nations. What manner of arrogance is this!

The earth in the firmament appears to be perfectly round, without edges or corners. However, everything exists in its natural bodily form, and our Divine Land is situated at the top of the earth. Thus, although it is not an extensive country spatially, it reigns over all quarters of the world. . . . The various countries of the West correspond to the feet and legs of the body . . . all according to the dispensation of nature.

In other circumstances, Aizawa's words would be significant, primarily as a fairly typical instance of a common, xenophobic and nativist reaction to foreign, particularly modern and Western encroachment. However, and here's the rub, the invention of the emperor-centred, Shinto-sanctioned polity, in response to the challenge of the West, froze this moment; institutionalised and reproduced it and finally, led to desperate and cataclysmic efforts to pursue the implications of a globally transcendent imperial authority.[32]

Notes

1. There is no comprehensive account of the Japanese state in either English or Japanese. A reliable political history is John W. Hall, *Japan: from prehistory to modern times* (New York: Dell, 1970).

2. With respect to the Meiji Restoration, the English reader is quite well served. W. G. Beasley, *The Meiji Restoration* (Stanford University Press, 1972) is a standard work. A more recent work, Marius Jansen and Gilbert Rozman (eds) *Japan in transition: from Tokugawa to Meiji* (Princeton University Press, 1986) deals competently with some important and neglected aspects of the state-building exercise.

3. Whereas commentators, particularly in the West, were persuaded that the Taisho period represented a 'natural' movement to democracy which was 'interrupted' by the militarist adventure of the 1930s, this view from the 1960s was never widely endorsed by Japanese academics and has lost popularity in the West in recent years. See P. Duus, 'The era of party rule, Japan 1905–1932' in J. B. Crowley (ed.) *Modern East Asia: essays in interpretation* (New York: Harcourt, Brale and World, 1970), pp. 180–205; and Edwin O. Reischaver, 'What went wrong?' in James W. Morley (ed.) *Dilemmas of Growth in Pre-war Japan* (Princeton University Press, 1971) pp. 489–510.

4. Some prefer to speak of 'transformation': that no fully satisfactory account of the Occupation legacy has been written in either English or Japanese is a comment upon the intrinsic difficulty of weighting the elements of continuity and change in the post-war political order.

5. Kyogoku Jun-ichi, *The political dynamics of Japan* (translated by Nobutaka Ike, University of Tokyo Press, 1987). Professor Kyogoku is, without doubt, one of the leading political scientists in Japan, and that great rarity, a political scientist who is not unduly burdened with respect for Western political science models and who is prepared to study Japan in its own terms. It is then excellent that Professor Ike has translated his *Nihon no Seiji* (Tokyo Daigaku Shuppankai, 1983). Sadly the new work is much abridged and the translation is not always successful.

6. The normative/pragmatic rule distinction is familiar thanks to F. G. Bailey, *Strategems and spoils: a social anthropology of politics* (Oxford: Blackwell, 1969).

7. These labels are not always helpful in the Japanese case. Both the JCP and the JSP have deradicalised their programmes in recent years, in a process which bears some comparison with 'Euro-communism'. See Shigeko N. Fukai, 'Beliefs and attitudes of the Japanese left during the early 1970s', *Asian Survey*, **xx**, 12 (December, 1980).

8. There are 512 seats in the lower house of the Diet. Typically 200–250 of these are shared by a minimum of 4 warring opposition parties. In the last election the LDP won 304 seats. Hans H. Baerwald, *Party politics in Japan* (Boston: Allen & Unwin, 1986).

9. For the case for including Japan in a category of 'Western' nations, see J. A. A. Stockwin, *Japan: divided politics in a growth economy*, 2nd ed (London: Weidenfeld & Nicolson, 1985) pp. 7–8.

10. Still of interest is the classic amount of G. B. Sansom, *The Western World and Japan* (New York, Knopf, 1950).
11. For a general discussion of the invention of tradition, as good a starting place as any is E. Hobbsbawm and T. Ranger, *The invention of tradition* (Cambridge University Press, 1983).
12. It is not possible to do more within the confines of the chapter.
13. An excellent, accurate and lucid account of the imperial institution is Herschel Webb, *The Japanese Imperial Institution in the Tokugawa Period* (Columbia University Press, 1968). I am grateful to colleagues and friends at Kokugakuin University and, particularly, to Professor Nagamori.
14. J. W. Hall, 'A monarch for modern Japan' in R. WE. Ward (ed.) *Political development in modern Japan* (Princeton University Press, 1968) pp. 11–64.
15. The phrase is E. P. Thompson's.
16. Hall in Ward, *op. cit.*, p. 23.
17. Webb, *op. cit.*, p. 264.
18. M. Jansen, 'The Meiji State: 1861–1912' in Crowley, *op. cit.*, pp. 95–119.
19. *ibid.*, p. 109.
20. Ishida Takeshi, *The introduction of Western political concepts into Japan*, Nissan Occasional Paper Series, no. 2 (1986).
21. 'Zenkoku yochi kunko no kengi' (May, 1872) Meiji Tennoki 2:674 cited by C. Gluck, *Japan's modern myths* (Princeton University Press, 1985) p. 74.
22. Precisely 99 more trips than his predecessors had made in the 260 years of the Tokugawa period.
23. Gluck, *op. cit.*, pp. 74–5.
24. A much quoted extract from Fukuzawa Yukichi, *Bunmeiron no gairyaku*, 18th edn (Tokyo, Iwanami Shoten, 1983) p. 195.
25. Helen Hardacre, 'Creating state Shinto: the great promulgation campaign and the new religions', *Journal of Japanese Studies*, **12**, 1 (1986) p. 31.
26. Hardacre, *op. cit.*, pp. 33–4.
27. D. C. Holtom, *The national faith of Japan* (1938; repr. New York, Paragon Books, 1965) and *Modern Japan and Shinto nationalism* (1943; repr. New York: Paragon Books, 1963).
28. Perhaps, the most perfect statement of this identity in the constitution is the following, 'The rights of sovereignty of the State, We [i.e. the Emperor] have inherited from Our Ancestors [principally Amaterasu] and We shall bequeath them to Our descendants.'
29. Hardacre, *op. cit.*, pp. 43–4.
30. M. Howard, *The causes of war, and other essays* (London: Unwin Paperbacks, 1983).
31. Ryusaku Tsunoda, Wm Theodore De Bary, Donald Keene (eds) *Sources of Japanese tradition* vol. II (Columbia University Press, 1985) pp. 85–6.
32. The words of Aizawa echo down through to the 1930s. An extract from Tokutomi Iichiro's commentary on the Imperial Declaration of War illustrates the point,

The virtue of sincerity is represented by the Mirror, the virtue of love is represented by the Jewels, and the virtue of intelligence is represented by the Sword . . . the basis of the Imperial Way lies in truth, in sincerity, and in justice. . . . The august virtue of the divine imperial lineage has not a single instance when it did not arise from these three virtues . . . they form the national character of Nippon, and, at the same time, the national trait of the people of Nippon. Combining them all, we call it the Imperial Way. . . . Herein lies the core of our theory. In Nippon resides a destiny to become the light of Greater East Asia and to become ultimately the Light of the World (Tsunoda, DeBary and Keene, *op. cit.*, p. 291–4).

Part II
The International Dimension

6 States and Revolution in the South

Fred Halliday

The period since 1945 has been characterised by a series of revolutionary waves in the Third World, each of which has led to the assumption of power by revolutionaries in a number of Asian, African and Latin American states, as well as to defeats for other movements aspiring to take power in this way. If the first wave, that immediately following World War II, produced revolutionary regimes in the Far East – in China, North Korea and Vietnam – the second, in the period between 1958 and 1962, led to the overthrow of *anciens régimes* in Iraq and Yemen and to the revolutionary triumphs of Cuba and Algeria. It was, however, in the third period, that between 1974 and 1980, that the greatest number of revolutionary victories occurred, in no less than fourteen states, ranging from Indo-China, through Central Asia, to several parts of Africa and the Caribbean. The list of failures could be as wide-ranging – from the Philippines, Malaya and Iran in the first period, through the Congo and the Dominican Republic in the second, to Chile in the third. Yet to add to the picture those states in which such revolutionary upheavals were unsuccessful is only to underline the extension, geographical and temporal, of this phenomenon, one of the major constituents of post-war international relations.[1]

The importance of these upheavals for international relations has, in broad terms, been twofold. First, they have occasioned a series of crises and conflicts which, albeit rooted in specific states and their historical conditions, have stimulated and focused global conflicts, and particularly East–West conflicts. One has only to think of the impact of the Chinese revolution, the Korean war, the Cuban missile crisis, the Vietnam war, Angola, Afghanistan and, more recently, Central America, to see how important these individual Third World crises have been to the course of the East–West conflict as a whole. In Europe the strategic dividing line and the general socio-political character of the states has been constant: major deviations – a Hungary or a Czechoslovakia in the East, a Portugal in the West – have proved to be unsustainable. In the Third World, on the other hand, no such stability of boundary or orientation has prevailed. One does not have to subscribe to the idea that the great powers have 'exported' their contest to the Third World, or that Third World combatants are in any sense 'proxies' of these great powers, to see that the two dimensions have intersected, with the USSR promoting change, within its strategic and diplomatic limits, while the USA has sought to prevent or manage change in such a way as to protect its strategic interest.

The very list of the 'Doctrines' which US Presidents have proclaimed since 1945 is a striking index of the importance of Third World upheavals, since each has been concerned with the maintenance of stability in the Third World and the intersection of Third World upheaval with East–West rivalry. The proclamations of Truman (1947), Eisenhower (1957), Kennedy (1961), Nixon (1969), Carter (1980) and Reagan (1985) all address this question. For all that the Third World is conventionally presented as secondary to the overarching strategic, i.e. nuclear, conflict between East and West, the fact that it is on Third World questions that US presidents have affixed their names to 'Doctrines' is a significant corrective.[2]

The second dimension of the importance of these revolutions is that they have brought into being a set of states that apparently pursue distinctive foreign policies and whose own internal political processes have had an enduring impact on that of other states in their region, and beyond. Revolutionary states cannot defy certain constraints of the international system, and are seriously limited by their own internal divisions and exiguous resources. But it is striking how far, within these limitations, the revolutions of the post-1945 period have had a distinctive impact upon the pattern of Third World politics and have sought to promote distinctive goals. They themselves take their goals seriously; their enemies too would appear to lend them credence, even if, at times, exaggerating their capacities and intentions.

The discussion which follows is an attempt to look, in inevitably broad and superficial terms, at the second of these two dimensions, at the foreign policies of revolutionary states and at some of the factors that may account for them. It treats states as distinctive administrative entities and tries to relate their foreign policies in the post-revolutionary period to the tasks and problems confronting such entities in this transformation phase. Recent theoretical work in historical sociology has brought to the fore a set of questions relating to the state that can contribute substantially to elucidating the relations between states, revolutions and foreign policy. By using the term 'state' to denote not the whole of a nation and its inhabitants, as is conventional in law and orthodox political (including international) theory, but rather the specific administrative and coercive apparatuses that control a particular society, this work has allowed new insights into how revolutions occur and what their goals are.[3] States are, in this perspective, not seen as representative of the societies and peoples over which they preside, but rather as discrete actors facing both outwards, towards other states and societies, and inwards, towards their own subjects. Their conduct of foreign policy is to be explained by this dual orientation and by the attempt to secure in the international sphere support for their internal policies. In what follows, this perspective on the revolutionary state will be applied to three aspects of post-revolutionary policy: (i) internal socio-economic transformation; (ii) the promotion of revolution externally; (iii) the search for new allies and socio-economic models.

SOCIO-ECONOMIC TRANSFORMATION

The central task facing any revolutionary regime is the consolidation of its internal position and the carrying through of those reforms to which it is committed, whether for ideological reasons or because these are necessary for the consolidation of its hold on society. As Theda Skocpol has shown so well in her comparative study of the French, Russian and Chinese revolutions, the most common result of revolutionary transformations is an increase in the power of states, in the intention and capacities of such ruling administrative and coercive entities to intervene in societies and control their activities.[4] Revolutionary movements come to power with a programme or project, a set of goals concerning what they would like society to look like, and they proceed to implement these on the morrow of their accession.

Three types of transformation are particularly relevant in this respect.[5] The first is the destruction of pre-existing property relations and the transfer of ownership, wealth and goods from one social group to the other. Such a radical expropriation and redistribution does not have to result in the creation of an egalitarian society for its consequences to be substantial. Land reform, nationalisation, the prohibition of certain service activities, the transfer of wealth in the form of income, housing, food to previously disenfranchised sectors – all constitute examples of such transformative policies. The second major type of transformation is the infusion of new values and ideas, through direct propaganda and educational campaigns and through other policy mechanisms ,including legal reform. Such changes may affect the ideas associated with work, but can also affect social status, the family, and religion. All societies require ideology and its reproduction for their continuation and stability; revolutionary states, realising the importance of ideology in sustaining the old and creating the new, lay great emphasis upon their domain. The third main area of transformation is in the creation of new political institutions, these being designed both to consolidate the power of the new regime over society and to serve as a means of mobilising support and distributing goods amongst the population. Again, it is not a question of supposing that such new institutions – parliaments, parties, local committees, mass organisations, security units – serve a democratic function, of articulating popular wishes, to see that they serve an essential role in the establishment of a new system of political power.

All three of these policy domains have important consequences for the formulation and implementation of foreign policy. Socio-economic reform affects international relations in a number of respects: expropriated groups may feel abroad and seek to recruit support from other states for the restitution of their new positions; homologous groups in other countries may believe, with greater or lesser realism, that the example of transformation in the revolutionary state will make such transformations more probable in their own state, either through force of example, a revolutionary demonstration effect, or through direct encouragement by the revolutionary state of parallel developments in other countries; processes of expropriation may also encompass interests of foreign companies and states (e.g. canals, bases, raw materials) and so provoke anxiety and reaction from the holders of such interests in other states, who may seek for their part to have their lost goods restored and who may also believe that, if left unchallenged, such expropriations will reproduce themselves elsewhere. In sum, despite the division of the world into distinct states and societies, it is almost impossible to insulate a process of socio-economic transformation in one society from others.

A similar, almost inescapable, transnational process applies to the change in values. Ideas are in one sense easy to export, and long before the modern communications system was established the spread of ideas, of reformation and revolution, constituted a striking example of the internationalisation of change within one state: one need only think of the reformation in the sixteenth century and the spread of revolutionary ideas from the North American continent after 1776 and from France after 1789. Whatever the capacity of revolutionary states to provide material (military, financial) assistance to sympathetic or allied forces elsewhere, the spread of ideas to other societies that are to a degree receptive of them, albeit often in a most distorted form, has constituted a major dimension of the spread of change from one society to another. Such ideas may be ones that identify and delegitimise an oppressor, or ones that validate the struggle and expression of a specific social group, or ones pertaining to the kind of alternative society which the revolution purports to be bringing about. In the spread of the ideas of the Iranian revolution to parts of the Third World where there was no direct influence by the Iranian state it is possible to see a striking, and recent example of this tendency: but it was equally true of the Chinese and Cuban revolutions whose 'models' and 'lessons' were adopted, often on the basis of a few political texts and little concrete evidence, in many parts of the world.[6]

The establishment of new political institutions by the post-revolution-ary regime can also involve widespread international repercussions, and be stimulated by the impact on the society concerned of external events. This is most evidently the case in the realm of security, where the consolidation of state power over the population concerned is often legitimised as being necessary to mobilise resources against a foreign menace. At the centre of the state, such a process involves the growth of a military apparatus capable of repelling an invader and the mobilisation of large numbers of people to participate in such a venture. Equally, however, the pressures of security, real, imagined or invented, can play a decisive role in shaping the local administrative bodies created by such regimes: the CDRs in Cuba, the CDSs in Nicaragua, the *kebeles* in Ethiopia and other similar bodies have served both as organs of local administration, dealing with housing, sanitation, educational cam-paigns and the like, and as security organs, running regular night-time patrols, keeping an eye on the movement of individuals within the district concerned, and conveying instructions from the central auth-orities to the population.

The interaction of socio-economic transformation with the inter-national dimension can be seen in many other aspects of the revolution-ary process, with the external factors at times accelerating the process of internal change, and at other times inhibiting it. The Chinese and Cuban revolutions, for example, are evident cases in which external confronta-tion produced a more rapid internal radicalisation than was initially intended and acted as a catalyst on domestic change. Alternatively, external pressure, or more precisely the need to reduce its impact, may lead revolutionary leaderships to postpone changes that they consider to be desirable: this was certainly the case in Nicaragua during the early part of the 1980s, where official caution on such matters as the private sector and the role of the Catholic Church was at least in part due to the desire not to augment the already substantial hostility to the Nicaraguan revolution from the USA. The retreat from radical reform on sensitive issues, especially women and land, by the People's Democratic Party of Afghanistan after its initial disastrous two years, i.e. from 1980 onwards, is another evident, if rather unsuccessful, example of such refraining from social reform as a result of a combination of pressure from without and within.

PROMOTION OF REVOLUTION

Neutral observers are often puzzled by what they see as a revolutionary state's unwise and dogmatic support for similar movements elsewhere and its tendency to become involved in the internal affairs of other countries. For all the compromise and constraints that have marked the foreign policies of revolutionary countries, this internationalist perspective has recurred in the foreign policy of many revolutionary states in the postwar period, from China, to Algeria, Cuba and Iran. Each has sought not only to present itself as a model for the Third World, but also to assist revolutionaries of similar suasion in other countries and to build an international network around its own revolution. Nicaragua has been constrained in what it can do in practice, but there is no doubt, from the early documents of the Frente Sandinista de Liberación Nacional (FSLN) onwards and the writings of its major theorist Carlos Fonseca, that it sees itself as part of a broader Central American revolutionary movement, uniting the peoples of that area against domestic rulers and their American supporters alike. Given the costs that such internationalist policies entail, the question which arises is why such states should, with such repetition and at such cost to themselves, engage in these policies.

One element is ideological: the fact that those who make revolutions do so in the name of universal values that must therefore be relevant to other societies as well. This is as true of the ideologies of the Chinese, Vietnamese, Cuban and Iranian revolutions as it was of the French and Russian. A second factor is theoretical: revolutionary analyses of the system that they are challenging posit an international structure of oppression (be it on the basis of class, race, imperialism or religion) that they are combatting. This means that if their own endeavour is to survive, this internationally-defined system of oppression must be broken and the struggle against it continued. A third element is more directly practical: revolutionary states, like others, seek allies. The prospect of like-minded regimes coming to power is one that holds out to revolutionary states a prospect of support from other states in the international system and which encourages them to extend support to those in other states seeking to attain power. These are, therefore, substantial reasons why it is worth taking seriously the commitment of revolutionaries to encouraging comparable changes elsewhere.

There is, moreover, a further source of the tendency of revolutions to promote international change, and that is the response of other states. To approach this problem by attributing initial or prime responsibility to one or the other is usually pointless, since both the revolutionaries and those opposed to them, for their respective reasons, engage in an international struggle over the fate of the revolution concerned. The timing of the confrontation may well be determined by one or the other side, but the fact of an interlocking commitment to internationalisation cannot be avoided. The reasons why other status quo powers feel compelled to act to intervene against, or at least contain, revolutions include, as we have seen, both the international impact of socioeconomic transformation and the commitment to encouraging revolution abroad: but there is an autonomous impulsion from the side of the counter-revolutionary state, born of its perception that its own legitimacy and power will be undermined if revolutions elsewhere are permitted to survive. As Aron argued, the international system presupposes a degree of homogeneity in the way states are composed, and heterogeneity is a factor leading to conflict.[7] Many is the expert who has tried, with greater or lesser sympathy, to understand why Nicaragua, an impoverished state of three million people, is perceived as a threat by the USA. Factors such as US economic interests, security of sea lanes, promotion of revolution, and the potential military gains of the USSR have all been mentioned: but none of these add up to a convincing explanation. In the face of such a mystery, liberal critics have argued that US policy has been based on misperception or the idiosyncrasies of a president. Yet the answer may lie not so much in identifiable rational concerns, or in the vagaries of the subjective, as in the manner in which revolutions, by undermining the homogeneity that states prefer, can provoke such hostile responses in others.[8]

The tendency of revolutions to promote similar changes elsewhere, and of other states to seek to suppress them, is a recurrent feature of international politics, from the early 1790s onwards. The same proclamations and responses recur again and again. That such a pattern should recur suggests that more than just errors of judgement, on either side, are involved. Yet if this interaction does recur, it is almost equally the case that neither project succeeds, at least not in the manner initially expected. Revolution cannot be 'exported' in the sense of transferred from one state to another, and the failure of revolutionaries to do so is striking. Equally, it has proved very difficult to overthow revolutions, as distinct from making them pay a very high price for remaining in power. Some cases of successful counter-revolution have occurred, but these have involved invasion by the armies of other states and have usually been made possible only by grave errors of judgement on the part of the revolutionaries themselves (in Hungary in 1919 and Grenada in 1983, as much as in France in 1815). Both parties to the internationalisation of revolution and counter-revolution therefore appear committed to a process that is costly and preoccupying to them, but which is rarely crowned with success.

THE SEARCH FOR ALLIES

Many revolutionary movements come to power proclaiming their independence from the prevailing alignments of international politics and the distinctiveness, if not uniqueness, of their own revolutionary process. This may be a result of the fact that, as in Cuba or Iran, the revolutionaries had originated from very specific political backgrounds, and it may also be a reflection of the nationalism which revolutionaries invoke as part of their overall legitimacy. It may also reflect a hope that by prudent downplaying of international links the full force of hostility from status quo states may be avoided. Communist parties are, of course, the exception here, since they come to power with an already proclaimed set of international alignments: but they too can often play down the degree to which they rely on international supports and the extent to which their programmes for transforming particular societies are influenced by, if not derivative of, what other already established revolutionary states have implemented. Not only in Cambodia, but also in China, North Korea, and Yugoslavia among others can such assertions of individuality be noted.

In some respects, such proclamations of originality and autonomy are, however, difficult to sustain in the longer run. First of all, given the prevailing divisions in international affairs, and the hostility which revolutions attract, even if they play down their longer-run goals, revolutionary states are forced to seek for international support, if only to guarantee their own security. It may be possible for Third World revolutionary movements to come to power through their own indigenous efforts, but it is not possible for them to stay in power without acquiring arms and, in many cases, a degree of strategic support from outside. The military pressures to which these states – be they Cuba, Nicaragua, Angola, Mozambique, South Yemen or Vietnam – are subjected pose the securing of military support as a vital necessity. In the post-1945 world this has meant that, whatever their suspicions of the USSR, it has been the Soviet Union which has provided these arms, and while the USSR has been careful not to give any formal military guarantees to its third world allies, even to Cuba (the Warsaw Pact being confined to European states), the presence of Soviet warships and advisers, and the demonstration of a rapid resupply capability, have to a significant degree linked the USSR to the security of these regimes.

Similar, if less obvious, pressures apply in the economic field. All Third World revolutionary regimes have faced severe economic difficulties in the aftermath of revolution, because of the turmoil of the revolutionary process itself and because of the pressures to which these societies have been subjected from without. To remedy these problems, Third World states have sought for substantial economic aid from the Soviet bloc – even China did so in the 1950s, until Khrushchev terminated Soviet aid agreements. Yet here the problems of securing support have been much greater than in the military sphere, because of the limited resources and often poor quality of Soviet aid. The USSR has given substantial aid to a core of Third World communist states (Mongolia, Vietnam, Cambodia, Laos, Afghanistan, Cuba), but has encouraged other states to diversify their sources of capital and trade, and, as much as possible, to rely on their own efforts. With theoretical revisions in the Soviet view of capitalism, it has become possible to argue that some relations with multinational corporations and with the World Bank may be beneficial for Third World states. The problem which many Third World states have faced is that this Soviet policy on economic aid cannot be compensated for by support from other sources. Neither China, nor the multilateral aid agencies, nor the multinational corporations can provide either the quantity of aid, or the alternative international trading and financial system that these countries require, quite apart from the openings to western pressure which participation in such relations permits. The result is that Third World revolutionary states often find themselves in a no-win situation: they oscillate between adoption of Soviet foreign policy lines, in the hope that this will lead to increased Soviet economic aid, and concessions to western sensibilities, in the hope that aid will be available from that source.

Nicaragua, Angola, Mozambique have all illustrated this trend; Ethiopia, which has not done so, has adhered to its pro-Soviet orientation at a very high price in terms of official western aid foregone.

Beyond questions of military and economic aid, however, there is a third dimension in which revolutionary states are compelled to look at other, post-revolutionary, states for support, and that is in providing guidelines on how to implement a programme of socio-economic transformation.[9] It is true that, in the initial post-revolutionary period, the new leaderships may proclaim that they have discovered an indigenous path of development, that the mistakes made in earlier transformations will not be repeated, and that the experiences of other revolutions may not be relevant. All sorts of national 'traditions' and 'experiences' of the revolutionary struggle itself can be invoked as answers to the problems of state policy in the consolidation period. In rare cases, the most striking in recent history being that of post-1979 Iran, revolutionary regimes persist for quite some time in this posture, whilst in other cases, such as China, where the regimes begin by asserting loyalty to another model, the subsequent strains may lead to exaggerated demonstrations of 'originality'. But there are, at the same time, a number of pressures upon Third World revolutionary states that do lead them to reproduce, in part, the patterns of administration and state policy seen elsewhere.

There are, first, the basic pressures of coming up with an answer to a whole range of practical questions – from how to run a ministry or prepare a government committee meeting, how to administer a hospital or a university, or train an army, or present news in the press; when it comes to more complex political issues, such as the running of a party, or policy on women, or the treatment of nationality issues, then such models are equally pertinent. Given the shortage of personnel, resources and time confronting many of these regimes they may be all too glad to take, off the shelf, some available answer to such questions. A second mechanism by which such reproduction takes place is that of training: personnel sent to more developed revolutionary states or trained in their own countries by experts from the more developed countries, and on the basis of teaching materials which these experts bring in, are likely to contribute to the reproduction of the administrative and political practices of the more developed states. Beyond these two dimensions, there is the more direct pressure resulting from the failure on the part of Third World states to do without the 'experiences' of more developed revolutionary regimes. Thus the failure of the Cuban attempt to pursue a non-Soviet path of economic development in the 1960s, including an attempt to abolish money and reliance on voluntary labour and moral incentives, culminating in the disaster of the attempt to grow 10 million tons of sugar in 1970, was followed by a more willing acceptance of Soviet advice and models from the early 1970s onwards.[10] The search for allies is therefore dictated not only by international factors as such, but also by the internal needs of the post-revolutionary transformation period. If for many Third World revolutionary states the USSR has fulfilled this role, Eastern European states have also done so in specific fields (e.g. the GDR in security, the media and education) for Soviet allies in the Third World, China for some of its allies (Cambodia, Albania), and Cuba for some of the African and American cases (Ethiopia, Angola, Grenada, Nicaragua).

CONCLUSION

Revolutions are not, as is rather too often supposed, aberrations or interruptions in an otherwise 'normal' pattern of national and international political life. They are, rather, important formative periods in the history of most great states, and their repercussions have shaped much of international relations as we know it, from the Dutch and English revolutions of the seventeenth century to the Iranian, Nicaraguan and southern African upheavals of the late twentieth. Revolutions are in both cause and effect international events, and they represent a dual challenge to the concept and practice of that most sacrosanct of political values, sovereignty: they challenge the power and legitimacy of established states *within* their own frontiers, and they simultaneously challenge the boundaries *between* states by proclaiming transnational ideals and by, within their objective limits, encouraging comparable challenges to state sovereignty elsewhere.

If revolutions have repeatedly been of such national and international significance, there is little reason, despite continued refinements in the art of suppressing them, to believe that they will not continue to be as influential. The international system will remain under their influence, just as the ability of individual societies to experience revolutions and to pursue post-revolutionary paths of transformation will to a considerable degree be affected by the international system itself. Here, indeed, it may be important to underline that for all that the international system can do to contain and divert revolutionary states, it is too easy to argue that such states, after an initial period of rebellion and conflict revert to more conventional state behaviour. While the initial enthusiasms of revolution may wear off, and attempts to export revolution are curbed, the very fact of the revolutionary regime surviving and of others believing that it does embody a distinct political and social system, can be sufficient to ensure that the international system remains hetereogeneous and that a considerable measure of international conflict results from them. The USSR today may not be as optimistic about world revolution as the Bolsheviks were just after 1917, but it remains a source of encouragement and support to anti-systemic forces throughout much of the Third World. Cuba failed in its attempts in the 1960s to promote guerrilla war in Latin America and Africa, but a quarter of a century after Castro entered Havana, Cuba was actively engaged in supporting its allies in Nicaragua and Angola. Whatever the outcome of the Iran-Iraq war, few can believe that Iran's distinctive character will not continue to affect the politics of west Asia, as long as an Islamic Republic survives.

Inevitably schematic as it has been, this analysis suggests two broader implications for the study of international relations, and for policies designed to reduce the risk of war in the international system. The first is that the international repercussions of revolutions and the conflicts they promote are not the result solely of illusions, misperceptions or policy mistakes on either side: they reflect deeper international tensions generated by revolutions, ones that must be seen as a result of what are substantial transformations of the societies in question and the international results of such transformations. The second conclusion is that, given the genesis of such international conflicts, and given the likelihood that revolutions and their consequences will remain an important part of international relations, a greater recognition of how and why revolutions promote international conflict may in part reduce the dangers which they pose. The goal of many practitioners of international politics has been, it would seem, to make the world safe *from* revolution. It might, in the longer run, be advisable to make it safe *for* them, so that what are important moments of transition and development for many societies should cease to be regarded as so menacing to international peace.

Notes

1. For one overview see Gerard Chaliand, *Revolution in the Third World* (Hassocks: Harvester Press, 1977); see also Geoffrey Barraclough, *Introduction to Contemporary History* (London: Watts, 1964).

2. I have gone into this in greater detail in ch. 4 of *The making of the second Cold War*, 2nd edn (London; Verso, 1986), and in *Beyond Irangate: the Reagan doctrine and the Third World* (Amsterdam: Transnational Issues, 1987).
3. As, for example, in Theda Skocpol, *States and social revolutions* (Cambridge University Press, 1979), and Peter Evans, Dietrich Rues-chemeyer and Theda Skocpol (eds) *Bringing the state back in* (Cambridge University Press, 1985). I have discussed some of the implications of this definition of the state for international relations theory in 'State and society in international relations: a second agenda', *Millennium* (summer, 1987).
4. Skocpol, *op. cit.*
5. I am particularly grateful to Maxine Molyneux for many helpful suggestions on these issues. For further discussion of the relationship between internal transformation and external factors see Fred Halliday and Maxine Molyneux, *The Ethiopian revolution* (London: New Left Books, 1981) ch. 1, Richard Fagen, Carmen Diana Deere, and Jose Luis Caraggio (eds) *Transition and development: problems of Third World socialism* (MR — CENSA Series on the Americas, 1987), and Gordon White, Christine White and Robin Murray (eds) *Revolutionary socialist development in the Third World* (Brighton: Wheatsheaf, 1983).
6. An early but still illuminating attempt to analyse the international impact of the Cuban revolution is Régis Debray, *Revolution in the revolution?* (New York: Monthly review Press, 1967).
7. Raymond Aron, *Peace and war* (New York: Krieger, 1966) pp. 373–81.
8. An excellent discussion of the international impact of revolutions is given in Richard Rosecrance, *Action and reaction in international world politics*, ch. 3. (London: Greenwood Press 1963).
9. For examples see the use made in Afghanistan and South Yemen of Soviet policy towards Islamic minorities, or the policy of Third World revolutionary states on organising their armed forces.
10. On the adoption of Soviet models in the 1970s see Carmelo Mesa-Lago, *The Economy of Socialist Cuba* (Albuquerque (N/M), University of New Mexico Press: 1981).

7 The State and Instability in Southern Africa

Tom Young

Southern Africa has never failed to attract attention, invariably accompanied by sweeping judgement. There has been no shortage of predictions of imminent catastrophe in the Republic of South Africa (whose persistent refutation by events seems to affect neither the prophets nor their popularity with the Western public) while more recently it has even been suggested that the region is a possible trigger for a global war.[1] While the extravagance and simple-mindedness of this rhetoric should be treated with considerable scepticism it does draw attention to some important features of the regional situation. Southern Africa has experienced and continues to experience considerable conflict both within and between states, conflict which has caused immense human suffering[2] directly and indirectly. Unhappily violent conflict and instability are not unique to Southern Africa yet the racial dimension of those conflicts ensures that they have implications for humanity as a whole. As ever the obligations of scholars are to try and explain and teach in the hope (usually forlorn) that this may also contribute to better debate and decision-making.

Political instability is a notoriously tricky concept and much of the discussion about it has been concerned with the problem of definitions and operationalising them.[3] While the literature may not provide a definitive consensus on these matters it does offer some guidance as to the usefulness of distinguishing the location and the forms of instability. For present purposes it will be assumed that instability can occur at any one of three different sites. Firstly, the political community in the widest sense, usually in modern terms the nation. Here instability includes violent communal conflict possibly also involving popular resistance to the central authorities, domestic insurgency, and at an extreme civil war and the collapse of the political community or the emergence of new ones. The second location of instability is what may be called the regime, defined as the legal and informal rules which govern the resolution of political conflict within a political order.[4] Here instability would include frequent shifts of regime, the occurrence of military coups, the abolition of parliamentary institutions and so on. Finally the third site of

112

instability is the government or the ruling group where instability may involve violent factional strife, succession crises, plots, purges and so on. In practice of course these various forms of instability overlap and may not be easily distinguishable, especially in polities with relatively low levels of institutionalisation and differentiation of their apparatus of government.

In trying to make sense of these phenomena it is important (though perhaps not wholly possible) to avoid the tendencies towards circularity in much of the literature. This particularly pertains to those analyses which ultimately point to the lack of legitimacy or institutionalisation as the cause of instability. Since stability is usually defined in terms of legitimacy and institutionalisation one often ends up saying little more than that instability is caused by an absence of institutions that create stability.[5] A more useful approach may be to examine what strategies ruling groups and states pursue. By and large in contemporary Africa[6] elites have seen themselves as engaged in nation-state building, a process involving attempts to achieve both institutionalisation and legitimacy in a situation of constraints and opportunities. These constraints and opportunities are not merely 'objective' but are also 'constructed' within a framework of policies and strategies, that is to say, what is construed as a constraint or an opportunity is largely a function of policy assumption. For example, ethnic heterogeneity may be perceived as a problem from a position which assumes that the normal nation-state is ethnically homogeneous or that such homegeneity is a desirable goal. Such assumptions will then affect all kinds of policies, from the construction of political institutions, to the cultivation of national symbols, even to attitudes towards indigenous languages. In what follows, then, it will be suggested that a great deal at least of the conflict and instability of Southern Africa can be explained as an effect of the policies pursued by political leaders and the kinds of states they have tried to create.

It is a commonplace observation about African states that on the basis of a notion of racial sovereignty they inherited territories that were characterised by arbitrary boundaries, that is to say boundaries that were fundamentally a result of a pattern of European conquest and later intra-European bargaining and accommodation. Because African elites have opposed self-determination in anything other than its anti-colonial sense, modern African states have usually comprised a variety of ethnic groupings, often with some sense of their own identity and not infrequently with collective memories of pre-colonial conflict, such memories and identities having themselves been manipulated by the colonial authorities to bolster colonial rule.[7]

Southern African states have generally shared this characteristic though there are obvious exceptions. Lesotho, Botswana and Swaziland (along with Somalia) are the closest thing to cultural nations that black Africa has, that is to say the Sotho, Botswana and Swazi are peoples with a common language and culture, occupying territory with which they have a lengthy historical connection. All other states in the region are characterised by considerable cleavages along ethnic, racial, linguistic and religious lines. That is to say that they are state-nations,[8] territories in which the political authorities find themselves having to forge a nation out of multiple loyalties. The precise mechanics of the attempts to deal with this problem have obviously differed with the ruling group in each country but all are to some extent trying to create some overarching national values, in a word to ensure the legitimacy of the nation-state. Nations and legitimacy are tricky concepts, both in theory and in practice. As de Jasay puts it 'legitimacy has been rare and elusive throughout history, needing ingredients simply not available at the snap of the state's finger. It took successful wars, prosperous peace, charismatic rulers, a great shared experience and perhaps, above all, continuity.'[9] Almost by definition most of these ingredients do not yet exist in Africa.

Thus the problems associated with national legitimacy have not by and large concerned boundary disputes between states (though Malawi, for example, does make claims on its neighbours) or secessionist movements, with the notable exception of Cabinda. Rather they have concerned the management by the state of tensions between the different groups that constitute the nation. To meet these difficulties African rulers have resorted to familiar strategies. There has been much activity at the symbolic level – the altering of colonial names, the projection of the Leader as the Father of the Nation or some such similar term, the cultivation or invention of pre-colonial historical identities and glories and so on. One of the more frequently offered justifications of the one-party state is that it represents a national will or feeling and this in turn authorises the designation of political division or disagreement as unpatriotic. Behind their rhetoric many African regimes practise various forms of ethnic balancing in appointments within state bureaucracies and other public sector posts.[10] What is noticeable is that the ruling groups of Southern Africa, as elsewhere in the continent, have been reluctant to concede the legitimacy of ethnic politics in an open political arena. Their attitude has been that, as Crawford Young puts it, 'National integration was a categorical imperative, requiring only the application of the skills of statecraft to remove impediments to the inexorable forces of historical progress and political development'.[11] Thus in Mozambique the insistence in the 1970s on a mass literacy programme in Portuguese and the disinterest in indigenous tongues was in part due to fears of a revival of ethnic particularism. In Zambia the move to a one-party state was precipitated by the beginnings of political expression of ethno-regional interests.[12] The widespread destruction or emasculation of systems of local government in Africa and the refusal to consider the possibility of decentralised systems of government also bear witness to this tendency.

Despite these strategies (and in some cases, it might well be argued, because of them) ethnic identities continue to be a factor in conflict and instability, as can be seen in Angola, Mozambique and Zimbabwe. As always it is necessary to avoid the Colonel Blimp notion of ethnicity as some sort of primordial or atavistic throwback without falling into the view popular in some circles that ethnicity is 'really' something else like class. The fact that ethnic groups stuggle for economic resources does not make them classes. It remains however difficult to make sense theoretically of the effects of ethnic identity. We know, for example, that the ruling group in Angola is characterised by racial and ethnic division. We know that the Popular Movement for the Liberation of Angola (MPLA) politburo does not contain a single Ovimbundu despite their being some 40 per cent of the population. Likewise in Zimbabwe not only are the differences between Shona and Ndebele speakers important so also are those between different groups within the Shona speaking population.[13] Yet these are differences which are officially denied and about which enquiries are not encouraged. Deprived of any 'official' mode of expression they surface nonetheless in the form of intrigue and cabals vying for influence.[14] It has to be said that we do not really know how these identities function in politics but what is clear is that ethnic identities are highly emotionally charged and easily aggravated where people feel their security or right to exit is threatened.[15]

South Africa, in this as in most other things, is a special case, in that the ruling group has been a racial caste which, rather than seeking to create a nation out of a plethora of ethnic units, has sought, at least until recently, to keep them separate in a system of compulsory ethnic partition, even taking it to the logical point of setting up somewhat implausible, and entirely unrecognised, 'national' entities within the territory of the Republic. As a form of institutionalisation this hasn't really worked in that all the Bantustans, with the possible exception of Boputhatswana, appear to be desparately unviable and dependent on Pretoria's handouts. Nor have these entities attained much legitimacy amongst a mass population, tainted as they are by their association with Pretoria's divide and rule policies.

As far as conflict and stability at the national level is concerned it may be concluded that the picture is mixed. Several states have quite high levels of national homogeneity, others have developed ad hoc systems of ethnic balancing especially in the public sector and there are yet others in which ethnic identities remain highly charged and a potential threat to the unity of those states.

Turning now to the sphere of the regime it is clear that broadly speaking the early optimism about African regimes that prevailed in the post-independence period has evaporated to be replaced by something approaching despair. The judgements of political scientists have taken on a harsher tone as in Jackson's remark that, 'Black Africa probably contains the largest concentration of decrepit states to be found anywhere'.[16] While this judgement is possibly a little unreasonable it can be suggested that something of a consensus among scholars is emerging round the following propositions.[17] Firstly that the inheritance of liberal democratic institutions or ideas from colonial rule, insecurely anchored as they were, was rapidly abandoned after independence – not merely in the formal institutional sense but in the sense of a depoliticisation of the public sphere, leading on to increasingly authoritarian forms of rule, usually via one-party states, often with party or mass organisations with mobilisational and/or conveyor belt functions. Secondly African rulers have attempted to strengthen and extend highly authoritarian central-ised administrative structures partly to confront the various particular-istic identities contained within the society and partly as a vehicle for highly ambitious developmental policies involving elaborate controls over a wide range of economic activities. Thirdly African states have been characterised by highly personalist forms of rule and administra-tion, involving the centralisation and concentration of state power in presidential offices. This general assessment might be summarised in Rothchild's remark that 'paradoxically the modern African state is overcentralised and consumes extensive resources, yet is fragile and lacks the ability to carry out is ambitious programs'.[18]

While the diversity of regimes in Southern Africa makes generalisa-tion difficult it is clear that these general propositions are pertinent. The particular mix of circumstances obviously varies. In Angola and Mozambique, for example, independence was partly a result of armed struggle against a colonial power which had itself long been a dictator-ship. Not only then was there no intellectual tradition or (even rudimentary) institutional machinery of democracy but both the MPLA in Angola and Frelimo in Mozambique identified 'liberation' with their own exclusive control of power and made it clear that they had no intention of sharing power with others or of permitting the functioning of other political forces. They have crushed all opposition by force in the name of Marxism-Leninism. The experiences and traditions of an authoritarian and centralised state were available however. To them were added the conventional mobilisational organisations familiar in Communist states for young people, women and workers. Despite the much trumpeted *poder popular* or people's power, the mass organisations are tightly controlled by senior members of the party leadership. The National and Provincial Assemblies, widely proclaimed at their inception to be vastly superior to mere bourgeois parliaments,[19] are treated in an almost offhand fashion, rarely meet, and have a role almost entirely restricted to the retrospective ratification of decisions already taken by the senior leadership. These regimes then offer very little participation in politics outside the elite even on their own terms. The political arena is a highly orchestrated and authoritarian one in which the political line is laid down by a very small group.

This in itself was entirely congruent with trends towards personalism in these regimes, which, given their Marxist-Leninist colouring, is rather different from that of, say, President Kaunda or Dr Banda. But the tradition in both countries of presidential offensives and arbitrary actions against officials attests both to the enormous power concentrated in the hands of the leader and to the lack of institutionalisation in the bureaucracy. Such leaders invariably claim a rapport with the common people, and in the case of Samora Machel many observers, not always sympathetic to the regime, attest to this being the case. But such relationships remain ultimately abstract – the people must play the role prescribed for them by the ideology.

Some of the effects of this pattern of structures have been visible in both countries. In both, the rural areas and agriculture are critical. The pursuit of state farm strategies has been a disaster, stretching these states' bureaucratic resources beyond their limits. Successive ministers of agriculture in Mozambique have been unable to resolve the confusion of state agriculture policy or to implement it. The massive neglect of the non-state rural sector has shattered the economy yet not until 1983 was publicly orchestrated criticism of agricultural policy allowed. There is no doubt these policies have contributed to severe disaffection in the rural areas with the ruling groups in Luanda and Maputo. It has only been under the pressure of widespread domestic insurgency threatening the collapse of the state that both governments have begun to dismantle some parastatals and decentralise some economic decision-making. It is true that in both countries resistance is fomented from outside yet it is also true that the operation of state institutions and the implementation of certain policies have produced widespread alienation from these governments which is easily fanned into open defiance.

Zambia, Malawi, and Lesotho are all countries which by contrast began their independent political life with elections or Parliaments and in which subsequently leaders have consolidated a personal form of rule by the steady destruction of independent political institutions, the incarceration, deportation or even murder of political opponents, though also, periodically, via tactics of cooption. This steady abandonment of parliamentary institutions is sometimes accompanied by proposals of alternative or even superior forms of democracy. In Zambia, for example, President Kaunda proclaimed in 1968 the national goal of participatory democracy to be practised in all Zambian institutions. It is clear however that levels of attachments to participatory institutions are low. Membership in the sole political party has declined to less than 5 per cent of the population. In relation to central government, Tordoff explains that, 'There is an obvious contradiction between the President's style of increasingly personalised decision-making and his own stress on participatory democracy.'[20]

Malawi is perhaps the clearest Southern African example of an autocratic state. Coming to Independence in 1964 Dr Banda's already high-handed methods precipitated opposition which was dealt with by dismissal of those concerned. When this opposition turned to violence it was crushed and Dr Banda consolidated his position. Since that time he has elevated himself to Life President, makes virtually all important decisions and important appointments, enjoys sole right to appoint members of the national executive committee of the country's only political party, selects candidates for parliamentary elections, nominates the Speaker of Parliament as well as nominated members of that institution. He appoints all cabinet ministers and from time to time occupies a number of portfolios himself – indeed briefly in 1984 he took over all the portfolios. Perhaps the most succinct analysis of his rule is his own comment to a group of visiting British businessmen, 'Anything I say is law. Literally law. It is a fact in this country.'[21]

Lesotho began independence in 1966 with a parliamentary system and the majority party of Chief Leabua Jonathan forming the government. But when it became clear that his party was losing the election in 1970, the election was suspended, government by decree established, opposition leaders imprisoned and their supporters throughout the country intimidated. By the end of the year Chief Jonathan proclaimed ingeniously a five-year 'holiday from politics'. Since this holiday the country has been wracked by more or less permanent crisis with successive attempts at reconciliation with his political opponents by Chief Jonathan breaking on the rock of how to re-establish some form of parliamentary institution. These unresolved tensions have periodically exploded into violence to the point that the Basutoland Congress Party has set up an armed wing, the Lesotho Liberation Army, which has been allowed to operate from South Africa.

It may be concluded that in many Southern African states ruling groups have attempted to set up state structures or regimes which while they may be strong in the despotic sense lack infrastructural power.[22] That is to say that while they may be able to deploy some degree of force and remain in office, their form of rule is one that is characterised by limited administrative capacities and a relative failure to attract popular approval and support. These two characteristics tend of course to reinforce one another. It is an almost inevitable effect of these kinds of rule that politics is little more than a succession of rotations, dismissals and punishments of subordinates on the inside and plots and conspiracies on the outside.

These characteristics are clearly related to the third instance of instability, namely, instability among the political elite or ruling group. While in states still in the process of institution building the difference between regime instability and elite instability may often be difficult to draw it is clear that one cannot assume that the two necessarily correlate. To take only the most obvious example the Marxist–Leninist MPLA in Angola has experienced severe internal strife and purges whereas the Marxist–Leninist Frelimo in Mozambique has shown a coherence and continuity of its senior leadership of a quite remarkable kind. In Angola, at least since 1975, the MPLA had had its critics on the left, both inside and outside the organisation. During 1976 the Neto leadership moved to crush these opponents and, in particular, to separate them from the genuinely popular organisations which had sprung up in 1974–5 around the slogan *poder popular* (popular power), and which had never really been under full MPLA control. A paradoxical effect of this was a strengthening of the position of Nito Alves, who, for a period, was minister of the interior. Although much of this political conflict took place in conventional Marxist jargon, it also involved rather more prosaic resentments and ambitions, running along ethnic lines. During 1976 Alves managed both to place many of his close allies in key positions in the party, state and army apparatuses, and to articulate a certain black African resentment against the white and *mestiço* (mixed) elements which form a disproportionate number of the party leadership. In late 1976 the Neto leadership began to move against him, initially by abolishing the ministry of the interior. In May 1977 he and his closest supporter, José van Dunem, were removed from the MPLA central committee. This event, in turn, precipitated an attempted coup, in which rebellious army units stormed the main Luanda jail and briefly took over the radio station, but were quickly suppressed by loyal troops. Despite the ease with which the coup was put down, its failure revealed widespread support for the 'Nitistas', and led to a considerable purge of mass organisations (the trade union federation, the women's organisation and the youth organisation), provincial administrations and sections of the armed forces. These developments were followed in December by the first MPLA congress, at which the now completely dominant Neto leadership marked out for itself a rigorously orthodox Marxist–Leninist road, changing the organisation's name to MPLA-PT (Partido de Trabalho). As a result of this reorganisation, the MPLA felt strong enough to show some clemency towards former opponents – prisoners were released and appeals were made to exiles to return – though to none associated with UNITA or the Alves group.

Nor is such elite instability restricted to more or less 'modern' regimes, as the contrasting example of Swaziland shows. Under the rule of King Sobuzha II the country experienced political stability though it also saw the abolition of effective parliamentary institutions precipitated by some electoral success on the part of a non-royalist party. The death of King Sobuzha in 1982 ushered in a period of intense struggle for power in which rival factions have tried to manipulate both 'traditional' and 'modern' parts of the Swazi polity in their own interests, in a perfect exemplification of what Jackson and Rosberg term, 'the political process [of] "palace politics", an elite activity of jockeying for power and place among big men and their collaborators who are usually concerned only with their own narrow interests'.[23]

These features of the political systems of the Southern African region explain a great deal of the nature of the regional conflict there. The nature of the domestic political order largely determines perceptions of threat. States perceive various aspects of their political order as making them vulnerable and are prepared to exploit such vulnerabilities in others. That said, the violent intensity of regional conflict is clearly dominated by one overriding confrontation, between South Africa on the one hand and the other states in the region, and this conflict is about one issue, namely apartheid and white minority rule in the Republic.

The evolving tragedy is witness to the durability both of Afrikaner nationalism and of black African determination to be rid of white rule. Although white rule is formally condemned by African governments in the idioms of human rights and democracy the real objection to apartheid and the white regime is that it is a racial affront. Few states in Southern Africa, or indeed the rest of Africa, can point to impressive records of democracy or human rights but this should not blind us to the real hatred for apartheid and white rule throughout Africa which ensures that even if particular governments forbid the use of their territories by black South Africans or even as in the case of Malawi have diplomatic relations with the Republic the pressures towards sympathy with Black South Africans remain and will sooner or later come to the fore.

In assessing regional conflict it is important to bear in mind the Republic's overwhelming predominance in the region – e.g. the Republic produces 80 per cent of the region's GNP, has about 60 per cent of its tarred roads and railways and produces about 75 per cent of generated electricity.[24] In the military sphere proper similar disparities exist in terms of equipment and spending and so on. Not only is South Africa a strong power but it is also a strong state in the sense of bureaucratic capacity, means of policy making and implementation and so on. Yet the Republic is an eloquent reminder of the necessity to distinguish institutionalisation from legitimacy. The Republic's legitimacy lies in its Afrikaner and wider white base – the rest of the population is more or less disaffected and this has produced periodic episodes of severe unrest of increasing duration and intensity. Thus within the population of South Africa as a whole both national and state legitimisation is weak. The structural problem the South African government faces is that it cannot rely solely on coercion for long periods of time, though in the short-run it will – it must therefore shift the basis of both national and state legitimacy. Its chosen way of doing that of the past two decades – i.e. the almost openly cynical manipulation of state-imposed ethnic identities in the form of the Bantustans – has manifestly failed to resolve the socio-political position of urban blacks. There is a recognition in Pretoria of the need for movement here but the availability of overwhelming force and the habits of decades ensure that the current leadership group perceives this and deals with it as an essentially administrative problem, i.e. they cannot yet accept black South Africans as political actors to be negotiated with.

The stage is set then for a quite complex set of mutual threat perceptions. Those between black African states, which undoubtedly exist, are massively overshadowed by the divide between the Republic and the surrounding states. The situation approximates what Buzan has termed one of 'structural political threats' – that is to say a situation 'when the organising principles of two states contradict each other in a context where the states cannot simply ignore each other's existence. Their political systems thus play a zero-sum game with each other whether they will it or not. . . . The achievements and successes of one automatically erode the political stature of the other, and this often leads naturally enough to more intentional forms of political threat'.[25]

On its side, despite the exaggerations of its 'total onslaught' rhetoric, South Africa clearly feels and is threatened by an unusual coalition of forces including extra-regional ones. Despite the Soviet bloc countries' generally low profile approach to South Africa, their involvement in arms supply and ideological solidarity with Angola and Mozambique as well as arms supply to SWAPO and the ANC and the presence of Cuban troops in Angola is a constant reminder that their involvement has grown and could grow further. The removal of the buffer zone of white states with the collapse of the Portuguese empire and the Smith regime in Rhodesia exposed all of South Africa's borders to infiltration – these are borders which even if black African states were determined to police are very difficult to control. South Africa cannot really be hurt by these states, except perhaps Angola, except insofar as they allow themselves to support SWAPO and the ANC or allow their guerrillas to cross borders. Given the Republic's massive legitimacy problems and the more or less chronic unrest of the last three years the possibility of increased levels of sabotage or the supply of some arms to black township populations is one that must worry the South African authorities.

The other weapon black African states in the region have in their armoury is positive support from some quarters in the West. These states have played an important role in mobilising the hostility of the international community towards South Africa and perhaps less successfully mobilising resources to try and escape at least partially the Republic's regional economic embrace. Western support, rooted in public opinion genuinely concerned about a moral issue rather than the cynical calculation of self-interest by governments is consequently unpredictable and, as recent events have shown, beginning to have real effects. In these circumstances South Africa has for some years pursued an increasingly aggressive strategy to establish herself as the dominant regional power and to be acknowledged as such. She has done this along the fault lines of the neighbouring states. Where there are ethnic or political dissidents these can be supported – this applies in Angola,

Mozambique, Lesotho and to some extent Zimbabwe. South Africa has adjusted this strategy to local circumstances as an irritant in Lesotho and Zimbabwe, as support for a fairly substantial but lightly armed force in Mozambique but in Angola there has been major direct involvement with aircraft to protect Unita against, by regional standards, a heavily armed Angolan government.

Where such vulnerabilities are less in evidence other more direct threats can be used as in the punitive raids against Botswana in June 1985 and against Lesotho in December 1982 and December 1985. These raids also illustrate the close connection between domestic and regional politics. The Gaborone operation for example claimed in the South African press to have been the result of months of painstaking preparation netted a fearsome group of ANC terrorists including a pregnant Dutch woman and a six-year-old boy from Lesotho. It is plain that this raid was very little to do with hurting the ANC and much more to do with cowing the Botswana government into submission and demonstrating the South African government's strength for domestic consumption. Opinion survey evidence consistently shows high levels of support for these raids amongst whites in South Africa, including amongst opponents of the government on its right and left. This is no more than an example of the frequently observed phenomenon of the promotion of external conflict as a means of maintaining the cohesion of a fragile state.

Complementary to this strategy of the selective use of armed force against neighbouring states has been a strategy to reinforce and if possible extend South Africa's as it were 'natural' predominance in the regional economy. The peculiarities of regional geography are poignantly illustrated by the position of Lesotho, which is entirely surrounded by South Africa. In addition to the raids already mentioned South Africa has persistently subjected the country to a variety of pressures by preventing the passage of goods or people in and out. This culminated in 1986 in a virtual blockade halting supplies of food and fuel across the border. Delegations from the paramilitary force and some opposition politicians visited Pretoria and shortly afterwards there occurred Southern Africa's first military coup as the military removed Chief Jonathan, pledging loyalty to the King Mosheshoe II.

Less overtly brutal policies have been pursued elsewhere. The dissident movements South Africa supports frequently attack economic targets which has the effect of increasing the dependence of these countries in South Africa, particularly as far as regional transport is concerned. Even without such attacks the Republic can manipulate freight rates and the availability of railway rolling stock and other facilities to the detriment of some of its neighbours. The other main area of vulnerability is in the field of labour, a number of countries benefiting from repatriated earnings of their nationals. This also is an area which Pretoria has used against Mozambique for example and has threatened to use against others.

Faced with this Leviathan black African states have reacted in different ways, partly depending on their degree of vulnerability and the political orientations of their leaders. Some states, notably Malawi and Swaziland, have been prepared to have bilateral dealings with the Republic, the former at full ambassadorial level, the latter in all but name. Notably they seem to be prepared to actually go along with the more hawkish demands of the south African government. Despite denials, Malawi has undoubtedly been used as a new sanctuary for the MNR (anti-Frelimo force) and Swaziland has ruthlessly rounded up and deported ANC activists, possibly even killed some of them. No other state has been prepared to go that far, not even the most vulnerable ones, Lesotho and Botswana. There continue to be signs of an alternative and more coordinated response amongst most countries but here again domestic factors intrude. Coordination at the diplomatic level is the easiest to manage and in the various fora of which they are members, notably the UN and Commonwealth, black African states have pushed for measures to be taken against South Africa and demanded resources and assistance for themselves. There has been some mileage in this but it is limited. Economic and especially military coordination amongst these states has proved much more difficult and here again differences of regime and ideology intrude. All Southern African states jealously guard their sovereignty and hard-won independence. They are, as already pointed out, quite politically diverse, with consequently different economic policies. Although they have grouped themselves together in a core regional association, the Southern African Development Coordination Conference, it is by no means clear that all the members share all of SADCC's objectives or take it seriously. The most criticial question for these countries in the economic sphere is the regional transport network and all landlocked SADCC members have a common interest in alternative transport routes which do not go through RSA. This concern with transport and in particular the vital position of the Beira corridor for Mozambique and Zimbabwe has in turn led to the beginnings of military cooperation between those two states with the involvement also of Tanzania. That military cooperation has not been without difficulties and clashes on the ground. It has also precipitated a new development in the region in the sense of joint military pressure being placed on another state, Malawi. Documents retrieved from the plane of the late President Samora Machel indicate there were serious discussions between Zimbabwean and Mozambican authorities about joint military action against Malawi if that country did not desist from support for the MNR.[26]

The rather depressing conclusion of this brief survey must be that since the domestic and regional politics of Southern African states are so interlocked, until the central question of the South African socio-political order is resolved there will be continuation of instability and conflict which, while falling short of all-out war, will not only be immensely destructive in human terms but will continue to obstruct the search for the kind of political institutions that can provide good government.

Notes

1. See, for example, Klaus Baron von der Roop, 'Power sharing versus partition in South Africa', *Australian Outlook*, **35** (1981) 158–68 and J. Webster, introduction to D. Tutu, *Crying in the wilderness: the struggle for justice in South Africa* (Grand Rapids, Mich.: Eerdmans, 1982).

2. For a useful overview, albeit from an anti-South African viewpoint see J. Hanlon, *Beggar your neighbours* (London: Catholic Institute for International Relations, 1986).

3. See D. Sanders, *Patterns of political instability* (London: Macmillan, 1981); K. M. Dowding and R. Kimber, 'The meaning and use of "Political Stability"', *European Journal of Political Research*, **11** (1983) 229–43. Also useful is S. Errson and J. Erik Lane, 'Political stability in European democracies', *European Journal of Political Research*, **11** (1983) (254–64) and R. Pinkney, 'The search for stability: can the Third World learn from the First?', paper presented to the UK Political Studies Association Conference 1987.

4. See Sanders, *op. cit.*, pp. 58–9; D. Easton, *A systems analysis of political life* (New York: Wiley, 1965) ch. 12.

5. On this point see L. Sigelman, 'Understanding political instability: an evaluation of the mobilisation-institutionalisation Approach', *Comparative Political Studies*, **12** (1979) 205–28, and Claude Ake, 'Explaining political instability in new states', *Journal of Modern African Studies* (1973) 347–59.

6. Though one should not forget the limit cases. One wonders to what extent Nguema, Amin and Bokassa had any societal projects at all. See S. Decalo, 'African personal dictatorships', *Journal of Modern African Studies* **23** (1985) 209–37.

7. See B. Neuberger, *National self-determination in post-colonial Africa* (Boulder, Colo.: Lynne Rienner Inc., 1986) and R. H. Jackson, 'Negative sovereignty in Sub-Saharan Africa', *Review of International Studies* **12** (1986) 247–64. See also C. Geertz, 'The judging of nations', *European Journal of Sociology*, XVIII (1977) 245–61.

8. For a useful discussion see H. Seton-Watson, *Nations and states* (London: Methuen, 1977).

9. A. de Jasay, *The state* (Oxford: Blackwell, 1985) p. 72.

10. See D. Rothchild, 'State ethnic relations in Middle Africa' in G. M. Carter and P. O'Meara, *African independence: the first 25 Years* (Bloomington: Indiana University Press, 1985) and for an example see D. L. Dressang, 'Ethnic politics, representative bureaucracy and development administration: the Zambian case', *American Political Science Review*, **68** (1974) 1605–17.

11. C. Young, 'Ethnicity, the colonial state and post-colonial state in Africa' in P. Brass (ed.) *Ethnic groups and the state* (London: Croom Helm, 1985) p. 83.

12. See W. Tordoff (ed.) *Politics in Zambia* (Manchester University Press, 1974).

13. See M. Sithole, 'Class and factionalism in the Zimbabwe Nationalist Movement', *African Studies Review*, **27** (1984) 117–25.

14. See *Africa Confidential*, 21 January 1987.

15. See A.L. Epstein, *Ethos and identity* (London: Tavistock, 1978).

16. R. H. Jackson, *op. cit.*, p. 257.

17. For a useful overview see T. M. Callaghy, 'Politics and vision in Africa: the interplay of domination, equality and liberty' in P. Chabal (ed.) *Political domination in Africa* (Cambridge University Press, 1986).

18. See D. Rothchild, 'Interethnic conflict and policy analysis in Africa', *Ethnic and Racial Studies*, **9** (1986) 73.

19. See, for example, P. Fauret, 'Mozambique at the Polls – "bourgeois electoral force"' (*New Africa*, December, 1977).

20. Tordoff, *op. cit.*, p. 384. See also C. Gertzel (ed.) *The dynamics of the one-party state in Zambia* (Manchester University Press, 1984) ch. 4.

21. Quoted in R. H. Jackson and C. G. Roberg *Personal rule in black Africa* (Berkeley, University of California Press, 1982) p. 166.

22. For this usage see M. Mann, 'The autonomous power of the state: its origins, mechanisms and results', *European Journal of Sociology*, XXV (1984) 185–213.

23. R. H. Jackson and C. G. Rosberg, 'The marginality of African states' in G. M. Carter and P. O'Meara, *op. cit.*, p. 53. For Swaziland see *Africa South of the Sahara* (London: Europa, 1987).

24. For a useful overview see E. Leistner, 'Economic Interdependence in Southern Africa', Supplement to *Africa Institute Bulletin*, **26** (1986) 1–16.

25. B. Buzan, *People, states and fear* (Brighton: Wheatsheaf, 1983) p. 78.

26. It should be noted that some observers have expressed doubts as to the authenticity of these documents.

8 The US Response to Political Instability in South Korea

Chintamani Mahapatra

After the downfall of the authoritarian regime of President Ferdinand E. Marcos of the Philippines with the tacit support of the USA, the Chairman of the Foreign Affairs Committee of the House of Representatives, Dante Fascel, remarked that President Marcos lost his mandate to rule because he frustrated the popular desire for democratic rule, and added sentimentally that 'Americans fought and many lost their lives to preserve the freedom of [South] Korea. The time has come – indeed is overdue – for the [South] Korean government to restore to its citizens the control of their own destiny.'[1] President Ronald Reagan, on the other hand, congratulated himself on his success in dealing with the Philippine situation, and within weeks of this success brought about a change in his earlier policy – known as the Reagan Doctrine – which had singled out leftism as the sole foe of freedom and democracy. The change in the policy was clearly reflected in the President's statement made on 14 March 1986: 'American people believe in human rights and oppose tyranny in whatever form, whether of the left or the right.'[2]

Although the Philippines and South Korea have very few things in common, both have been under the rule of an authoritarian regime. Furthermore the USA is indubitably a strong link between them as a common ally, guarantor of security and the most important source of military assistance. It was indeed symbolic of Washington's connection with Manila and Seoul that the US Congressman Tom Foglietta brought a personal message of encouragement from the new Philippine President, Corazón Aquino, to the South Korean opposition leader Kim Dae Jung. As such, the overthrow of the Marcos regime could not go unnoticed in the Republic of Korea, where opposition to the authoritarian regime of President Chun Doo Hwan was rapidly building up. As Marcos was about to make his exit from the Malacanang Palace after twenty years of authoritarian rule, President Chun made a conciliatory gesture towards the opposition from the presidential residence Chong Wa Dae or Blue House. The opposition leader, Kim Young Sam, on the other hand, congratulated the Philippines on achieving a peaceful transfer of power, and remarked that 'dictatorial regimes always fall', and the 'road to democracy is now an irreversible trend in the world'.[3] Kim probably referred to the fall of the military dictatorships in a few Latin-American countries since 1979, and the fall of the Marcos regime in the Philippines and that of Duvalier in Haiti in 1986. The Korea Catholic Justice and Peace Commission issued a prompt statement which said, 'At least the people of the Philippines are free of their chains, and we watched the role of the Christian Church there with some guilt.'[4] A Roman Catholic Church circular called the 'democratic revolution' in the Philippines 'a lesson' for South Korea.

However, unlike Marcos, Chun repeatedly made promises to step down from the Blue House after the completion of his constitutional term of office. The real bottleneck in the process of political transition was apparently the deadlock over the issue of the revision of the constitution. While Chun and his Democratic Justice Party were pushing for the adoption of a parliamentary form of government, the opposition parties were demanding a presidential form of government with the direct election of the head of state. As political compromise on constitutional issues appeared elusive, President Chun took a risky decision and suspended all debates and discussions with the opposition parties on 13 April 1987 and the Democratic Justice Party went on to choose its chairman, Roh Tae Woo, to run for the presidency in an election that was to be held under the existing electoral system. Roh was Chun's candidate, and his nomination clearly indicated that Chun was determined to resolve the political future of South Korea in his own way. Chun's hope was soon belied by his actions which sparked off a massive popular uprising of unprecedented character throughout the nation. All these events culminated in a 'political miracle', reflected in Roh's surprise political move of accepting almost all the principal opposition demands, an action which was subsequently endorsed by President Chun in a nationwide television broadcast.

While domestic factors undoubtedly play a significant role in political transition processes in any state, the role of the external factors in many is no less. The role of the USA in the recent Philippine political transition, for instance, is no secret. South Korea, like the Philippines, has close security and economic ties with the USA. The US, in fact, served as 'midwife' at the birth of South Korea in the post-war period, and has since influenced the shape of Korean history in more than one way.[5] The level of strategic cooperation and growing economic ties between the USA and South Korea have created a situation where the former has to keep track of the political developments of the latter and exert its influence whenever necessary to protect as well as enhance its interest. What are USA's interests in South Korea? How were these interests threatened by the recent political unrest in the country? How did the USA react to political violence in South Korea? What steps did it take to protect its interests? How did the Philippine situation differ from the Korean one? Whither South Korea? Whither the USA's South Korea Policy?

STRATEGIC SIGNIFICANCE

Although during the period between the end of World War II and the outbreak of the Korean War, South Korea was far from being regarded as an important strategic area by American strategists,[6] the Korean War brought about a complete reversal in the American perception of and policy towards South Korea. The US sent its troops under the banner of the UN to defend South Korea from 'aggressive communism', and ever since then has developed a security interest in the Korean peninsular that has increased over the years.[7] On the second day of the war, the USA signed a Mutual Defence Assistance Agreement, and soon after the war entered into a Mutual Defence Agreement with the South Korea which came into effect on 17 November 1954 and was to remain in force *indefinitely*, unless terminated by either party one year after notice had been given to the other.[8]

Today South Korea constitutes an important part of the US security system in the Asia-Pacific region by housing a number of US naval and air bases at places such as Saechon, Chinhae, Osan, Chongju, Taegu, Suwon, Pusan and Inchon. As the US military left the Cam Ranh Bay in the aftermath of the Vietnam War, these bases in South Korea assumed added importance by being 'the only forward' US bases in continental Asia.[9] About 40 000 American troops are stationed in South Korea, not only to protect the host country from a possible invasion from communist North Korea, but also as part of an overall strategic plan to face up to any possible challenge to US interests in the whole of the Asia-Pacific region. US troops in South Korea constitute one of the significant symbols of Washington's commitment to the security of the non-communist countries of the region. The importance of this symbol is reflected in the fact that when the Nixon administration decided in 1973 to withdraw one of the two US infantry divisions from South Korea, it caused an immediate alarm in governing circles in Japan; and the talks of troop withdrawal during the early Carter administration evoked even more intense reaction in Japan and other friendly countries of Asia. The US government went on record to reassure the Japanese that Washington would fulfil its 'standing treaty commitment to Japan'.[10] After the unification of North and South Vietnam and the communist takeover of the whole of Indochina, the mainland Chinese and the North Koreans are believed to have an eye on Taiwan and South Korea respectively. There has been decades-long allied planning to defeat any overt North Korean invasion of South Korea, and if there is less possibility of a North Korean attack, it is partly due to the 'high-level' readiness of the Korean and US armed forces in South Korea.[11] It is noteworthy that besides NATO's central front, South Korea constitutes the only other theatre where US forces are forward-based. And the South Korean theatre is even more vulnerable to the 'cry-wolf' syndrome than the NATO's central front. The Reagan administration has therefore strengthened the 'trip-wire' role of the US forces in South Korea in recent years.[12] It goes without saying, that in the event of the loss of South Korea, either politically or otherwise to the North Koreans, the USA would have to pay a heavy price in terms of losing its remaining credibility in the region as a guarantor of the non-communist nations' security. The South Korean military establishment, on the other hand, which did not even exist before World War II, owed its birth to the US occupying forces in the post-war period. The South Korean military was trained and equipped by the USA and by 1981 had become one of the largest armed forces in the world. With a view to strengthening the joint and combined operations of the South Korean armed forces and the US troops in the event of an emergency, the two countries have been conducting the annual 'Team Spirit' exercises since 1976, involving troops and equipment from the US military bases in Hawaii, California, Okinawa, the Philippines and South Korea.

Over the years, US-South Korea security relations have taken on the appearance of a responsible partnership instead of the earlier image of a patron–client one. However, the United States continues to be the stronger ally and the 'ultimate stabilizer' of the Korean conflict. Notable is the fact that the operational command of the South Korean forces is vested in the commander-in-chief of the United Nations Command in South Korea, who is none other than the commanding general of the US Eighth Army in Korea.

Although during the period of *détente*, and subsequently in the post-Vietnam War period, American security policy towards South Korea grew a little ambivalent due to the changes in the international environment and the compulsions of US domestic political pressure, 'there have been both a sustained [US] commitment to the defense of Korea and clear-cut actions to support that commitment'.[13]

The proposal for the phased withdrawal of the US troops from Korea during the initial years of the Carter administration was in no way an indication of Washington's declining interest in South Korea. Jimmy Carter had made this proposal during his election campaign in the backdrop of the traumatic Vietnam experience, but as he assumed office, the US army requested of Congress to double the military construction funds for Korea. President Carter, furthermore, clarified in various news conferences that his proposal was not meant to reduce the US commitment to defend South Korea in the event of a communist attack.[14]

The proposed withdrawal of the US ground troops was in fact promptly dropped when intelligence reports in 1978 and 1979 revealed that North Korea had greater military strength than was previously estimated. In addition, a Korean-US Combined Forces Command was inaugurated in 1978 for efficient integration of the functioning of Korean and US forces.

Moreover, South Korea has been the largest recipient of the overall US foreign military aid to East Asia in the entire post-war period (if Vietnam is excluded from the list).[15] More recently, in January 1987, President Reagan asked Congress to approve $311 million worth of US military construction projects in the Far East. In the proposed plan South Korea drew the maximum of $149 million for the construction of 15 army projects at camps and elsewhere, and 17 air force projects at Kunsan, Kwang-ju, Osan and Suwon.[16]

The importance of South Korea to the USA, both as a strategic location from which Moscow is only a few minutes flying time north, and as a close ally, has increased greatly in recent years in the wake of the US withdrawal from Indo-China, increasing military presence of the Soviet Union in the region, and the beginning of troubles in the ANZUS alliance. After the communist victory in Vietnam, the Soviet Union managed to get access to the military facilities at the former US base, Cam Ranh Bay, which has enabled them to undertake electronic surveillance of US bases in the Philippines and other US military activities in the Pacific Ocean. Moscow is also the 'potential beneficiary' of the trouble in the ANZUS alliance created by New Zealand's Labour government, which banned the visit of US warships unless Washington disclosed the type of weapons carried by the ships.[17] North Korea, the main adversary of South Korea, is regarded by Moscow as part of a strategic line linking itself with Indo-China, and thus the growing closeness between Moscow and Pyongyang in recent years has created added concern, both in Seoul and Washington. Consequently, the Reagan administration, with its 'assertive' foreign policy marked by its anti-communist style of functioning, has upheld 'the spirit of Cold War alliance with South Korea'.[18] South Korea, above all, is one of the few Asian countries that enjoys the privilege of being under the US 'nuclear umbrella'.

THE 'NEW JAPAN'

When South Korea became an integral part of Washington's global strategy for the containment of communism, it was economically one of the poorest nations on earth. A strategic prize was an economic liability. The division of the Korean penisula in 1945 left it with limited agricultural resources and a large pool of unskilled labour, while North Korea inherited the abundant amount of natural resources and most of the then existing industrial base built by the Japanese during colonial rule.[19] As a strategic ally, the USA considered the economic development of South Korea to be as important to its own interest as to that of the South Korean people. The USA channelled liberal aid and provided favourable trading opportunities to South Korea which has since evolved from a major recipient of economic aid to a nation at the threshold of joining the fully industrialised nations of the world. The USA over the years has successfully encouraged Japan to increase its participation in the South Korean economy, and today South Korea is regarded in some quarters as one of the 'new Japans' of the Far East, the others being Taiwan, Hong Kong and Singapore. However, Hong Kong and Singapore are simply city-states. Although Taiwan is credited with its higher national income, better foreign exchange reserves and more widely distributed industrial ownership, South Korea has better control and direction of its production activities. The South Korean economy is also regarded as a model of Third World development in many South East Asian countries. In other words, South Korea's gigantic enterprises 'have captured Third World imaginations to a greater extent than Taiwan's economic success'.[20]

In addition to being a development model for Third World countries, South Korea has achieved the distinction of being the largest producer of colour television sets, and the second largest ship-builder in the world. The South Korean conglomerates, such as Samsung, Daewoo, Lucky

Goldstar and Sunkyung, not only compete successfully with multinational companies in the First World, but are also engaged in research and development in such high technology fields as bioengineering, semiconductors and computers.[21] South Korea indeed has moved from being one of the poorest nations of the earth to one of the few Newly Industrialising Countries (NIC), to one of the very few Rapidly Industrialising Countries (RIC), and today it is the twelfth largest exporter in the world, and the seventh most important trading partner of the USA. The Americans buy almost one-third of all Korean-made goods exported abroad, and send about one-fifth of all the merchandise imported into South Korea.[22] Moreover, about 2000 US companies do business on South Korean soil. Although Japan is more prominent in direct foreign investment, the USA also has a substantial investment in South Korea – approximately $471.4 million in 1983.[23] South Korea, as a matter of fact, is one of the few countries that provides a lucrative field for foreign investment. Currently 76.3 per cent of 999 business areas under the Korean Standard Industrial Classification are open to foreign equity investment, and the foreign investors are permitted to hold up to 100 per cent of shares of the companies and remit profit abroad without restriction.[24] It is to be noted that US trade with the Pacific region overtook its trade with Europe by 1978, and it was up by 24 per cent in 1983.[25] How true was Charles Denby when he predicted in 1898 that the Pacific Ocean was 'destined to bear on its bosom a larger commerce than the Atlantic. As the countries in the Far East and Australia develop their resources, the commerce of the United States with them will assume proportions greater in their direction and scope, than over commerce with Europe.'[26] Along with the rising thrust of Washington's involvement in the Asia-Pacific region, South Korea has assumed increased significance in the calculations of US policymakers not only as strategic bases, but also by dint of its own economic achievements. The strategic significance of South Korea's alliance with the United States has in fact gained 'its economic dimension to an extent that the US has to consider its commitment to South Korea increasingly on its own right'.[27]

POLITICAL STABILITY

The high level of US security and economic interests in South Korea finds its reflection in the increasing interest in Korean affairs among scholars as well as in the general public in the USA. Korean studies find an autonomous representation in the programme committees of the

Association for Asian Studies (the largest professional organisation of Asian specialists in the world), the Social Science Research Council, and the American Council of Learned Societies in the United States. While Harvard University, the University of California at Berkeley, the University of Washington and the University of Hawaii have well-established programmes on Korean studies, other universities, such as the University of Illinois, Indiana University, the University of Chicago, and the University of California at Los Angeles, are in the process of either introducing or expanding their Korean studies programmes.[28] The US government, on the other hand, evinces a great interest in the internal political developments in South Korean, which is but a natural consequence of its vital strategic and economic interests. In order to fulfil those interests political stability in South Korea and a friendly regime in the Blue House have always been considered a minimum requirement by the United States. From the US point of view an extreme nationalist in the Chong Wa Dae is hardly a desirable substitute for a communist ruler.

The very first government in South Korea headed by Syngman Rhee was the product of Washington's determination 'to create in Korea a government friendly and responsive to American interest'.[29] After the Japanese surrender Rhee returned home in one of the private planes of General MacArthur, and quickly organised a coalition known as the Central Council for the Society for the Promotion of Korean Independence (SPKI). The US occupying forces found Rhee to be more friendly than Lyuh Woon-Hyung, who had already formed a national group called Korean Peoples Republic much before Rhee's arrival in Seoul. With the full backing of the USA, Rhee rose to power in 1948 to become the first president of the Republic of Korea,[30] and continued to rule over South Korea in an authoritarian fashion until a major student uprising against his regime in 1960 virtually forced him to step down from office. He received support and assistance from Washington as long as he was able to maintain political stability in his own country. When his government could not control the student movement, and violence disrupted peace, the USA played a significant role in Rhee's downfall.[31]

When Ho Chong became caretaker prime minister, a parliamentary system of government was adopted replacing Rhee's presidential system, and a general election was held in July 1960. A new government under the prime ministership of Chang Myon was soon inaugurated. The democratic experiment was, however, very short-lived. The country soon plunged into unrest and anarchy, and the inept leadership was incapable of restoring stability. As a result, a military group under the leadership of Major-General Park Chung Hee and a retired colonel, Kim John Pil, took over the government by staging a bloodless coup. The coup leaders were a 'new and different breed from the civilian and more senior military people' with whom the USA had had most contact.[32] The State Department made an assessment that the coup 'undermines stability', and recognised the desirability of restoring the authority of lawful government against the 'reckless challenge' of military 'cliques'. But Washington refrained from exerting any influence on behalf of the civilian prime minister because of the 'strange unwillingness of the president, armed force leaders and other key officials' of South Korea to take any action to suppress the coup attempt.[33] The general public, likewise, remained almost completely passive. Thus Washington adopted a 'cautious attitude of wait-and-see' instead of overtly siding with an almost 'lost cabinet'. Eventually, in the absence of an alternative, it took steps to protect its interests by accepting the new regime as the *de facto* government of South Korea. The new regime, headed by Park Chung Hee, who subsequently became the president, continued to rule over South Korea in an authoritarian fashion until he was assassinated in 1979.

Park Chung Hee was a complete dictator. But he was able to maintain political stability, and was thus rewarded with US assistance and support. His sweeping economic reforms received massive economic aid from Washington, and eventually brought about the much talked-of South Korean 'economic miracle'.

The Rise of Chun Doo Hwan

For a time, after the assassination of President Park, political life in South Korea was enlivened as the Democratic Republic Party and the New Korea Democratic Party increased their political activities in anticipation of presidential and National Assembly elections. The interim president, Choi Kyu Hah, who was prime minister under Park, managed to maintain stability and promised rapid reform. But the Korean army continued to become the dominant factor in the political scene. Hardly six weeks after the Park assassination, however, a power struggle within the military came to the surface. General Chun Doo Hwan, charged with investigating the assassination, arrested his superior, Chief-of-Staff General Chung Seung Haw, and rose to power.

There was widespread protest against Chun's activities, climaxing in the popular revolt in Kwang-ju province. Chun sent in Korean troops to suppress the revolt, which resulted in the killing of hundreds of people, although the government put the death toll at 189. Chun then declared martial law, got rid of his opponents through arrests and imprisonments, manipulated the constitutional procedures, and finally, in August 1980, got himself elected as the president by the National Conference for Unification acting as an electoral college. The troops that went to suppress the Kwang-ju uprising were part of the ROK-US Combined Forces Command which was under the command of US General John A. Wickham Jnr. The US-based human rights organisation, Asia Watch, pointed out in its report that the Kwang-ju massacre became a 'symbol of US support for dictatorship', and that General Wickham 'either permitted or condoned the transfer of Korean forces from the front line to aid in the suppression of Kwang-ju civilians'.[34] In any case, General Wickham made a highly political statement supporting the rise of Chun Hoo Hwan to power. He told the *Los Angeles Times* in an interview on 8 August 1980, 'Peace and stability are important to the United States here, and national security and internal stability surely come before political liberalization. . . . I'm not sure democracy the way we understand it is ready for Korea or the Koreans ready for it. . . . Korea seems to need a strong leader.'[35]

The USA in the past had supported many dictatorial regimes in various parts of the globe, with the rationale that a rightist dictator was at any time better than a leftist totalitarian regime. To quote a former US president, Jimmy Carter, 'There were times when right-wing monarchs and military dictators were automatically immune from any criticism of their oppressive actions. Our apparent commitment was to protect them from any internal political movement that might result in the establishment of a more liberal ruling group. . . .'[36]

In the case of South Korea, US Ambassador Richard L. Walker went a step further, and described the Korean opposition leaders and the anti-government student demonstrators as 'spoiled brats' in an interview in Columbia, South Carolina, on 14 February 1981.[37] President Carter was at least 'determined' to promote human rights in the countries ruled by Washington's 'authoritarian allies and friends', but Chun Doo Hwan occupied the Blue House at a time when US politics were at some kind of crossroads. Jimmy Carter lost the election in 1980, and Ronald Reagan, the new president, had already made it clear during the campaign days that he would abandon Carter's human rights policies. And indeed he did. The Reagan administration went to the extent of urging congress to reinstate military aid to countries under military/authoritarian regimes, which had been denied such aid by its predecessor. Chun Doo Hwan, furthermore, became the first foreign head of state to meet the new US president. The Reagan administration delayed the release of the 1980 edition of the State Department's *Country Reports on Human Rights Practices* to avoid any embarrassment to Chun.[38] President Chun returned to Seoul with assurances of US support, which were further reinforced two years later when President Reagan returned a visit to Seoul in 1983.

The Crisis

Seeds of political and civil unrest had taken root in South Korea when Park Chung Hee was still in power. But they assumed serious proportions when Chun Doo Hwan rose to power by brutally suppressing a popular uprising in Kwang-ju in 1980. Kwang-ju became a symbol of n ational protest against the dictatorial tendencies of the government, such as suppression of political dissent, curtailment of freedom and misuse of governmental power. Park Chung Hee justified his authoritarian rule on the grounds of maintaining social stability and achieving economic success for a long time. The Korean economic achievements under the Chun administration were no less great. In fact, when Chun came to power the national economy was in bad shape with a negative growth rate of 5.2 per cent, and inflation for consumer prices running at about 32.2 per cent.[39] But the Chun government was not only able to bring the economy back to the path of positive development, but also registered a spectacular growth rate of about 12 per cent in 1986.[40] Nonetheless, the economic growth hardly made any contribution to political stability in South Korea.

One of the most serious challenges to the Chun administration came from student political activism. Students in Korea have been politically active since the Yi Dynasty. During the Japanese colonial administration they constituted a significant section of the forces fighting for independence. Their strong opposition to the autocratic practices of President Syngman Rhee contributed to his downfall in April 1960. Students were violently opposed to the dictatorial practices of President Park Chung Hee, and the Chun regime was unable to neutralise them. Just one statistic will perhaps suffice to give a clear indication of the seriousness of the student problem in South Korea. During the period between March 1984 and August 1985, there were 3924 cases of student demonstrations, in which 994 000 students from 86 universities participated.[41] Moreover, many secret cells were created by the students with the object of overthrowing the Chun government. According to South Korean police sources, 72 such cells at 22 different universities were functioning under two radical underground organisations known as Chamintu and Minmintu.[42] Likewise, 24 other dissident labour and religious groups were organised under Mintongnyon. The well-organised Christian churches also registered their opposition to authoritarianism in South Korea. Although Buddhism is most widespread, Christianity, with more than seven million followers, is the most organised and influential religion.

The opposition political parties on the other hand, especially the New Korea Democratic Party and the Korea National Party, intensified their activities from 1985 onwards, demanding the adoption of democratic institutions. Although the opposition parties in South Korea have all along been elitist in nature and personality-based, lacking any grassroots support, they – especially the NKPD – were encouraged by the result of the 1985 National Assembly elections to strengthen their struggle against the present regime and its Democratic Justice Party. The 1985 election almost transformed the political scene in South Korea with the fledgling New Korea Democratic Party scoring a 'stunning upset victory' in the cities, and garnering a solid minority bloc of seats.[43] While the opposition parties were not particularly concerned that Chun should resign immediately, and seemed to have believed that he would step down from office in 1988 following his oft-repeated promise to do so, they nonetheless strongly opposed the government's proposal for the adoption of a parliamentary form of government. The opposition leaders perceived the government proposal as a tactic of the ruling elites to perpetuate the *status quo*. Since the ruling parties in South Korea have all along been the institutional frameworks for one-man rule, and have risen or fallen with their leaders, Chun seemed to be planning to retain his power, directly or indirectly, in a parliamentary set-up in which his democratic Justice Party was most likely to dominate the political scene. As a matter of fact, the DJP has no parallel in the nation's history in terms of its strong base and organisational structure as a political party.[44] The opposition parties, on the other hand, pleaded for the adoption of a presidential form of government with the direct election of the president (under the present system the president is elected by an electoral college). President Chun and his party rejected the opposition demand outright. After a prolonged deadlock, the NKPD threatened 'to topple the government if it continues [its] blind plot to extend dictatorial rule'.[45]

The counter-threat came from the government side. President Chun declared that in the absence of a consensus, he might 'make a grave decision to ensure the smooth implementation of the political timetable'.[46] He did not define the term 'grave decision'. However, his suspension of talks with the opposition parties regarding constitutional revision in April 1987 was a no less grave decision. More serious repercussions were created by the selection of Roh Tae Woo by the DJP as the presidential candidate less than a month after the scuttling of talks on constitutional reforms by Chun. And the problem assumed crisis proportions.

Roh was prominent among the persons whose names figured in the political speculations on the likely successor to President Chun. A classmate of Chun in the Korean Military Academy, Roh Tae Woo, had assisted Chun a great deal during the December coup of 1979.[47] Consequently Roh's nomination as the DJP's presidential candidate led to widespread protest demonstrations, in which thousands of people including students, religious groups and even a large section of the Korean middle class took part. The demonstrations often took violent turns, especially when the students engaged in street battles with the police. After more than two weeks of violent demonstrations and rallies, an apparent 'political miracle' occurred in Seoul. Roh Tae Woo made a public acceptance of nearly all the opposition demands, including a direct presidential form of government, and simultaneously announced an eight-point blueprint for the democratisation of the Korean polity. A few days later President Chun appeared on television and endorsed Roh's political proposals. What were the reactions in the USA to political violence in South Korea? What role, if any, did Washington play in the events that culminated in a political miracle in Seoul?

REACTIONS IN THE USA

Political instability in South Korea causes worries in Washington because it hinders the smooth maintenance of the military installations and the peaceful operation of economic activities, and it increases the chances of communist infiltration from the North. Although the rise of a South Korean version of the Viet Cong is a distant possibility at present, growing radicalisation of the student movement, increasing ties between the students and the working class, and a gradual appearance of anti-American feeling unknown before in this country, have created additional concern in Washington. The cause of anti-Americanism is a perception, right or wrong, that the authoritarian administration of Chun Doo Hwan is able to sustain itself in power because of American support for the regime. In 1982, for instance, South Korean students set an American Cultural Centre on fire. And just before the incident, leaflets were distributed among the people which read, 'The United States has supported the military regime which refuses democratization, social revolution and development and unification. . . . Let us stage the anti-US struggle to eliminate the US power which is rampant in this country. . . .'[48] In 1985, anti-US sentiment in South Korea grew stronger with the slogan-shouting students occupying US Government office buildings one after the other.

Events in South Korea drew considerable attention of concerned persons in congressional, diplomatic, bureaucratic and scholarly circles in the USA – almost all of them urging some kind of a positive action from Washington to protect US interest in South Korea. William Gleysteen, a former US Ambassador to Seoul, expressed his surprise at the extent of anti-US feelings harboured by certain sections of the South Korean population, especially the students, and said that if anti-US sentiment grew significantly after 1988, it would affect key relations between the two allies.[49] The House Appropriations Committee of the US Congress noted that the growing political turmoil in South Korea 'could lead to instability which could harm the interests of the United States'.[50] It objected to the Reagan administration's reluctance to criticise the government of South Korea, and suggested that the USA should publicly advocate political and human rights reforms in South Korea. The Senate Committee, likewise, said that it would be more receptive to future aid requests if South Korea 'proceeds towards full democratic freedom' that would include a national election in 1988.[51] A former assistant secretary of state for East Asian and Pacific Affairs, Richard Holbrooke, suggested that 'American influence in the process between now and 1988 must be exercised with great skill and an absolutely clear-eyed understanding of the US national interest. . . .'[52] Edwin O. Rieschauer, a Harvard University professor and former Ambassador to Japan, pleaded for American support for the democratic forces fighting against the authoritarian regime. 'The dangers are great now. People are trying to settle things . . . we should make quite clear our support at the moment for Korea's democracy . . .' said the Harvard professor.[53] Richard Walker, former US Ambassador to South Korea, on the other hand, said in a speech at the Centre for Asian Studies at Clairmont Institute in Ontario, that Washington should not attempt to teach or instruct the Koreans in their democratisation, emphasising that Koreans should solve their problems in their own way.[54] Walker, however, had been a known supporter of the Chun regime ever since his appointment as Ambassador to South Korea. Alan

D. Romberg, a Senior Fellow for Asia at the Council on Foreign Relations, was also of the view that the United States should not withdraw its support for President Chun, and suggested the exercise of 'patience' and avoidance of pressing for 'quick fixes'.[55]

As dictators in South Korea, Chile and Pakistan began to face rising domestic opposition in the wake of the downfall of dictatorships in the Philippines and Haiti, the State Department's Foreign Service Institute's Centre for the Study of Foreign Affairs organised six symposia 'to search for clues that might help prevent future Irans and encourage future Spains'.[56] This in itself indicated the US administration's concern about worsening political situations in countries ruled by Washington's authoritarian allies in general, and events in South Korea in particular.

Careful Adjustment

As political instability in South Korea began to threaten US interests, Washington carefully responded to the changing situation there. The USA would certainly prefer a systemic stability in South Korea, but it could not ignore its short-term interests there. At the same time it had to work slowly for the achievement of long-term goals. Consequently, a carefully calculated adjustment in the Reagan administration's policy towards the Chun regime appeared in 1985 when the State Department began paying some attention to the opposition leaders of South Korea. The US policy of opening the lines of communication to the opposition groups had begun in 1983 in the case of the Philippines.[57]

The Reagan White House moved slowly with regard to the Korean situation in view of the strong position of President Chun, and did not allow Kim Dae Jung to develop high-level contacts with the US executive branch. Indeed, Kim had much earlier tried to establish contacts with US officials during his exile in Washington to hasten his attempts to end the military dictatorship. He was granted meetings with officials at only the assistant secretary level. However, as political unrest in South Korea grew intense in 1985 and Kim decided to return to Seoul, the Reagan administration successfully exerted pressure on the South Korean government not to arrest the opposition leader when he returned in February 1985.[58]

A group of prominent US citizens, including some congressmen, accompanied Kim to ensure his safety and probably to prevent a replay of an Aquino-type incident. The return of Kim apparently had some positive impact on the National Assembly elections which led to the emergence of the NKDP as a significant opposition force. However, the

Reagan administration continued to keep its contact with the South Korean opposition at a lower level to avoid antagonising President Chun who still had full control over the administration. In 1985, the US Secretary of State, Assistant Secretary of State and Deputy Assistant Secretary of State all visited Seoul. Secretary Shultz declined to meet the opposition leaders, but Deputy Assistant Secretary William Clark did meet the NKDP president Lin Min Woo, and Kim Dae Jung.

The dramatic downfall of the Marcos regime in Manila and the USA's successful role in the event apparently encouraged the Reagan administration to pursue further its policy of putting pressure on the authoritarian regimes to make way for democratic rule. On 27 March 1986 the State Department publicly opposed Chun's refusal to accept the NKDP's drive for a signature campaign to petition the government for early democratisation of the polity. It said: 'We believe that it is inconsistent with the basic democratic principles to deny citizens the right to petition the government. . . . We will continue to do all we can to emphasise our support for democratization in [South] Korea.'[59] Private prodding accompanied public statements. The US Embassy in Seoul badgered the Chun administration into providing better medical treatment for the opposition leader Kim Dae Jung. In the same month the White House issued a policy statement entitled 'Freedom, Regional Security and Global Peace'. It was geared to Reagan's vociferous campaign to raise military aid for the Nicaraguan rebels. But it also expressed support for US allies around the world, such as the governments of Pakistan and Thailand. Noticeably absent in the eight-page document was any mention of South Korea. The political significance of this fact was perhaps underlined even more by the White House's denial of the political significance of the omission. Another important development in 1986 was that the US Embassy in Seoul sent invitations to the opposition leaders Kim Dae Jung and Kim Young Sam to attend the reception celebrating US Independence Day. Neither Kim had been invited to such a reception since Chun assumed power in 1980.

In October 1986, James R. Lilley arrived in Seoul as the new US Ambassador to South Korea. Lilley, a veteran of the CIA in which he had worked for 27 years, had once served as Deputy Assistant Secretary of State for Asian and Pacific Affairs. Upon his arrival Lilley began making and keeping regular contacts with the moderate opposition leaders.[60] By opening up lines of communication with the opposition leaders, Washington not only attempted to minimise criticism of its unqualified support for the ruling authoritarian regime, but also tried to build up contacts with persons who might one day form the government. However, it did not mean that the US deserted Chun. Secretary of State George Shultz, visiting Seoul the same year, gave effusive support to the Chun regime to the extent that Kim Dae Jung called it 'very disappointing to the Korean people'.[61] The time was perhaps not ripe for Washington to take sides in the domestic political conflict in South Korea.

However, as time passed the political turmoil in South Korea became worse, and the impasse over the issue of constitutional reform began to irritate the policy-makers in Washington. The US Assistant Secretary of State, Gaston Sigur, expressed his annoyance at the lack of progress on constitutional reform in South Korea in a speech he delivered in New York. The United States' concern over the domestic political uncertainty in South Korea was quite apparent in the first few months of 1987 in the shape of more frequent visits to Seoul by many high-ranking US officials and dignitaries, and in their speeches and interviews. In March 1987, William Clark, the Deputy Assistant Secretary of State, paid a visit to Seoul to make preparations for Secretary Shultz's scheduled visit, and met several key politicians to exchange views on Korea's political situation. He also met opposition leaders Kim Dae Jung, Kim Young Sam, Lee Min Woo and Lee Man Sup. Clark seems to have suggested to the Korean political leaders that democratisation measures be taken regardless of the deadlock over the issue of constitutional reform. Then came the visit of the Secretary of State, George Shultz. His message was, however, more direct. A senior US official put the message Shultz delivered to Chun more bluntly: 'You have an historic opportunity here. You've got the chance. Do it.'[62] The 'historic opportunity' perhaps referred to Chun's own expressed desire to go down in South Korean history as the first president to transfer power peacefully after the completion of his constitutional term of office.[63]

Chun received Shultz's message, but in his own way. He suspended the talks on constitutional revision with the opposition political parties, and went on to democratise the Korean polity in a way that would serve his purpose best. No criticism against Chun's action came from the Reagan White House. When Roh's nomination as a presidential candidate sparked off violent protests all over the country, President Reagan sent a letter to President Chun through Ambassador Lilley advising him to maintain restraint in dealing with the demonstrators. However, as there was no sign of an end to the violence, and stern military action against the demonstrators seemed imminent, the State Department issued a strong warning: '. . . we urge Korean military commanders to concentrate on the defense of [South] Korea and allow the political process to develop in a manner agreeable to the people.'[64] Under-Secretary of State Edward Derwinski soon arrived in Seoul to persuade the Chun administration to refrain from imposing martial law. In the last week of June 1987, President Reagan sent Assistant Secretary of State Gaston Sigur as a troubleshooter. Sigur's visit was successful. He returned to Washington and reported to the president on 26 June that there was a 'time in Korea full of opportunities for progress toward a political compromise . . .'.[65] After just three days, on 29 June, the so-called 'political miracle' took place. The role of domestic factors was substantial in the occurrence of this miracle, but Washington's influence on the course of events, especially Sigur's warning against military intervention, seems to have been considerable.

ANOTHER PHILIPPINES?

As Marcos accepted Reagan's strongly worded message delivered by Senator Paul Laxalt in 1985, and conducted the presidential election without delay, so Chun accepted Reagan's message delivered by Sigur in 1987, and perhaps agreed to hold a direct election for the presidency.

Will South Korea go the way of the Philippines? Unlike in the latter, the South Korean military has dominated the political life of the country ever since the first military coup of 1961 which brought Chun's predecessor, Park Chung Hee, to power.[66] In the aftermath of World War II, both the South Korean and Philippine economies were bordering on bankruptcy, but today, while the South Korean economy has reached the threshold of an industrialised country, the Philippine economy is still in a state of utter dependency. Another major difference lies in the nature of the communist threat to the Philippines and South Korea. An ever-expanding communist insurgency has been seriously threatening the political stability and the fabric of the Philippine society. South Korea has no such major domestic problem. However, it is a divided nation which perceives a perennial threat to its independent existence as a non-communist nation from the communist North. Thus communism threatens the Philippines from within and South Korea from without. Consequently, while the South Korean regime attempts to consolidate its position by involving the threat from the North, the Philippines government faces a challenge to its continuation in office from a section of its own population.

Moreover, where Marcos failed utterly, Chun succeeded resoundingly. The areas were economic achievement and political manoeuvrability.

In 1980, the rate of economic growth in the Philippines went on a downwards slide, and by 1985 the country was in the grip of sky-rocketing inflation, a crippling foreign exchange crisis, choked mon-etary growth, and a growing unemployment and under-employment problem. South Korea on the other hand, under the Chun administra-tion, reversed the negative growth of the national economy in 1980, and in 1985 achieved a 5.2 per cent gross domestic product (GDP) growth, which is a low growth rate in light of the country's recent record, but is quite commendable if compared with the growth rates of Singapore, Hong Kong and Taiwan in the same year, which were 1.8 per cent, 0.8 per cent, and 4.1 per cent respectively.[67] Politically, the alleged assassination of the Philippine opposition leader Benigno Aquino in August 1983 is considered the biggest blunder committed by the Marcos administration. Aquino's death stirred the people's blood, and brought thousands of them on to the streets demanding the president's resigna-tion. Chun Doo Hwan, on the other hand, did not repeat Marcos' folly, and allowed the South Korean opposition leader Kim Dae Jung to return to his homeland from the USA. In spite of twenty years of continuous rule and recent political and economic set-backs, Marcos showed no signs of quitting his throne willingly. But Chun in Seoul declared his opposition to 'one-man rule', limited the presidency to a single, non-renewable, seven-year term in the new constitution, and time and again announced his resolve to leave the Chong Wa Dae after the completion of the prescribed term of his office. He is most likely to step down, and there is no reason why South Korea should go the way of the Philippines. But will democracy dawn in South Korea in the post-Chun period?

UNCERTAINTY AHEAD

Korean history is devoid of democratic institutions. The first Western-style constitution of 1948 in post-war South Korea was alien to most of the Koreans. The first elected president of South Korea, Syngman Rhee, soon turned into an authoritarian ruler. The collapse of his government in the wake of student protest demonstrations against him made way for a democratic experiment, but it survived for only a very short time. A military coup took place in 1961 which brought Park Chung Hee to power. General Park ruled South Korea autocratically until he was assassinated in 1979. However, South Korea achieved an 'economic miracle' under his administration, and with a considerable rise in the standard of living of the people, there appeared a popular aspiration for political freedom and political rights – 'revolution of rising expectations', as Richard Holbrooke calls it. After Park's assassination, active and open political activities began, and for a moment it seemed as if elections for the presidency and the National Assembly would take place and democracy would dawn in South Korea. However, it was hope against hope. Another military coup took place, and Chun Doo Hwan came to power. But Chun could not swim against the tide of new popular expectations. People were simply not satisfied with the economic success story of his administration. It seemed as if authoritarianism's economic achievements gradually became the cause of its own destruction. The result of the 1985 election indicated this trend. A DJP moderate, Lee Jong Chan, remarked that one of the lessons of the election was that it was no longer possible 'for economic development to dominate political issues' in South Korea.[68] Will the recent 'political miracle' fulfil the popular aspiration? Prospects seem to be bleak. While the opposition parties are still unable to organise themselves under one leader, or to put an end to the rampant factional fighting, a large-scale labour movement threatens to turn the economic miracle into an economic collapse. Even if the opposition forces manage to form a coalition under one leadership, presumably Kim Dae Jung or Kim Young Sam, there is no certainty that either of the Kims will win the election. If Roh wins the election, the opposition may not accept the verdict, and may cry 'Fraud!' by the ruling party. As Kim Dae Jung told an American journalist, 'If the elections are fair, we will win. But if the government side wins, it only means they cheated.' And thus political stability may not come to South Korea. On the other hand, the South Korean military may not accept a civilian president, especially if it feels that its present privileged position in society is likely to be threatened. The dawn of democracy in South Korea thus remains a question mark.

CONCLUSION

Whenever there is civil strife in a country, the successful foreign policy of a powerful external ally depends on making a careful analysis of the situation and backing the right horse at the right time. The external power becomes helpless if the alternative horse is politically unacceptable, and the one it supports is weak and feeble. The US policy makers perhaps faced such a situation at the time of the Chinese, Cuban and Nicaraguan revolutions. But if the external ally continues to back the wrong horse (which may be in power) and does not switch its support to the right horse in time, it generally fails to protect its interests. In the case of Iran, the US had to pay a heavy price as it continued to support the dictatorial Pahlavi regime, and could not build up a rapport with the opposition forces at a suitable time. However, Washington's policy towards the Philippines in the first half of the 1980s was successful, because the White House continued to put gentle pressure on the Marcos regime to undertake economic and military reforms as long as the political situation remained uncertain, and once it was clear that Marcos was no longer capable of maintaining his position, Washington carefully switched its support to the opposition forces who soon achieved victory in the political conflict. Unlike in Cuba and Nicaragua, where the forces fighting against the dictatorial regimes were dominated by leftist elements, the US had no such difficulties to face in the Philippines as Corazon Aquino and her supporters presented quite an acceptable alternative front with their moderate democratic stand. Chile has now been witnessing an anti-authoritarian movement against the present regime of Augusto Pinochet Ugarte, who first came to power by staging a military coup in 1973 that overthrew the elected government of Salvador Allende Gossens. The USA has begun putting token pressure on the Pinochet government for early democratisation of the polity, but has not yet been able to intensify the pressure in the absence of an acceptable alternative.[69] Added pressure on Pinochet, it is feared, might actually benefit the left-wing forces there without strengthening the democratic forces which are less organised and more faction-ridden.

Unlike in the Philippines and Chile, South Korea has no problem with communists within its territory, where the opposition parties represent a moderate democratic ideology. As the USA opened the line of communication to the South Korean opposition, the opposition leaders have also been enthusiastically trying to build up contacts with the ruling circles in the USA with a view to expediting the process of democratisation with Washington's support. And thus both the ruling circles and the opposition forces in South Korea realise the value of their cooperation with the USA. The USA could benefit from it, as the available alternative to authoritarianism does not present an unacceptable front. However, Washington cannot support and oppose both sides at the same time, nor can it remain indifferent. It will, perhaps, try to maintain a modicum of relations with both, which is not always easy. But the real problem lies in the uncertain future of South Korean politics, with the military, strongly entrenched in politics, trying to safeguard its position, and a rising tide of popular aspiration for political freedom struggling to break into the *status quo*.

Notes

1.   *Far Eastern Economic Review*, 27 March 1987. Such an utterance assumes substantial significance as the United States is planning its first ever national war memorial, to be built for the Americans who died in the Korean War.

2.   *International Herald Tribune*, 15–16 March 1986.

3.   *Far Eastern Economic Review*, 6 March 1986.

4.   *Far Eastern Economic Review*, 27 March 1986.

5.   Hong N. Kim, 'US archival materials in Washington, DC, for the study of Korea', *Korea Observer*, **188** (1987) p. 117.

6.   The US policy makers who considered South Korea a liability before the Korean war seriously debated the use of nuclear weapons, if necessary, to defend South Korea by the closing days of the war. See, Top Secret, Eyes Only, Memorandum of Discussion at the 179th Meeting of the National Security Council, 8 January 1954, Papers of the President, Whitman File, *Foreign Relations of the United States*, **15** (1952–54) p. 1704.

7.   For background information on US security policy toward South Korea see Claude A. Buss, *The United States and the Republic of Korea: background for policy* (Stanford: Hoover Institution Press, 1982).

8.   *Encyclopedia of the Third World*, rev. ed. (New York: Facts on File, 1982) vol. 2.

9.   Joo Hong Nam, 'US-ROK security relations towards the 1990s: the role of US forces in Korea', *Korean Journal of International Studies*, **18** (1987) p. 117.

10.   News conference of the Vice President, 2 February 1977, *Public Papers of the Presidents of the United States: Jimmy Carter, 1977* (Washington, DC: Government Printing Press, 1977) p. 64.

11.   For a detailed analysis see Edward A. Olsen, 'The arms race in the Korean Peninsula', *Asian Survey*, **26** (1986), and Tong Whan Park, 'Political economy of the arms race in Korea: queries, evidence and insights', *Asian Survey*, **26** (1986).

12.   Joo, *op. cit.*, p. 179.

13.   Gerald L. Curtis and Sung-joo Han, *The US–South Korean alliance* (Lexington, Mass.: D.C. Heath, 1983), p. 54.

14.   For details see, *Public Papers of the Presidents of the United States: Jimmy Carter, 1977, op. cit.*

15.   The scale of US assistance between 1962 and 1983 was more than $6000 million for South Korea out of about $30 000 million earmarked for the East Asian region as a whole. See *Statistical Abstracts of the United States*, 1985 (US Department of Commerce).

16.   *Summary of World Broadcasts*, second series FE/8465, 14 January 1987.

17.   Chintamani Mahapatra, 'Marcos' Exit: A US-engineered Change?, *Strategic Analysis*, **10** (1986), p. 608.

18.   Nam, *op. cit.*, p. 178.

19.   *Countries of the world and their leaders yearbook, 1983:* A Compilation of US Department of State Reports (Detroit: Gale Research, 1983).

20.   William H. Overholt, 'Korea's international roles: a move towards prominence', *Korea and World Affairs*, **2** (1987), p. 14.

21. Byung-Foo Ahn, 'Korea: a rising middle power in world politics, *Korea and World Affairs*, **2** (1987) p. 14.
22. *The Far East and Australasia, 1987* (London, Europa, 1987).
23. Evelyn Colbert, 'Japan and the Republic of Korea', *Asian Survey*, **26** (1986) p. 286.
24. *Korean Newsreview*, 16 August 1986.
25. Girijesh Pant, 'Political economy of the Korean miracle', *Social Scientist*, **144** (1984) p. 23.
26. Letter from Charles Denby to John Sharman, 31 January 1898, in Ruhl J. Barlett (ed.) *The record of American diplomacy: documents and readings in the history of American foreign relations* (New York: Knopf, 1950) p. 408.
27. Nam, *op. cit.*, p. 178.
28. *Korea Herald*, 21 March 1987.
29. For details see Bruce Cummings, 'American policy and Korean liberation', in Frank Baldwin (ed.) *Without parallel: the American–Korean relationship since 1945* (New York: Pantheon, 1974) p. 44.
30. Lee Shin-bom, 'South Korea; dissent from abroad', *Third World Quarterly* (London) **9** (1987) 132–3.
31. Curtis and Han, *op. cit.*, p. 43.
32. Secret, Report by the Director of the Central Intelligence Agency, concurred by the US Intelligence Board, 31 May 1961, Special National Intelligence No. 42–2–61, declassified documents series of the US Government, BLPES, London.
33. Secret, telegram, from the Department of State of American Embassy in Seoul, 16 May 1961, declassified documents series of the US Government, BLPES, London.
34. Asia Watch, *Human Rights In Korea* (New York: Asia Watch Report, 1986) p. 43.
35. Quoted in Shin-bom, *op. cit.*, p. 134.
36. Jimmy Carter, *Keeping faith: memoirs of a President* (Toronto and New york: Bantam Books, 1982) p. 578.
37. 'Our opposition concerning the arson at the USIS in Pusan', Korean Christian Organization Resolution, 15 April 1982, in Wonmo Dong (ed.) *Korean–American relations at the crossroads* (New Jersey, Korean Christian Scholars in North America 1982) pp. 171–2.
38. Tamar Jacoby, 'The Reagan turnaround on human rights', *Foreign Affairs*, **64** (1986) p. 1069.
39. *Korea Newsreview*, 28 February 1987.
40. *Korea Newsreview*, 3 January 1987.
41. *Korea Youth and Students* (Pyongyang) **9** (1986).
42. *Far Eastern Economic Review*, 15 January 1987.
43. Alan D. Romberg, 'New stirrings in Asia', *Foreign Affairs*, **64** (1985) pp. 132–3.
44. Ahn Byung-Young, 'Industrialization and political parties in Korea', *Korean Social Science Journal*, **13** (1986–7) p. 34.
45. *Far Eastern Economic Review*, 11 December 1986.
46. *Korean Times*, 15 January 1987.
47. *Far Eastern Economic Review*, 4 June 1987.
48. Dong, *op. cit.*, p. 113.

49.   *Korea Times*, 14 January 1987.
50.   *Congressional Quarterly Weekly Report*, **34** (1986) 9 August 1986.
51.   *Congressional Quarterly Week Report*, **34** (1986) 27 September 1986.
52.   Richard Holbrooke, 'East Asia: the next challenge', *Foreign Affairs*, **64** (1986) p. 746.
53.   *Korea Herald*, 8 March 1987.
54.   ibid.
55.   Romberg, *op. cit.*, p. 537.
56.   Hans Binnendijk, 'Authoritarian regimes in transition', *Washington Quarterly*, **10** (1987) p. 153.
57.   Gary Hawes, 'United States support for the Marcos Administration and the pressures that made for change', *Contemporary Southeast Asia*, (1986) pp. 18–19.
58.   *New York Times*, 24 and 25 January 1985.
59.   *Far Eastern Economic Review*, 27 March 1987.
60.   *Newsweek*, 13 July 1987.
61.   Edward A. Olsen, 'South Korean Political Uncertainty and US Policy', *Washington Quarterly*, **10** (1987) p. 175.
62.   *Korea Herald*, 8 March 1987.
63.   *Korea Newsreview*, 16 August 1986.
64.   *Far Eastern Economic Review*, 2 July 1987.
65.   *Korea Herald*, 3 July 1987.
66.   For details see Nena Vreeland *et al.*, *Area handbook for South Korea*, 2nd ed (Washington, DC: Government Printing Press, 1975).
67.   *The Far East and Australasia, 1987* (London: Europa, 1987).
68.   *Far Eastern Economic Review*, 13 March 1987.
69.   Chintamani Mahapatra, 'Whither Reagan's Chile Policy?', *Strategic Analysis*, **10** (1986) p. 971.

9 International Law, Conflict and Stability in the Gulf and the Mediterranean

George Joffé

The stability of states in the Middle East and North Africa is threatened both by domestic unrest and interstate conflict. Conversely, one of the techniques that states in the region use to combat their inherent instabilities is to exploit interstate tensions so as to unify domestic public opinion. A common arena for this type of behaviour, particularly for littoral states, is in the maritime areas associated with the states concerned – not least, no doubt, because it avoids recourse to direct threats to national sovereignty. As a result, it has become common practice to exploit the opportunities inherent in international law to attempt to gain national advantage, thus avoiding the use of military force until all other avenues have been exhausted.

The aim of this chapter, therefore, is to consider the significance of international law for conflicts in the Gulf region and the Mediterranean. The conflicts themselves have been selected because they represent disputes in which economic considerations powerfully buttress the issue of national sovereignty and thus make the potential significance of international law in their eventual resolution greater than it might otherwise have been. Furthermore, although legal considerations may have played little part in the genesis of the conflicts themselves, the factors which did generate them may well have important implications for the future evolution of international law.

The conflicts in question are connected with states which have not usually been considered to be prepared to respect international legal principles but which have in fact done so in recent years in certain specific domains at least – Iran, Iraq and Libya. Furthermore, the conflicts have had significant implications for neighbouring states, particularly in the Gulf, leading them to evaluate relevant legal factors in determining their responses. The conflicts are, firstly, the Gulf War and the implications for oil exports through the Gulf and, secondly, the issue

151

of freedom of navigation in the Gulf of Sirt, where Libya has ever since 1973 claimed exclusive rights despite opposition from other states, most notably the USA.

As far as the Gulf War is concerned, the dominant consideration is the role played in the genesis of the conflict by the Shatt al-Arab delimitation dispute[1] and the way in which this has reflected the internal stability of the states involved. However, there are many other areas of dispute over maritime delimitation in the Gulf region[2] and some of these have resulted in active conflict in recent years. The Shatt al-Arab issue involves consideration of the use of rivers as international boundaries, particularly when such a boundary is intimately linked with historical conflict and contemporary issues of access to crucial national economic centres such as Basra in Iraq, or Khorramshahr and Abadan in Iran.[3]

Other conflicts in the Gulf relate to issues of maritime delimitation of the continental shelf[4] and access to offshore oil, as well as to rights of freedom of navigation for third parties in a situation of conflict – particularly when such access is of vital importance to third party states in the region and to states outside it. Behind all of these conflicts, in short, lie acute concerns over national security and national economic interest by all the states in the region,[5] whether riparian or littoral. On occasion, these disputes, such as that between Qatar and Bahrain,[6] can break out into open conflict, as occurred in 1986. These concerns have been intensified in recent years by the development of the 1982 Law of the Sea, as a result of the UN Conferences on the Law of the Sea, particularly UNCLOS 3, and the concept of the exclusive economic zone (EEZ) – although the Gulf itself is too small for explicit application of EEZ precedent.

The Gulf of Sirt issue has been chosen because the dangers of conflict have been publicly emphasised in August 1981 and in March 1986, when Libyan forces and US naval and carrier-borne aircraft came into conflict during US military exercises in the Gulf or close to the unilaterally proclaimed Libyan 1973 closing line. The Libyan action in attempting to close off the Gulf on historic and security grounds has been treated as a preposterous claim by several interested observers and at least fourteen states have publicly rejected the Libyan claim or expressed reservations about it. Yet the US naval action in March 1986 implicitly justified Libyan's action, if not its rationale, for in attacking SAM missile batteries along the shoreline the USA made it clear how vulnerable that coastline is to attack from enemy forces within the closing line areas.

Libyan sensitivity on this point is rendered more understandable by the fact that the vast majority of Libya's economic activity is also located along the Gulf coast. It should be remembered here that economic activity is one of the two major pillars for the stability of the Libyan state, the other being the control exercised by the radical components of the Qadhafi regime on Libyan's political institutions. No wonder, then, that the Libyan authorities have sought some basis in international law for ensuring not only Libya's sovereignty but also the protection of its vital economic interests. Indeed, in using established legal precedent for what is, in effect, a new purpose, it may well be that the Libyan action will help in the evolution of international legal practice in defining the rights of states over waters along their coasts.

IRAN, IRAQ AND THE SHATT AL-ARAB DISPUTE

The boundary between Iran and Iraq is, in many respects, unique in the Middle East.[7] It evolved over a thousand years and was the subject of detailed discussions concerning its delimitation for over fifty years – from the 1840s to 1913 – both because of the confrontation between two decaying empires, the Ottoman and Persian, and because of intense Anglo-Russian rivalry for control over the region. The 65-mile-long Shatt al-Arab riverine portion of the border, however, is even more unique and more complex. The complexity arises not only from problems of locating an actual boundary in a wide river – along a low water shore line, along the median line, along the line of greatest depth or 'main channel' (the *thalweg*), or any combination of these – but also because of the interplay of national economic interest and national prestige. Largely because of this, the problem of the delimitation of the Shatt al-Arab has come to embody many of the issues that led to the outbreak of the Gulf War in September 1980.[8]

The Evolution of a Frontier

Extremely detailed discussions of the formation of the Shatt al-Arab boundary are provided by several authors.[9] The basic elements in its evolution are relatively simple, however. The first attempt at a formal allocation of a boundary between the Ottoman and Persian empires occurred in May 1555, when the Amassia treaty was signed. This, however, really only created a tribal march or frontier zone between the two empires. It was not respected, in any case, and was replaced by a new treaty – the Zuhab treaty – in 1639 in the wake of a major Ottoman victory.

Although an uneasy peace was restored to the region, the two empires indulged in continuous squabbling, particularly over the allocation of the Shatt al-Arab region.[10] In 1727, after an Ottoman agreement with the new power of Russia to the north to divide the Persian empire and a consequent invasion of southern Persia, large areas were ceded to the Ottomans in the Treaty of Hamadan. These, in turn, were returned to Persia under the terms of the Treaty of Kherden in 1746.[11]

A major problem was that in the south the riparian boundary proposed (initially along the Bahmanshir river) did not correspond to ethnic divides, for Arab-speaking populations had extended into Khuzestan and may groups were in any case migratory. Eventually, a further treaty – the First Treaty of Exerum – was drawn up in 1823, which added little in precision to its predecessors in boundary delimitation. The upshot of this uncertainty was that in 1837 the Ottomans destroyed Khorramshahr because they feared that it would become a commercial rival to Basra, just a little further up the Shatt al-Arab. The Ottoman authorities, on the basis of the ethnic spread across the river, also maintained their claim to large areas of Khuzestan.

Great Power Intervention

War was averted, however, because Britain had by then come to realise the commercial and strategic potential of the Gulf region and Persia – steam had made the Tigris navigable and thus allowed British commerce to penetrate into the heart of the Ottoman empire, while Russian advance southwards from Muscovy had made Persia into an imperial concern because of the potential threat to India.[12] Britain, therefore, enforced negotiations over the tricky question of the border on both protagonists and, together with Russia, the Ottoman empire and Persia delimited the border in the Second Treaty of Ezerum in May 1847. A major Ottoman concession was that the Shatt al-Arab became the effective riparian boundary, a concession which was acceptable because the Arabic-speaking Muhammarah region on the eastern bank was effectively autonomous from Persian control.

As far as the Shatt al-Arab was concerned, the 1847 treaty gave the Ottoman empire sovereignty over the river, although Persia had acquired control of Khorramshahr (the first Farsi name for Muhammarah) and the east bank of the river. Persian vessels were, however, to have freedom of navigation up the river. Although the treaty provisions were never properly delimited on the ground, an informal agreement appears to have developed along the Shatt al-Arab, whereby the boundary was assumed to be a median line and each state controlled its own navigation along the river.[13]

This comfortable situation of informal compromise was to change radically, however, at the start of the twentieth century, for two reasons. The first was the ever-growing British interest and presence in the head of the Gulf and the Shatt al-Arab. Linked to this was the second reason – the discovery of oil at Masjed Sulaiman in Iran in 1908 by the Burmah Oil Company.[14] Furthermore, the use of steam ships had made oil prospecting in Iraq possible as well and work began in 1904, although oil was not to be struck in commercial quantities until 1923. In addition, Britain and Russia had plans to control Iran, while London viewed with alarm German attempts to penetrate the Ottoman empire as part of its *Drang nach Osten* policy which included the construction of the Berlin to Baghdad railway and an extension into the Basra area.

All these factors persuaded London and St Petersburg that the time had come to resolve all outstanding disputes over the Persian–Ottoman border and, in 1913, a protocol was signed in Istanbul which granted the Ottoman empire control of the Shatt al-Arab waterway, up to the low water line on the Persian bank with certain islands including Abadan island remaining in Persian hands. This was modified in 1914, given the growing importance of Khorramshahr as an oil supply port, so that a mile above and below the port a riverine median line was followed.[15]

British Pre-eminence

Although it was not evident at the time, the 1913 protocol marked a profound change in the nature of control over the Shatt al-Arab. Until then, the issue had essentially been one involving the riparian Persian and Ottoman empires, even if outside powers had acquired a growing interest in the region. Now, however, colonial interests were to dominate the disposition of the boundary and, furthermore, these interests were to be tied to the development of the oil industry in Iran and Iraq, the post-World War I successor states to the pre-war empires.

Britain, in fact, was to be the dominant power, even after Iraq was granted nominal independence in 1922. Indeed, even before the Iraqi mandate was granted by the League of Nations to Britain in 1920, the British military commander in Iraq issued a statement – the Basra Declaration – which unilaterally declared that the port of Basra extended over the Shatt al-Arab, including the Iranian ports of Khorramshahr and Abadan for ninety miles down to the mouth of the estuary. Furthermore, Britain acquired a *de facto* protectorate over the autonomous region of Muhammarah inside Iran and covering both the ports mentioned above, so that it could protect its new oil interests in Iran as well. This convenient situation, in which the more legalistic aspects of control of the Shatt-al-Arab became irrelevant, was to come to an end in 1924, as the new ruler of Iran, Reza Shah, annexed the Sheikhdom of Muhammarah and began to insist on respect for Iranian sovereignty. The 1913 protocol now meant that all Iranian river traffic came under Iraqi control and had to pay dues to the Basra Port Directorate. This situation was quite unacceptable, both to Iranian pride and to its perceived security and economic requirements. In fact, insofar as the Basra Port Directorate acted independently from the Iraqi government, despite its nominal integration into the new Iraqi administration when Iraq was granted nominal independence in 1924, the situation became even more irksome to Iran and complaints and incidents came thick and fast.

By the 1930s, it was obvious that the dispute over delimitation of the Shatt al-Arab waterway was *the* crucial bone of contention between the two states, because the 1913 delimitation effectively granted control of all the waterway to Iraq and the Basra Port Directorate, soon to be renamed the Basra Port Authority, and meant that access to the Iranian ports of Khorramshahr and Abadan was effectively under Iraqi control. Furthermore, earlier provisions under the 1847 Ezerum treaty which guaranteed freedom of navigation for Iranian shipping in the river – as provided for by international law[16] – had been completely overridden by the 1919 Basra Declaration. Finally, Iran repudiated both the 1847 treaty and the 1913 protocol.[17]

Despite Iraqi appeals to the League of Nations in 1934, little was done to defuse the tensions. It was only after a coup in Iraq in late 1936 that the issue began to be reconsidered and negotiations between Iran and Iraq began during 1937. The resulting treaty conceded the *thalweg* principle to Iran for the first time, providing for a six mile stretch from the No. 1 jetty at Abadan down towards the edge of Shutait island to be divided by the *thalweg*. The treaty also provided for Iranian warships to use the river – although Iraq considered the Shatt al-Arab to be an inland waterway because of the general alignment of the boundary along the east bank low water mark.[18] There were also provisions for free navigation of merchant ships of all nations, as provided for in international law. Although the treaty was extremely unpopular in Iraq and led to a change in government, it remained in force with no significant objections from either state throughout the British occupation of Iraq and most of Iran during World War II.

The Struggle for Hegemony

In 1953, however, in the wake of the Mussadaqh crisis in Iran, and the restoration of the Shah under aegis, the problem of the Shatt al-Arab delimitation arose once again. Iran, however, did not seek to enforce its legal claim that a *thalweg* delimitation was the proper method of establishing an equitable international boundary – its pre-war argument – but instead argued that it was unreasonable for Iranian and Iran-bound vessels to fund the activities of an Iraqi entity – the Bhasra Port Authority, which used the funds exclusively for Iraqi port improvements and which employed only Iraqi pilots.[19] The issue remained dormant until the Iraqi revolution in 1958 which overthrew the Iraqi monarchy and brought the Qassim regime to power.

The radical changes in Iraq highlighted the underlying role played by the Shatt al-Arab dispute in acting as a surrogate for nationalist sentiment in both Iran and Iraq for, in response to the Shah's renewed complaints over the status of the border, the new Iraqi government laid explicit claim to the whole of the Shatt and even to Iranian territory in Khuzestan. For the first time since 1847, too, the dispute was to pit Iran and Iraq against each other without any interference from outside powers, whether Russian, Turkish, British or – latterly – American.[20] The dispute was also to develop gradually into a test of strength for both regimes over their relative hegemonies within the Gulf region and the Middle East over the next twenty years – a development which was ultimately to culminate in the Gulf War. During this period, three crises directly related to the Shatt al-Arab underlined the worsening relations between the two states.

The first crisis revolved around the explicit issue of Iranian sovereignty over the Shatt al-Arab. It broke out in 1961 when Iran insisted that ships entering Iranian ports on the Shatt should use Iranian pilots. The Iranian action was provoked by the Iraqi refusal to allow Iran to treat the port of Khosrowabad, halfway down the Shatt from Abadan, as the latter's outport – just as Faw was for Basra – and thus allow shipping arriving there as under Iranian sovereignty as they moved up the Shatt towards Ábadan. The Basra Port Authority called a strike of all pilots, thus halting all Iranian oil exports from Abadan, and Iran decided not to push the issue pending negotiations which never actually took place.[21]

Eight years later, the issue blew up again, this time because of Iranian support for the anti-government rebellion in Iraqi Kurdistan.[22] The only area in which Iraq felt strong enough to retaliate was over control of the Shatt al-Arab and over its irredentist claims to Khuzestan. As a result, it insisted on Iranian vessels in the Shatt not flying Iranian flags – an insult to Iran that the Shah was not prepared to accept. The result was that Iran abrogated the 1937 treaty on the grounds that Iraq had not fulfilled its obligations under it. The grounds for the Iranian action were that a bilateral navigation convention had never been negotiated, as required by the treaty, and that, under the doctrine of *rebus sic standitus*, Iran was disadvantaged by the treaty and that it was therefore null and void.[23] Iraq successfully rejected this, arguing that the correct principle was *pacta sunt servanda* – that treaty had a legal sanctity and could not be challenged in this way. Iran countered by asserting that it had really signed the treaty, as it had all preceding treaties, under duress (from Britain).

In reality, however, the 1969 confrontation underlined the growing dominance of Iran in Gulf and regional affairs. It was already evident that Britain would soon abandon its bases in the Gulf, for the Gulf states had been briefed on British intentions in 1968.[24] Iran was determined to replace British influence, despite similar ambitions in Riyadh and, most importantly, Iraq, where the arrival of the Ba'athist party to power introduced a new desire for regional integration under Ba'athist hegemony. However, given its impotence in the face of Iranian aggressiveness, the disarray in the immediate aftermath of the Ba'ath coup in 1968, the tensions of a major struggle with international oil companies and the continuing war in Kurdistan, Iraq was not able to resist the growth in Iranian power. The Shatt al-Arab thus became the focus of these wider concerns, particularly when Iran mustered considerable forces at the mouth of the river to ensure that it could impose an effective *thalweg* solution to the demarcation of the river and control its own shipping.

For the next six years the situation in the Shatt al-Arab remained unresolved, with diplomatic relations between the two neighbouring states broken off and frequent incidents in the river itself. Meanwhile, Iraq's position, particularly in Kurdistan, continued to worsen, due in no small part to Iran's support for the *pech merga* Kurdish guerrillas. By 1975, the situation had become critical for the government in Baghdad and, in order to relieve its domestic pressures, the Ba'ath regime turned to the Shah in a deal whereby Iranian support for the Kurds was to be abandoned in return for a settlement of the Shatt al-Arab dispute in Iran's favour, according to the *thalweg* principle – the Algiers Agreement of 1975.

The Run Up to the War

The loss of nationalist face for Iraq – however necessary it might have been for the sake of domestic survival – involved in the Algiers Agreement was considerable. Even more important, Iraq had to accept that Iran had established its hegemony over the Gulf and sought an ever increasing role in Middle Eastern affairs through its position inside Opec and its access to Washington. Inevitably, therefore, Iraq was to seek an opportunity to redress the situation.

The opportunity came in 1979 with the fall of the Shah and the arrival of a radical Islamic regime to power in Tehran under Ayatollah Khomeini. On the one hand, the Iraqi leadership feared the implications of a Shi'a regime in Tehran – which, in contradistinction to Iraq's irredentist nationalist and Arab nationalist claims to Khuzestan, would make claims of religious affiliation to southern Iraq where the majority Iraqi Shi'a population lived. On the other hand, Iraq believed Iran to be militarily weak in the aftermath of the revolution and saw an opportunity to seize the initiative in Gulf affairs. Once again, the Shatt al-Arab dispute was to provide a focus when, on 22 September 1980, Iraq invaded Iran, five days after having unilaterally abrogated the Algiers treaty.[25]

The Shatt al-Arab delimitation and demarcation have, therefore, acted as a focus for a series of disputes between Iran and Iraq over the past 63 years, since Reza Shah seized power in Iran. Although the dispute began as an issue of Iranian national pride and sovereignty, the primary cause was economic in that Iraqi hegemony over the river prevented Iran from servicing its nascent oil industry properly. In the wake of British departure from the region, the dispute became primarily one of national sovereignty and regional hegemony, culminating in the Iraqi humiliation of the 1975 Algiers Agreement and its revenge in 1980. Not surprisingly, the issue remains as alive as ever, and one of the four Iranian conditions for an end to the current hostilities is the restoration of the Algiers Agreement and the *thalweg* principle of delimitation, both to demonstrate Iran's regional status and to guarantee protection for future shipping movements into Abadan and Khorramshahr, once war damage has been repaired.

INTERNATIONAL LAW AND THE GULF

International law in the Gulf relates to three different kinds of problems, all of which have acquired importance in recent years both because of the Gulf War and because of national anxieties to preserve access to economic resources. The Gulf, particularly along the Arab side, is relatively shallow, with the average water depth being around 46 metres, and has many islands scattered through it. It is also relatively narrow and has been a region of cultural confrontation between the Arab and Persian worlds for centuries, as well as, more recently, an environment for colonial control, particularly when it was discovered to be rich in petroleum reserves.

Irredentist Claims

Not surprisingly, therefore, the first and the most longstanding of these problems has been the issue of irredentist claims to islands in the Gulf – Iraq's claim to Bubiyan island as part of its claim to Kuwait and its attempt to improve maritime access to the virtually landlocked port of Umm Qsar; Iran's claim to Bahrain and its occupation of Abu Musa and the Tunbs islands, claimed by the UAE, in 1971; Kuwait's and Saudi Arabia's disputes over islands off the Neutral Zone; and Qatar's dispute with Bahrain over the sovereignty of the Hawar islands.

The Iraqi claim to Kuwait and, by extension, to Bubiyan island, stemmed from Kuwait's role as part of the Ottoman *vilayet* of Basra. Although the claim was virtually abandoned under the Treaty of Lausanne of 1923, irredentist sentiments lingered and the claim was reasserted in 1961 by the Qassim regime in Baghdad. The claim received virtually no support and, in 1963, when the Qassim regime was overthrown, Iraq acknowledged Kuwait's independence. A claim was retained to Warba and Bubiyan islands, however, not least because they control access to Umm Qasr port. The claim led to incidents in 1973, but pressure from other Arab states forced Iraq into negotiations with Kuwait.[26] The detailed delimitation of the frontier between the two countries and the sovereignty over the islands was only finally resolved, however, in November 1984 when Kuwait finally rejected Iraqi demands for a military presence on Bubiyan island. Nonetheless, Kuwait is forced to keep a wary eye directed towards Baghdad because of irredentist sentiment there. This, indeed, is part of the reason for Kuwait's continued support for Iraq in the Gulf war, even at the cost of virulent hostility from Iran and the threat of Shi'a dissidence within the Emirate itself. This has now become so institutionalised in the relations between the two states that Kuwait's support for Iraq has become a positive component of national policy.

The issue of control of the islands of Qaru and Umm el-Maradim off the Neutral Zone between Kuwait and Saudi Arabia has never been satisfactorily resolved. Delimitation of the Neutral Zone was laid down in the 1922 Uqair Convention and was confirmed in the 1965 agreement.[27] However, although the two islands were supposed to pass under Kuwaiti sovereignty according to an exchange of letters in 1923 and another in 1932, Saudi Arabia has never formally abandoned its claim to them.

The Hawar island dispute – the archipelago is only 2.4 km from the Qatari coast – has persisted despite attempts by Saudi Arabia and Kuwait to mediate. The problem has arisen because the British resident in Bahrain unilaterally allotted them to Bahrain in 1939. Since then, Bahrain has asserted its claim, despite Qatari protest, by granting petroleum prospecting concessions on them in 1965 and 1980.[28] Despite the fact that both states are now members of the Gulf Cooperation Council and thus engaged in integration of their economies and defence forces, the sensitivity of the issue is such that, when a Dutch company dredged an artificial island to serve as a base for prospecting on the concession in 1986, Qatar invaded the site and took the workers involved capitve because of the threat it perceived to its claim.

The issue of Iran's claim to Bahrain was ostensibly resolved by UN mediation in 1970, when the principle of self-determination was given precedence to Iran's historical claim to the archipelago as its fourteenth province. The historical claim was based on arguments that Bahrain had traditionally been under Persian control since about 1300, except for a period of Portuguese occupation between 1507 and 1602, until Britain established an effective protectorate over the archipelago in 1820. In fact, the archipelago had been wrested from what was only nominal Persian control in 1783 by the ancestors of the current ruler and the Iranian claim has always been resisted, with the first British protest dating from 1844.[29] Since the Islamic republic has come into being, however, the claim has been revived for propaganda reasons and, although there is little likelihood of any formal attempts being made to put it into effect, the propaganda combined with growing Arab anxieties over the Gulf War, has done much to destabilise the political climate in the Upper Gulf. This is particularly important in view of the 70 per cent Shi'a majority in the population that has provided Iran with a receptive audience for its attack on Bahrain's Sunni rulers.

One Iranian claim that has been satisfactorily resolved has been the delimitation between Iran and Saudi Arabia. Indeed, the 1968 agreement resolved two problems – that of delimitation between the two states in the Gulf and a quite separate issue of sovereignty over two islands on the proposed delimitation line. The basic assumption was that the border should consist of a median line between defined baselines along each coast designed to smooth out the coastal irregularities. Kharg island, in Iranian waters, was treated as if it had a 'half-effect' and thus provided for an indentation in the median line equivalent to half its maximum extension from the Iranian mainland coast. The most striking feature was the allocation of two disputed islands – Jaz Farsi and Jaz al-Arabi. The former was granted to Iran, the latter to Saudi Arabia, with a 12-mile territorial water zone obtruding into the median line division for Saudi Arabia and a local median line between the two islands themselves.[30]

More serious has been the Iranian claim and occupation in 1971 of the islands of Abu Musa and the Tunbs, which are also claimed by the emirate of Al-Sharjah, part of UAE. The Iranian claim is based, like that to Bahrain, on historical precedent, bolstered by arguments over national security, since the islands dominate the Lower Gulf and access to Iranian ports and offshore oil fields there. Although Abu Mausa is 69 km from the Iranian shore and well on the Arab side of any median line through the Gulf, the two Tunbs islands are much closer to Iran, being only 24 km from Qeshm island[31] and the Iranian claim to them is more easily explicable than that to Abu Musa.

Both claims have been resisted – only diplomatically – by the UAE, with support from Saudi Arabia and, more significantly, Iraq, which made the return of the islands to the UAE one of its original war aims. Iraq's attitude – formally a consequence of its pan-Arabist Ba'athist ideology – reflects the need of the Ba'athist regime to legitimise its role inside Iraq by demonstrating its pan-Arab orthodoxy in the Gulf and elsewhere. The issue, in short, has been subsumed into the wider issue of regional hegemony which has pitted Iraq against Iran ever since the late 1960s and played no small part in the initiation of the Gulf War. At the same time, the issue of offshore oil and gas has undoubtedly played a large part in the calculations of both Iran and the Arab states opposed to its occupation.

Maritime Delimitation

These disputes clearly acquire considerable importance because of the large amount of offshore oil and gas in the area in addition to any question of national sovereignty or political irredentism. Indeed, this is a factor that has also made the second type of problem a particularly acute issue – maritime delimitation between contiguous and opposed states in the Gulf. Indeed, of the 29 identifiable maritime boundaries in the Gulf, only 2 adjacent boundaries and 5 opposite boundaries have been delimited, while 13 adjacent and 9 opposite boundaries are still not agreed and thus represent a fertile source of potential conflict.[32] The Gulf War has admittedly put many of these issues into abeyance, but they will certainly reassert themselves once hostilities die down.

Over the past two centuries, particularly since the Second World War, an elaborate system for delimiting the rights of littoral states and of ships at sea over rights of passage has grown up. In the Gulf, given its extremely crowded marine environment and restricted space, these considerations have become particularly important for they affect issues of national sovereignty and access to oil and gas deposits. In the context of the Gulf War and the practice of the belligerents of declaring exclusion zones, together with the UN Treaty on the Law of the Sea in 1982, an added urgency has been given to the issue of delimitation, particularly as all the states in the region will want to renew offshore oil concession options once hostilities die down.

Generally accepted principles of international law today recognise six different zones of sea, depending basically on the distance of each zone from the shoreline of the state concerned. Internal waters consist of those waters which are of interest only to the state concerned – bays and estuaries. Limitations on such waters were laid down under a UN convention for contiguous zones and territorial seas in 1958. In addition to the convention, there is always the alternative claim that the state concerned had traditionally had exclusive use of them in the past – 'historic rights'. Territorial seas, extending for 12 miles from the coast in the case of Gulf states, except for Bahrain, Qatar and the UAE, are those waters adjacent to the coast in which the state in question claims sovereignty over the waters, the sea bed, the subsoil and the airspace above – although it cannot deny ships of other nations the right of 'innocent passage' through them. The contiguous zone extends from the outer edge of the territorial sea for 12 miles according to the 1958 convention to allow control for customs, fiscal, quarantine or pollution purposes.[33]

Most important, perhaps, from the point of view of maritime delimitations in the Gulf, is the continental shelf, for states have exclusive rights to exploitation of the seabed and subsoil in this region – a matter of considerable concern, given offshore oil and gas deposits, such as Qatar's North Gas Field of the shared oil fields between Kuwait and Saudi Arabia and Iran. The problem is that, until 1982, there was no effective definition of the continental shelf. Under another UN convention in 1958 designed to define the continental shelf, it was basically defined as being bounded by the 200-metre isobath, largely because at that time the technology to work mineral resources at greater depths did not exist. However, there was a further provision that extended the definition to deeper waters if technology permitted exploitation of minerals. According to the convention, the continental shelf was limited by the 200-metre isobath or beyond this limit to where the depth of the superjacent waters admits of the exploitation of the natural resources of the seabed or the subsoil.

This situation has changed during the intervening years and, under the 1982 UN Treaty, the continental shelf limitation has been redefined and augmented by the concept of the exclusive economic zone which extends for 200 nautical miles from the coast. The continental shelf concept has been expanded so that it now extends from the shore, for a minimum of 200 miles and a maximum of 350 miles, to the edge of the continental margin.

In the Gulf, however, the whole sea area forms a single continental shelf and is thus subject to division between the littoral states according to 'equitable principles'.[34] In the Gulf, this has usually been taken to mean a median line delimitation, according to the 'equidistance principle', with other methods only being used if this creates an obviously inequitable result.[35] The most obvious cause of inequitability is the role played by islands and adjustments to median lines have often been made as result. The roles played by Qeshm and Larak islands in the Straits of Hormuz, or of Kharg island in the Upper Gulf, are good examples. Delimitations have occurred, however, and have been achieved by negotiation, without reference to supranational bodies, such as the International Court of Justice at The Hague.

Nonetheless, given the plethora of different definitions and the complexity of the sea bed in the Gulf, it is hardly surprising that relatively few delimitations have been concluded. Active and potential disputes abound as a result. Iran and Kuwait and Iran and Iraq are in dispute over their adjacent boundaries, quite apart from the role played by the Gulf War. In the case of Iran and Kuwait, the problems arise because each state allows for its own island in unilaterally setting a median line but ignores the islands of the other – Faylakah in the case of Kuwait, Kharg in the case of Iran. Agreements between Iran and the UAE has been formalised, apart from a section opposite to Dubai, because of the disputes over ownership of islands and the effect to be given to them in modifying the median line.

As far as opposed boundaries are concerned, the UAE-Omani maritime boundary almost led to war in 1977 when offshore oil was discovered, although the issue was said to have been settled in 1979.

Many such boundaries are only delimited when provision is made for joint exploitation of oil and gas reserves. Qatar and Abu Dhabi deliberately located their common boundary so that each had equal access to the Al-Bunduq oil field. A similar approach had to be adopted by Saudi Arabia and Iran in dividing the Marjan-Fereydoon field, while Bahrain ceded its interests in the Abu Safah field to Saudi Arabia in return for half the revenues from the field in perpetuity.[36]

It is clear that the problems of delimitation in the Gulf are complex, largely because of the large numbers of states clustered around a semi-enclosed sea. The problems are worsened by the fact that all delimitations have a direct bearing on access to natural resources. Over the past seven years, they have been embittered by the Gulf War and their resolution in future will reflect the degree to which the states in question perceive their relative regional power. In this respect, the Arab states are likely to find themselves increasingly in confrontation with Iran, particularly as the Gulf Cooperation Council welds them into a single economic unit. Iraq, however, given its poor showing in the war to date, is unlikely to be able to improve its position or its access to the Gulf through maritime delimitation.

Freedom of Navigation

The third type of problem is currently the most acute – the issue of freedom of navigation for commercial vessels. It has become acute because of the Gulf War in which both protagonists have been prepared to attack neutral shipping, whether or not it was engaged in trade with one of the belligerents. To date, over 300 ships have been attacked. This has been particularly blamed on Iran which has also threatened to close the Straits of Hormuz on at least two occasions and has used derelict oil platforms in the Rostum offshore field as a helicopter platform to interdict shipping between the Straits and Das Island. Its justification has been Iraqi attacks on shipping, particularly on the shuttle service between Kharg island and Larak island, from where most of Iran's oil exports now occur. In fact Iraq, which initiated the attacks on shipping has been responsible for over 60 per cent of all attacks. Kuwait has been a prominent victim of Iranian hostility because Teheran has insisted that its shipping was being used to support Iraq's war effort.

The seriousness of the problem can be gauged by the fact that in late 1986 Kuwait felt obliged to seek protection from such attacks by asking four states – Britain, the USA, the USSR and China – for protection by allowing shipping travelling to Kuwait to travel under their national flags, so that any attack would then internationalise the Gulf conflict.[37] Initially, the USSR agreed to lease several tankers to Kuwait, while the USA actually reflagged eleven Kuwaiti tankers under its own colour, in an attempt to dissuade Iran from further attacks on shipping. Although the formal justification for this move, which involved the direct participation of US naval forces in the maritime aspects of the Gulf War, was to guarantee the freedom of navigation from Iranian attack, the real reasons appear to have been to counter the growth of Soviet influence in the Gulf and to protect US access to future sources of oil imports. The reality is that US policy might easily achieve the reverse of what it intended.

Prior to the 1987 crisis, however, the USA, Britain and France had stationed naval vessels in the vicinity of the Gulf since 1984 in order to enforce the right of freedom of navigation and the USA had warned Iran against the use of Chinese Silkworm SSM missiles which had been installed around the Straits area. However, there were many complaints from Gulf states and others that these naval units only protected their own nationals' vessels and thus added little to regional security. In any case, international concern in these sorts of circumstances has traditionally been with freedom of navigation of the high seas – all sea areas outside the contiguous zone, with interest in the more limited regions of sea area being tied to the concepts of 'innocent passage' and 'transit regime'.

Indeed, the issue of freedom of navigation is particularly acute at the mouth of the Gulf, given intermittent Iranian threats to close the Straits of Hormum. The Gulf is a semi-enclosed sea[38] and the Straits of Hormuz are narrow enough for there to be no high seas – seas outside territorial limits and contiguous zones – available for passage. However, under international law, the right of innocent passage – the right to pass through the region provided that the ship in question has hostile intent – still exists through the Straits, although Iran has threatened to interfere with this principle in the past. Its justification for doing so is that the shipping involved represented a threat to its own security[39] – no doubt because of the fact that it was to carry oil from states that support Iraq in the war and thus indirectly contribute to its continuation. Furthermore, Iraqi attacks on shipping were a direct threat to Iran's own right to freedom of navigation and thus had to be countered.

In fact, Iranian claims are still unacceptable under international law because straits, such as the Straits of Hormuz, are normally governed by a transit regime. Here the very fact that in the past shipping has used the straits for passage from one sea to another establishes a permanent right, whatever the purpose of the passage.[40] This is particularly important because of the exclusion zones declared both by Iran and by Iraq in different parts of the Gulf. In the case of Iran, the exclusion zone is designed to extend into the Straits of Hormuz up to the median line. Although this does not directly affect shipping because the shipping' lanes are with Omani waters,[41] it does underline the continual Iranian threat to attempt to close the Straits and thus to interdict the 10–13 million barrels of oil that passes through the Straits daily.

Furthermore, the crowded nature of the Gulf itself means that rights of freedom of navigation are particularly important because they can be so easily threatened, especially in view of its role as a major trade thoroughfare for oil exports to the developed world. Its maritime regime is, therefore, of considerable important to many nations. Perhaps the most striking aspect of the issue is the degree to which all states in the region seek to justify their actions by recall to international legal principles, even those states which are not normally considered to be particularly sensitive to such matters.

LIBYA AND THE GULF OF SIRT

One state which is rarely considered to have much interest in international law is Libya. In fact, this popular attitude is misleading for, since 1980, Libya has twice appeared before the International Court of Justice – on one occasion with Tunisia and on the other with Malta – to seek the court's help in maritime delimitation. Libya's interest in international law, at least as far as international boundaries are concerned, is not merely confined to maritime delimitations, however. Disputes exist over its land boundaries as well, over those with Algeria, Niger and Chad particularly, and the likelihood of a further appeal to the Court over the Aozou Strip issue has grown as a result of recent events in northern Chad. Indeed, Libya's border disputes have an acute bearing on domestic stability since they form a point of national consensus, particularly over Libya's claims to the Aouzou Strip, and because of the commitment of the Qadhafi regime to defend them despite the contradiction between this and its Arab nationalist ideals which would appear to argue that such manifestations of national sovereignty are irrelevant.

However, the most notorious case of a border dispute involving Libya – and one that has acute implications for domestic stability – is that with the USA as a result of Libya's unilateral decision to treat the Gulf of Sirt as part of its internal waters in 1973. Its 12 October 1973 declaration asserted that Libya had an exclusive historic title to the Gulf and that its control was essential for the country's security. The Gulf, south of the line of latitude 32° 30′N, was therefore to be treated as internal waters and Libyan territorial waters were to be deemed to exist to the north of that line.

The decision led to clashes between Libyan and US aircraft in August 1981 and to further incidents in March 1986, just before the US airforce bombed Tripoli and Benghazi in retaliation for Libya's supposed involvement in terrorism against US representatives in Europe. Furthermore, the Libyan decision has been generally treated with derision, particularly by Western nations, and the UK government, which described the Libyan declaration as 'eccentric' in debates at the UN, has regularly sent naval units into the Gulf to sustain its claim that it is part of the high seas, while twelve other states have registered their rejection of the Libyan claim.

Objections to the Libyan Claim

The basic objection to the Libyan claim was that the Gulf of Sirt did not conform to the conventional definitions relating to internal waters. These are three in number. According to the 1958 UN convention on the territorial sea and contiguous zone, a bay was any marine indentation on a coastline which had an entrance not wider than 24 miles.[42] The definition was widened by the 1982 UN treaty which, in Article 10, stated a bay would be so defined and thus to be treated as internal waters if its area is 'as large or larger than that of a semicircle whose diameter is a line drawn across the mouth of [the bay]'. The final definition predates both convention and treaty and derives from customary international law. Here a bay is a marine indentation in the coastline to which the state concerned can show exclusive historic title.

Those who objected to the closing line complained that the Gulf of Sirt met none of these criteria. Its width along the proposed closing line is 304 nautical miles – far in excess of the 24-mile restriction under the 1958 convention. Its maximum depth is 134.6 miles – too little to provide the required area to qualify under the 1982 treaty. Finally, no state appeared to treat Libya's claim to historic title seriously and Libya has, in consequence, been accused of abusing international legal principles.

Ironically enough, several of the states that have condemned Libya appeared to have acted in a similar manner. Italy, for instance, closed the

Bay of Taranto in 1977, although it too meets none of the criteria normally required, despite Italian claims of historic title. The practical reasons for the Italian action seem to relate to an important NATO naval base on the bay, however. The USSR closed St Peter the Great Bay, even though its width and depth completely preclude any such action. Once again, the real reasons seems to have reflected security concerns, since the naval base of Vladivostock is located on the bay.

There are many other examples of similar behaviour, with some of the most flagrant examples being found in the way in which Burma and Colombia have closed large areas of their coasts so as to redefine their territorial waters. Tunisia, Libya's western neighbour, has also closed off the Gulf of Gabes and the Gulf of Tunis without international protest. It thus seems that Libya's unilateral action was not so unusual, even if it did not conform with international legal usage.

The Role of the Gulf

In fact, the key to Libya's decision probably resides in its statement in the original 1973 declaration of concerns over security. The Gulf, the declaration stated, was 'crucial to the security of the Libyan Arab Republic'. A glance at a map soon reveals why this should be so. The peculiar demographic nature of Libya has ensured that population settlement has traditionally concentrated around Tripoli and Benghazi, with a subsidiary population centre inland, around the Fezzan. This has developed as the result of Libya's hostile geography and the development of its traditional economy, which depended either on seaborne trade or on trans-Saharan links. The Gulf, in short, virtually separates the populated regions of the country in two.

Since independence in 1951 and, more particularly, since the discovery and exploitation of oil in the 1960s, the Gulf has taken on a wholly new significance. Libya's major oil fields are located in the Sirtica basin and four of its five oil export terminals – As-Sidrah, Ras Lanuf, Al Brayqah and Az-Zuwaytinah – are located there. The other terminal, at Tubruk in Cyrenaica, is of minor importance. The result is that the Gulf of Sirt handles around 90 per cent of Libya's vital crude oil exports which conventionally provide 99 per cent of its export revenues, themselves virtually the sole source of development and import finance.

Even more significant is the fact that Libyan planning decisions during the 1970s – which were designed to provide the state with a degree of *physical* integration – have emphasised the significance of the Gulf. Refineries have been built at Ras Lanuf and Marsa Brayqah. A petrochemical complex is being completed at Ras Lanuf and another is planned for Maradah. A fertiliser plant has been planned for Sirt and another is being completed at Marsa Brayqah. Power stations are being constructed at Marsa Brayqah. Power stations are being constructed at Marsa Brayqah, Ras Lanuf and Az-Zuwaytina. The steel plant at Misuratah is partially constructed. New towns at Brayqah and Ras Lanuf will eventually house 120 000 persons and the Great Manmade River water pipeline, which brings water from the underground aquifers at Sarir, Tazirbu and Kufrah, will also provide irrigation for ambitious schemes in the Sirt region.[43]

Many of these plans and developments may well be misconceived and others may never reach fruition. However, enough has already been achieved for the Gulf of Sirt region to be able to contribute up to 70 per cent of Libya's total GDP. The region is, in other words, crucial to national unity and survival, even if it is not the location of the major population concentrations which are still found around Tripoli and Benghazi. It is hardly surprising, then, that the Libyan regime considers the Gulf to be central to Libyan security considerations, for penetration by alien naval forces into the Gulf of Sirt brings all of these economically strategic locations within range of modern weapons systems within minutes. Indeed, the US attack in March 1986 underlined this extremely effectively.

The Claim to Historic Rights

The consequence of this sensitivity by the Libyan authorities to the vulnerability of the crucial economic resources of the Gulf of Sirt has been a determination to limit rights of free navigation in the Gulf itself – a practice that has been introduced by other states when they felt vital economic or strategic interests to be threatened. The technique chosen to do this has been to assert a claim to 'historic rights' – to exclusive use of the Gulf on the basis that it forms part of Libya's internal waters.

The problem, then, is to determine precisely what an 'historic bay' means in terms of international legal principles. Superficially, the problem seems simple – historic rights relate to rights sanctified by long and exclusive usage. However, legal precedent suggests that this interpretation is too narrow. Indeed, one authority has suggested that the 1958 convention included' . . . bays which were vital to the security or economic needs of States . . .'[44] within the definition of historic bays, provided certain other conditions were met.

Implicit in this discussion is the suggestion that historic rights really involve the interplay of three sets of factors – specifically historical considerations; specific economic and geographic factors that make the bay in question of importance within the overall economy and geography of the state concerned; and vital national interest connected with the security of the bay that makes control of the bay essential. The Gulf of Sirt was treated by Libya's political precursors as of sovereign interest to Libya and subject to sovereign control which was not continuously contested by other states. Indeed, apart from the Christian corsairs of Malta, little attempt has been made historically to interfere with local power in Libya and the Gulf. Furthermore, it is evident that the Gulf is crucial for economic reasons, both as a centre of Libyan economic activity and as a vital transit point for exports. Finally, given the preponderant role played by the Gulf in Libya's economy, it clearly represents a region of vital interest to the Libyan state.

If indeed there is a growing tendency to reinterpret the term 'historic rights' in this wider context, then Libya's claim to the Gulf of Sirt as part of its internal waters becomes more understandable. It is undoubtedly vital to the unity and survival of the state, it is crucially involved with Libya's all important export trade and it has never been subject to continuous disputes over sovereignty by other states in the region. Furthermore other states have also implicitly used the justification of 'historic rights' as a cover for vital national interests in justifying the integration of bays into their own internal waters.

Indeed, it could be argued that the evolution of the concept of 'historic rights' becomes of increasing importance to developing countries where the economic legacy of colonial occupation has often emphasised littoral economic development and the role of concentrated coastal settlement in export patterns linked to a wider economic structure. This evolution in international legal principle becomes, in short, a means of protecting vital national interest and the developed world should, perhaps, view this evolution with more sympathy than it has shown to date. Freedom of navigation, after all, is still protected in such circumstances by the 'right of innocent passage' – without which essential trade could not occur. It is hardly necessary for rights to freedom of navigation without restraint for warships to be maintained in such circumstances – the underlying purpose, after all, of the US interventions in the Gulf of Sirt.

CONCLUSION

This analysis has attempted to illustrate the way in which international legal principles are both manipulated for the sake of domestic stability and, at the same time, are used to formulate relations between states in the Gulf and the Mediterranean. The Shatt al-Arab issue has come to embody the hegemonistic designs of two neighbouring states and has also become, in part, the symbol of the violent struggle in which they are now engaged. Delimitations in the Gulf emphasises the latent irredentism in littoral states over a region of economic importance and the ways in which they accommodate competing national interest. The issue of freedom of navigation indicates the ways in which interested third party states exploit international law in their own interests, a consideration that is underlined by the Gulf of Sirt issue.

The Gulf of Sirt issue, however, is the most speculative of the issues discussed here. It underlines the continuing vitality of international law in adapting to changing international economic and political circumstances as far as developing states are concerned. It demonstrates the flexibility of legal principle in absorbing concepts for which it was not originally designed, in accommodating vital national interest within the framework of historic rights. The arguments put forward here are, although speculative, now the subject of considerable debate for they do indicate ways in which the perpetual dialectic between legal principle and practice may continue to evolve and develop. At the same time they illustrate the way in which such legal approaches may find a relevance in the creation of stable and coherent regimes of domestic order for modern states.

Notes

1. K. S. McLachlan and E. G. H. Joffé, *The Gulf War, a survey of political issues and economic consequences* (London: EPL, 1984) p. 8.

2. A. Drysdale and G. Blake, *The Middle East and North Africa, a political geography* (Oxford University Press, 1985) p. 123.

3. K. Al-Izzi, *The Shatt al-Arab dispute, a legal study* (London: Third World Centre, 1981) pp. 25, 47; I. Delupis, *International law and the independent state* (New York: Crane Russak, 1974) p. 45.

4. S. H. Amin, *International and legal problems of the Gulf* (Wisbech: Menas Press, 1981) p. 97.

5. H. M. Al-Baharna, *The Arab Gulf states, their legal and political status and their international problems* (Beirut: Librairie du Liban, 1975) pp. 278–311.

6. A. J. Day (ed.) *Border and territorial disputes* (London: Keesings, 1982) pp. 212–13.

7. R. Schofield, *Evolution of the Shaff al-Arab boundary dispute* (Wisbech: Menas Press, 1986) p. 12.

8. McLachlan and Joffé, *op. cit.*, p. 36.

9. Schofield, *op. cit.*, pp. 42–66; Day, *op. cit.*, pp. 214–19; Al-Izzi, *op. cit.*, pp. 25ff.; Amin, *op. cit.*, pp. 65–96.
10. Al-Izzi, *op. cit.*, p. 26.
11. Day, *op. cit.*, p. 214.
12. Schofield, *op. cit.*, p. 44.
13. Day, *op. cit.*, p. 216.
14. R. W. Ferrier, *The history of the British Petroleum Company* (Cambridge University Press, 1982) pp. 86–8.
15. Schofield, *op. cit.*, p. 51.
16. I. Delupis, *International law and the independent state* (New York: Crane Russak, 1974) p. 45.
17. Al-Izzi, *op. cit.*, pp. 51–5.
18. *ibid.*, pp. 60–2.
19. Schofield, *op. cit.*, p. 58.
20. McLachlan and Joffé, *op. cit.*, pp. 10–11.
21. Schofield, *op. cit.*, p. 60.
22. McLachlan and Joffé, *op. cit.*, p. 11.
23. Schofield, *op. cit.*, p. 61.
24. Netton, *Arabia and the Gulf: from traditional society to modern state* (Lava: Croom Helm, 1986) p. 182.
25. McLachlan and Joffé, *op. cit.*, p. 38.
26. Day, *op. cit.*, p. 222.
27. Al-Baharna, *op. cit.*, pp. 173–227.
28. Day, *op. cit.*, p. 212.
29. Al-Baharna, *op. cit.*, pp. 192–3.
30. Amin, *op. cit.*, pp. 104–106.
31. Drysdale and Blake, *op. cit.*, p. 126.
32. *ibid.*, p. 124.
33. *ibid.*, pp. 120–2.
34. International Court of Justice, *Tunisia/Libya continental shelf dispute: judgement 24.2.1984* (The Hague: ICJ, 1984) p. 69.
35. Amin, *op. cit.*, p. 97.
36. Drysdale and Blake, *op. cit.*, pp. 124–30.
37. *Guardian*, 8 April 1987.
38. Amin, *op. cit.*, pp. 18–19.
39. Delupis, *op. cit.*, pp. 40–1.
40. *ibid.*, p. 42.
41. Drysdale and Blake, *op. cit.*, pp. 138–9.
42. Delupis, *op. cit.*, p. 45.
43. viz., Economist Intelligence Unit, *Libya – a country profile* (London: EPL, 1986).
44. D. O'Connell, *The international law of the sea* (Oxford, Clarendon Press, 1984) p. 424.

10 Conclusion: Southern Instability, Security and Western Concepts – On an Unhappy Marriage and the Need for a Divorce

Caroline Thomas

It is usually the case that Western security experts attempt to analyse Southern security by reference to concepts and tools of analysis which originate in the First World. Often, many of these tools are transposed onto Third World states in a wholly inappropriate fashion. This has led, and continues to lead, to confusion rather than enlightenment. Particularly significant here is the concept of 'national security' which has its roots in Western liberal societies, yet which has been adopted both by Western analysts and many leaders of Third World states to explain and legitimise certain policies. The first part of this paper questions the validity of the term 'national security' when used to analyse and describe the security problems of Third World states. A case is made for divesting the term 'state security' of the negative connotations associated with it in Western literature, and regarding it in a neutral fashion. This would be helpful since state security seems to be a far more appropriate tool of analysis for many Third World states when discussing security. It is suggested that some of those Third World states most admonished by Western politicians and analysts for the pursuit of state security are the very Third World states which come nearest to fitting the Western notion of national security. The second half of the paper discusses the 'strong and weak states' debate flourishing in contemporary Western social science, and suggests that for such a conception to be really useful in the context of Third World security, there is a compelling and urgent need for redefinition rather than inflexible application. We must divest ourselves of Western liberal notions of strong and secure states if we are interested in understanding the particular security concerns of Third World states and in advancing them.

174

NATIONAL SECURITY, NATIONS AND STATES

'National security' is primarily a Western concept of the post-World War II era. It was adopted by the USA, and exported not merely to other developed Western states but also to willing recipients in the Third World.[1] Its usage there became established by the habits of Western security analysts, the rhetoric of Third World elite governments with their natural proclivity for putting the cart before the horse now that often arbitrary territorial demarcations had been accepted, and importantly, the moral – almost ideological – use of the concept by Western governments which had a demonstration effect on their counterparts in the Third World. 'National security' developed an air of moral legitimacy, even obligation.

Before examining the implications of this on Third World states, their security, and relations between the Western states and the developing world, it is essential to clarify terms, since it is argued here that many of the problems and distortions evident in recent work arise partly from definitional obscurity. Hugh Seton-Watson's *Nations and States* is enlightening.[2] A state can be regarded as a 'legal and political organ with the power to require obedience and loyalty from its citizens'. A nation is a 'community of people, whose members are bound together by a sense of solidarity, a common culture and a national consciousness'. In international relations it is generally agreed that the optimal situation for local and international security is where the boundaries of state and nation coincide. Over most of the world, this situation does not exist; hence governments must undertake the task of building group cohesion and group loyalty, of building a national consciousness within the territorial boundaries of the state.

When the concept of national security first became fashionable in the USA, there were some empirical grounds in support of it. While many ethnic communities existed there, it is probably true to say that the process of forging a common culture and national consciousness among the immigrant communities was well underway. This is important because if there is no identifiable nation contiguous with the territorial limits of the states, then it is inappropriate to speak of national security. How can there be national security where there is no nation? Moreover, even if a nation exists, can security really be defined in relation to it? The existence of a nation does not preclude the possibility of class conflict, despotism, regionalism or a whole host of other divisions. This point is perhaps best illustrated by reference to the West European states.

These states have developed over several centuries, and are often held up as models of nation-states.[3] When compared with other areas of the world, the identification of nation with state seems applicable. Common language and culture are their hallmarks. Yet even some of these suffer from separatist movements, political polarisation and socio-economic divisions which challenge the notion of the existence of a single, identifiable conception of national security.[4] While in general terms, these states have been characterised in the post-World War II era by a high degree of domestic political consensus, which has made the pursuit of security for a national way of life comprehensible, present political circumstances have detracted from this. Even in these model nation-states, identification of 'national security' is not always clear-cut.

The Soviet Union does not make much use of the concept of national security, preferring the term state security. This makes sense both practically, since that state does not approximate a single nation, and ideologically, since to the extent that Marx and Lenin paid any attention to the question of nationalities, they felt that the development of societies would leave nationalism behind.[5] What matters to the leaders of the Soviet Union is the security of their state as a state, and then as a bulwark against capitalism. While some of the Eastern European states, notably Poland, approximate the Western nation-state model more than the Soviet multi-nation model, their security is still portrayed in terms of the state rather than the nation in official statements. 'The people' may be used as a term of reference, but 'the nation' is generally not. Again, there are strong ideological and practical reasons for this. The socialist commonwealth must be the higher level of identification than the state; there is no room for national identification, since this would be a divisive force in the socialist fraternity.[6]

THE DIVERSITY OF THE THIRD WORLD

The Third World is a huge and heterogeneous grouping of states.[7] The tendency to regard these states in a similar fashion and to apply Western terminology and categorisation to them has distorted our understanding of them, and nowhere is this more evident for the student of international relations than in the field of security. Most Third World states have become the recipients of the national security concept, while a few have adopted the notion of state security. This has serious implications for politics at the state, regional and international level, especially since the distinction between national and state security has become inextricably bound up with the value judgments of Western analysts, governments and in some cases publics. National security is generally portrayed in the West in positive, acceptable terms, which legitimise the pursuit of the national interest however the government chooses to define it. By contrast, state security is painted in essentially negative terms, which by implication cast doubt on the legitimacy of any pursuit undertaken in its name. Such thinking in the West is of course underpinned by the ideological East-West divide which facilitates a sharp distinction between liberal-democratic, capitalist states, and one-pary, centrally-planned states. One need only recall President Reagan's rhetoric to substantiate that such attitudes exist at the highest echelons of Western governments. When transposed onto the Third World, the distinction drawn in terms of legitimacy and morality between national security and state security has great ramifications for international alignments and security, as well as for local security.

While a few Third World states contain part or all of historic nations within them, these are the exceptions and not the rule. Most Third World states are the result of arbitrary colonial boundaries. In the case of the Latin American states, independence from the colonial powers was won earlier than for the Afro-Asian states, and more progress has been made at nation-building in the former. A characteristic of this has been that nation-building proceeded before industrialisation. In some cases, specifically Argentina, waves of immigrants from Europe led to the creation of settler-states almost on the lines of Australia, Canada, the USA and so forth. In others, such as Brazil, intermingling of settler with local populations created a new culture.[8]

The story in the rest of the Third World is very different. It was only in the late 1950s and early 1960s that decolonisation took off, and this led to the emergence on the international scene of a multiplicity of new states which did not contain a single nation within them. The nation-state model simply did not apply. Africa is the example par excellence of a continent ravaged by the artificial and self-serving territorial boundaries of the European colonisers. Hence the continent is left in a 'catch-22' situation: redrawing the boundaries to conform to ethnic realities would open up a can of worms; while adhering to colonial boundaries has led to irredentist and secessionist claims. The latter problem, exemplified in the Horn,[9] will not go away until either nation-building within states totally succeeds, or until the central governments of various states are strong enough to impose their will on all parts of their territory, or until certain states are strong enough decisively to take the land from their neighbours which they lay claim to on ethnic grounds.

The situation in South Asia is also problematic. A variety of nation-building bases of the state have been tried out, but success in making nation and state coincide has been very limited. India, with its secular ideology, has seventeen official languages and a myriad of others. In the Punjab, the secessionist Sikh movement calls and fights for an independent Khalistan. Kashmir remains a hotly disputed region with Pakistan, and the loyalty of the Kashmiris probably falls to Pakistan rather than India, especially if there is no hope of an independent Kashmiri state. Throughout India, communal rioting is a fairly frequent feature.[10] In Sri Lanka, it seems that the government polices for example in education, have caused greater divisions rather than greater unity and have reinforced ethnic differentiation in the Sri Lankan state.[11] General Zia of Pakistan, in making Islam the basis of the state, is trying to circumvent the social, political and economic problems faced by the state and to give it an identity in the Islamic world.[12] Pakistan has the memory of dismemberment to carry with it, with the Indian action which facilitated the creation of Bangladesh in 1971.

South-East Asia fares better in terms of nation-state building than Africa or South Asia. Taiwan, Hong Kong, Singapore and South Korea benefit from being relatively ethnically homogeneous, and have a Confucian tradition.[13] Vietnam, through anti-colonial war and social revolution, has created by Third World standards a highly mobilised population,[14] and the People's Republic of China has quite remarkably managed this also.[15]

Many Middle Eastern states benefit in terms of social cohesion from the dominance of the Islamic faith, but nation-building in several of them has been impeded by the presence of diverse ethnic and religious groups, the Lebanon being the most obvious and most tragic current example.[16] Added to this is the problem of the Palestinians, a nation without a state,[17] and the Kurds, another nation without a state.[18] These stateless nations also present problems for the concept of national security as promulgated by the West. It could well be argued that 'acts of terrorism' with which they are charged are carried out in the pursuit of national security – to secure the future of their own nations. To the extent that this is true, and that these nations exist in reality whereas other so-called nations within most Third World states do not, then the term national security has more relevance when applied to them. Aside from these difficulties, the experience of Iran also poses problems for the formulation of the national security concept. While it is true that only half of the inhabitants of Iran speak Farsi as their first language,[19] it is equally true that the Persian nation is not a creation of European colonialism but has historic foundations. Thus, there is a case for speaking of a national identity and national security in relation to Iran, but it should be remembered that the Persian identity which the Iranian state has largely come to represent has gained its primary position in Iran only at the expense of the other national minority groups within the physical boundaries of the state.[20] The Baluch, for example, have been discriminated against continually. In the days of the Shah, when Iran was perceived as one of the two pillars of security in the region in the Western scheme of things, massive internal repression was carried out in the name of national security. The justification made the widespread atrocities more palatable to the Western allies of the Shah. This did not make them any more palatable to the inhabitants of Iran. The reaction to rapid, enforced modernisation and widespread terror was social revolution in Iran. This did away with a monarchy which ignored the wishes of the population and brought in its place a theocracy which had a groundswell of popular support. Interestingly, the Western press and governments, and much of the Western publics, admonish the use of terror by the Khomeini regime, even though that regime has enjoyed more internal support than the Shah had; yet in contrast, they were willing to condone his repressive policies. The latter are justified by Western security analysts by reference to the sacred concept of national security; the former are branded as illegitimate by reference to the profane concept, state security, or to archaic religious fanaticism.

NATIONAL SECURITY AND STATE SECURITY: WESTERN PREJUDICE

Jeanne Kirkpatrick has drawn an unconvincing and self-serving distinction between totalitarian and authoritarian regimes:[21] the former are regimes hostile to the West, the latter are regimes friendly to the West; the former pursue state security, the latter, national security. While this may be a sop to the conscience of the faint-hearted in the West, it can do little for those who are eager to understand Third World security, and who want to unravel the notions of national and state security. If national security means nothing more than policies carried out by governments in the name of a non-existent nation, thereby legitimising those policies whatever they may be in the eyes of Western states, then let us recognise this quite clearly. If this is the case, how does national security in the Third World differ from state security as a governmental pursuit? What makes one legitimate and the other illegitimate? Are they not both the same thing?

An interesting paradox arises here. There are certain states which leading Western governments would earmark as purusing an unjust state security rather than just a national security. These would include the Soviet Union, Vietnam, Cuba, Iran, Nicaragua, Ethiopia and Mozambique. It is a supreme irony that in several of these states which have undergone some type of social and/or political revolution, domestic consensus-building has achieved a far greater sense of unity and purpose than was ever the case before the revolutions took place.[22] While certain groups have been displaced, the trend has been towards inclusion of greater numbers, rather than exclusion as was the case previously. Unfortunately, the Western notion of national security at this point gets inextricably linked with the idea of the operation of a competitive Western style democracy. These states, mostly in the Third World, do not fit the requirements of a liberal polity in the Western image, and hence it is automatically assumed that they belong to the communist camp and are thus inherently undesirable. Their greater approximation to the liberal goal of self-determination in post – as compared with pre-revolution days is quietly forgotten. By contrast, the concept of national security is divorced from the notion of a liberal democracy when it is applied to the states of the Third World whose governments are Western allies. The irony, therefore, is that the Third World states which have been targeted for criticism because of their pursuit of state security are often the vary states which have progressed the most along the road to forging a domestic consensus – or at the very least a stronger consensus than existed previously. While a few examples of relatively successful nation-building can be found in the ethnically relatively homogeneous states of South-East Asia, the pattern has certainly not been repeated in Africa, South Asia, the Middle East or Central America and the Caribbean, or even much of Latin America. With a few special exceptions, therefore, the post-revolutionary states have gone the farthest to creating united societies in the Western image, but without the Western value system. It is mostly those states whose security may best be understood by reference to the concept of national security, if that notion is to be applied at all to Third World states. A further irony is that the very hostility of the Western states has helped the latter forge a sense of internal unity, and has made it far more difficult to differentiate between nation and state. Vietnam and Cuba are obvious examples here, and Nicaragua is probably going the same way.

It seems strange that the national security concept still holds such sway. Some authors continue to attempt a global application despite all the empirical evidence which suggests that this is at present a futile task. Barry Buzan for instance argues that 'The case for attempting a global application of the term rests on the near universality of sovereign states as the principal basis of political organisation in the international system.'[23] Yet the universality of the sovereign state surely suggests a different line of global application – that of state security, rather than national security. When the Western colonisers divided the world between them, they may have sown the seeds of political entities in their own image (i.e. states, all be they far from sovereign in the Third World); they did not sow the seeds of Western-style nation-states. Given this, Third World governments must do what they can to preserve the territorial integrity of the state which they rule, and hopefully find a path by which the inhabitants of their state may secure less harsh conditions of life. They can hardly define and protect the interests of their nation when such a thing does not exist in the western sense of the term. They must instead define and pursue the interests of their state and its inhabitants, and attempt to forge a domestic consensus in a mechanical fashion when no national consensus exists.

Buzan's ideas are fairly representative of those mainstream Western analysts who have tended to downgrade the utility of the state security concept even though it is far more entrenched in the empirical reality of social and political formations in the Third World that the national security concept. The value judgments implicit in the national security/ state security division alluded to previously are explicit in Buzan's work:

> We need also to keep in mind that national security is not the only concept on offer. One can also approach the Third World using the concept of state security favoured by totalitarian regimes. In many respects state security is a less ambiguous term than national security. When compared with the idea of national security it puts more emphasis on the state as a centralised governing organisation, and less on the individuals and social groups existing within the state. State security is a simpler, and in some senses more primitive, concept than national security. For that reason it may be easier to apply to Third World conditions than a concept like national security, which was developed by and for states within which there is much less distance between the state organisation on the one hand, and society and citizens on the other.
>
> National Security means the security of a whole socio-political entity. It concerns the way of life of a self-governing people, including their social, cultural, political and economic modes of organisation, and their right to develop themselves under their own rule.[24]

Various points emerge from this quote. The good/evil conceptualisation which is implicit in much Western analysis and use of the concepts national and state security stands out in sharp relief. State security is rooted in totalitarian states; state security is less sophisticated than national security; it is more 'primitive'. National security on the other hand has its feet firmly in the Western liberal camp; it is concerned with whole socio-political entities, with ways of life and self-government. This conceptualisation is as ideological as those championed by the holders of government office here in the West who turn a blind eye to atrocities committed by a Third World ally so long as 'national security' is the justification. Also, it is ethnocentric. State security is simpler and more primitive than national security, and therefore it is more fitting for Third World states. Yet forging a nation-state where none existed previously is a highly difficult and complicated task. To use the word 'primitive' to describe state security is inappropriate. Having established state security as a more appropriate concept for the Third World, arguably for inappropriate reasons, the author then ignores his own deduction and proceeds to apply national security to the Third World, without offering an explanation. This is yet further evidence of the distortions which Western liberal bias may produce in analyses of Third World security, even though this is far from the author's intention.

Work being done by sociologists is of key relevance for students of Third World instability and security.[25] Michael Mann has devised a simple diagram (Figure 10.1) to illustrate his conception of strong and weak states, and this is especially appropriate for our purposes in analysing Third World states because it enables the variety in that group to become apparent.[26]

Mann argues that there are two types of state power: one is despotic, or the arbitrary power of rulers to impose their will on the inhabitants of their territory; the other is infrastructural, which could include a range of things such as provision of education and health services, the maintenance of transport and communications facilities, banking services, the collection of taxes and so forth. While social cohesiveness may be increased or decreased as a result of the development and exercise of these different state powers, the level of social cohesiveness may also make the exercise of state power easier or more difficult.

A major difference between Mann's scheme and Buzan's is that for Mann, social cohesiveness is a characteristic of a society, whereas for Buzan it is a characteristic of a state.[27] Hence under Buzan's classification, most Third World states would be weak states, because most fail to match up to the Western liberal model of domestic cohesion – most are not self-governing nation-states. I wonder whether black South Africans, or Lango and Acholi in Uganda in the 1970s, or people of the Bahai religion in Khomeini's Iran, or the peasants of Guatemala and

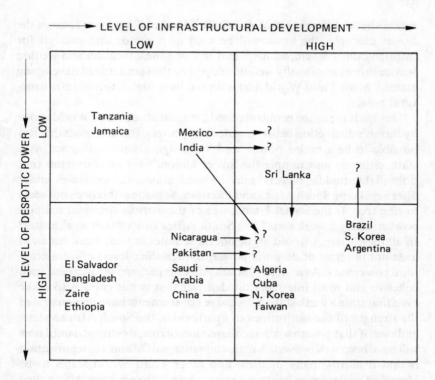

Figure 10.1   Adaptation of Mann's model to include Third World states

Honduras as who have been forced into refugee camps, or the intellectuals of Taiwan, Singapore and Hong Kong, who are afraid to criticise their governments publicly, or the Indians and Chinese in Malaysia, or the trade union leaders over much of Latin America, believe that they live in strong or weak states? Given the despotic power of their respective states over them, they would in all probability categorise them as strong. While the above examples refer to varying degrees of despotic power, some Third World states also exhibit a relatively high degree of infrastructural strength. The South-East Asian newly industrialising states spring to mind here,[28] but equally, some of the post-independence revolutionary states are making progress here too, albeit in the context of a different value system which of course establishes a different set of priorities.[29] Hence, if Vietnam follows the Soviet example, the army will be used as a motor and catalyst for infrastructural developments,[30] and in Cuba the education and welfare services are exceptionally well-developed by the standards of developing states.[31] Most Third World States do not have high levels of infrastructural power.

This leads me to the problem posed for students of Third World states by Buzan's distinction between states and powers. Buzan argues that it is possible to be a major power, and 'have significant weaknesses' as a state, citing as an example the Soviet Union.[32] He mentions too that 'formidable middle powers' may be weak states, the examples under offer here being South Africa and Pakistan. Somehow this does not seem to ring true. Is the Soviet Union, one of the world's strongest military powers, really a weak state? Are South Africa or Pakistan weak states? In all these cases, I would argue no; these states are not weak states, at least not in terms of despotic power, though their levels of infrastructural power vary. As a society, South Africa is perhaps the weakest, least cohesive and most internally divided, yet that is not enough to make even that state a weak state. Successive governments have demonstrated the strength of the institutions of apartheid in the South African state, and even if that system were to collapse tomorrow, its strength until now will have been well proven. A major advantage of Mann's categorisation is that it allows many of these and other Third World states to be identified as despotically strong states, even if the societies within their territorial boundaries may lack social cohesion. The distinction between state and society is also helpful because it helps minimise the Western liberal bias apparent in so much of the discussion of strong and weak states, thus making room for the requirements indigenous to Third World states.[33]

It is impossible to be a weak state and a strong power at the same time. The converse, however, is possible: a state can be a strong state and remain a weak power. Third World examples would be the city states of South-East Asia, possibly Cuba and Nicaragua. Even strong states which have cohesive societies may not be strong powers, if by power we are referring to the ability of the state to minimise significantly any undesired impacts from the external environments, or its ability to impose its will there. Indeed, the concept of strong powers is very fuzzy. The standard criteria are related to relative military might. Yet even these military criteria are not clear-cut, at least not in the current phase of international politics. Whereas in the nineteenth century, British military power was based on gun-boat diplomacy which could be put into operation effectively, current US military power is based primarily on its nuclear capability. Yet as the Vietnam war demonstrated, this is not always an effective capability. While that state has a massive armoury of the most sophisticated conventional weapons, again they do not much add to its power unless it is perceived by other members of the system that the US is willing to commit its own soldiers to battle. Buzan notes the difficulties inherent in the task of quantifying power, but rightly maintains that there is widespread agreement on a crude ranking system: 'Who would dispute that the United States is more powerful than France . . .?' While this is true, it is equally the case that issue-specific assessments of power can reveal glaring deficiencies in these generalisations. That there exists a global hierarchy of power in the international system, in which the Third World states occupy the bottom ranks, is generally accepted; but it is equally true that states like India, Vietnam and Israel demonstrate formidable power on a regional level, and also that on a local level the will of the superpowers can come under acute challenge, as in Afghanistan or El Salvador or Nicaragua. Military might is a primary indicator of power, but it is not necessarily the ultimate indicator, nor does it necessarily stand alone.

FUTURE DIRECTIONS FOR THIRD WORLD SECURITY

The formation of strong states with cohesive societies is the primary challenge facing the Third World. While many display characteristics of despotic strength, fewer display the characteristics of infrastructural strength. Most of these states display a great lack of societal cohesion. In states which are relatively young and which are artificial creations this is not surprising.

The Western liberal model of the nation-state stresses the importance of domestic political consensus, which is arrived at through open competition in multiparty elections. The aim for Third World states is also consensus, but the path for most will be different. While India has experienced democracy on the Western liberal model to a level possibly unmatched anywhere else in the newly independent states,[34] the resurgence of separatist tendencies suggests that the road to achieving domestic consensus is a very long and arduous one. Who would have thought that Sri Lanka, forty years after independence, would be in the midst of a civil war? The creation of a unified society is no easy task. In Jamaica, it seems that the operation of a Westminster-style democracy has deepened divisions rather than healed them.[35] In most Third World states practising this type of democracy, or rhetorically claiming to do so, electoral abuses are often the order of the day.

Given the nature of most Third World states, the operation of a Western-type democratic process is likely to emphasise differences rather than eradicate them. Competition all too often follows the lines of ethnic or religious differences as these become the bases, sometimes unspoken, sometimes explicit, of political parties. In these conditions, strong states in Buzan's terminology, are an impossibility. Within Mann's scheme, strong states are of course a possibility, because they are not dependent on societal consensus. It seems that through the development of infrastructural power, however, societal consensus will be increased in the long run (though aggravated in the short run – for example, development of transport systems in the Kurdish areas of Iraq). This will especially be the case where politics is played out not in a competitive arena but in an integrative one. Consensus in Third World states is far more likely to result from the integrative forces of one-party states, whether they are based on religion or secular ideologies, than from the operation of a competitive Western style democracy. This is of course unpalatable to the liberal democrat, but it is realistic. Domestic mobilisation for development is impossible in an environment where divisions are constantly being reinforced, and where that competition is the essence of the political process. To say this is *not* to downgrade the value of human rights in Third World states, which many in the West (and even in the Third World) would see as its logical deduction. Rather it is to argue that if development is desired, if the fulfilment of basic human needs such as entitlement to food, clean water, health care, education and so forth are priorities, then agriculture and industry must be developed; and a competitive domestic political process modelled on Western lines is not often going to provide the route whereby this can be achieved in these artificial states. Prime Minister Rajiv Gandhi has spoken of India taking a leap into the twenty-first century; for the majority of the inhabitants of the state of India and the rest of the Third World, a leap has yet to be made into the twentieth century. This is not to belittle the achievement of India to date, far from it; in many respects her economic achievements have been remarkable. It is meant rather to highlight the enormity of the challenge confronting Third World states which are faced with the basic tasks of feeding people, providing them with clean water, shelter, sanitation, health care and education, as well as the task of industrialisation. Given the technological advances being made in the rich industrialised states, the challenge for the poorer states becomes all the greater and more difficult of achievement.

One-party states are of course *not* a sufficient condition of mobilisation within Third World states, but in many cases the lack of competition may be a necessary condition. The Soviet Union as a developing state,[36] has undergone rapid industrialisation and general development this century. This multi-nation state has been transformed from a poor, deeply hierarchical agrarian state into a modern industrial one with a far more egalitarian social structure – albeit at a great human cost. China is another dramatic example of how the task of fulfilling basic human needs for a vast population can be achieved rapidly albeit in circumstances which would offend Western liberal sensitivities. The so-called free-market success stories of Singapore, Hong Kong, Taiwan, South Korea are very far removed from the liberal model in their domestic politics.[37] Equally, numerous examples can be offered of states where repressive policies have been followed in a political environment which does not tolerate competition or criticism, such as Uganda under Idi Amin, yet where no such developments have taken place, or where those that have have reached only a handful of people. Where are the examples of development in terms of social transformation and the meeting of basic human needs in Third World states which have followed the path of competitive electoral politics?

To argue that most Third World states are unsuited for the Western type of political process is not to say that they, or the political systems to which they are best suited at present, are 'primitive', a very unfortunate adjective quoted earlier. It is merely to acknowledge that they are *different* from Western states. They do not have the benefit of developing within the context of a nation-state; social cohesion is something that has to be forged, and very rapidly at that. The task of development is for them therefore all the greater. The acute differences in levels of development existing among the members of the present international system is an additional problem; when the European nation-states industrialised, the present gross disparities within the international system were not so marked in the European system of states.

All these things have enormous repercussions on the security of Third World states. National security is not an appropriate concept for most, since they do not form nations. State security is more suitable, since what is at stake in the first instance is the territorial integrity of the state. The culture and way of life of the people is something that can be protected only when it has first been established, and this will be achieved through mobilisation for development. The creation of an infrastructure, and of infrastructural state power which goes hand in hand with it, fosters this mobilisation. In some cases, notably the states where Islam is the dominant religion, the culture and way of life is already deep-rooted. It was the mistake of the Shah to ignore this. It will be instructive to see if the growing number of Islamic states utilise religion as a basis of domestic consensus to promote development; perhaps it will be shown that religion does not have to be an impediment to modernisation.[38]

While statehood itself will result in some common security concerns between *all* states, the context in which the debate on security takes place is dominated by the preoccupations of the northern industrialised states. Hence the emphasis is always on advanced weaponry, strategy, and the East–West divide. This hierarchy of priorities and world view is far too limited to be of great value for an analysis of the security needs of Third World states. It reflects the particular historical, political, economic and social development of those industrialised states, their technological progress and position within the international system. While all these factors are important, it should be stressed that Third World states can generally be defined by total insecurity in *all* aspects of their existence. Apart from the basic territorial insecurity created by their arbitrary boundaries, their vulnerability to the sophisticated weaponry of older, richer, predatory northern states and indeed, the fear of regional powers and proxies in the Third World, they are insecure in so many other fields which northern states, albeit to varying degrees, can take for granted. They have the insecurity of often totally incohesive societies, of undeveloped infrastructures, of the international regimes governing money, trade, food, conventional weapons, nuclear proliferation, information, technology transfer and a whole host of other things, which they see as being controlled by the North, and more particularly often by the Western states. Even a factor like the weather adds enormously to the basic insecurity of these states.

In discussing Third World security, therefore, there is an urgent need to move beyond the application of Western concepts, for this leads to limitations and distortions in the analysis. If we want to understand the security problems of the Third World, then we must first divest ourselves of our Western liberal assumptions and prejudices, recognise that while we created the present Third World state system in our own image, we did a very poor job of it, and approach the study with an open mind, ready to listen, look and learn rather than blindly impose concepts which are completely out of touch with the empirical reality which we have had a formative hand in creating. The solutions to the massive predicament of gross underdevelopment and insecure statehood already adopted with some success by certain Third World states may not be to the liking of our liberal political, economic and social tastes. Yet our liberal model has not offered a workable solution for overcoming the economic, social and political problems of the Third World states. Even the much-acclaimed economic development of the states of South-East Asia has been achieved more through state control and intervention than through the free market. What's more, these states have got away with this precisely because the USA considers them to be at the sharp end of the East–West divide and of great strategic significance to her. It is time for us liberals to take a back seat, in the knowledge that our own states' copy-books did not emerge unblotted from the birth pangs of modernisation. Domestic consensus is the goal of all states; to suggest that there is only one right way, that is the Western liberal method, to go about achieving this, demonstrates both ethnocentrism and an inability to learn from our own mistakes.

The author would like to thank John Hall, Avi Shlaim, Vanita Ray, Paikiasothy Saravanamuttu, David Knox and Julian Saurin for responding to an earlier draft of this paper.

Notes

1. See B. Buzan, 'People, states and fear: the National security problem in the Third World', paper presented at Southampton University and revised in E. Azar and C. Moon (eds), *National Security in the Third World* (Aldershot: Edward Elgar, 1988). Page references refer to revised edition.

2. H. Seton-Watson, *Nations and states* (London: Methuen, 1977). See also E. Gellner, *Nations and nationalism* (Oxford: Blackwell, 1983), and J. Breuilly, *Nationalism and the state* (Manchester University Press, 1985).

3. See M. Mann, *The sources of social power*, vol. 1: *From the beginning to AD 1700* (Cambridge University Press, 1986). Also J. A. Hall, *Powers and liberties* (Oxford: Blackwell, 1985).

4. For example, see A. D. Smith, *The ethnic revival* (Cambridge University Press, 1980); also T. Nairn, *The break-up of Britain* (London: New Left Books, 1977).

5. Marx did not write about nationalism; he felt it was dying and unimportant. Lenin saw it as retrogressive.

6. See C. Thomas, *New states, sovereignty and intervention* (Aldershot: Gower, 1985).

7. See the lengthy debate in *Third World Quarterly*, 1979.

8. See J. G. Merquior, 'Patterns of state-building in Brazil and Argentina', in J. A. Hall (ed.) *States in history* (Oxford: Blackwell, 1986). See also N. Mouzelis, *Politics in the semi-periphery* (London: Macmillan, 1986).

9. See J. Mayall, 'The battle for the Horn, Somali irrendentism and international diplomacy', *World Today* (September, 1978); and 'The national question in the Horn of Africa', *World Today* (September, 1983); also I. M. Lewis (ed.) *Self-determination in the Horn of Africa* (London: Ithaca Press, 1983).

10.   See M. J. Akbar, *India: the siege within* (Harmondsworth: Penguin, 1985).
11.   On the management of ethnic conflict in Sri Lanka see R. B. Goldmann and A. J. Wilson (eds) *From independence to statehood* (London: Pinter, 1984).
12.   On state-building in Pakistan, see A. Khan (ed.) *Islam, politics and the state* (London: Zed, 1985).
13.   G. White and R. Wade (eds) *Developmental states in East Asia*, IDS Reports, no. 161 (1984).
14.   See William J. Duiker, 'Ideology and nation-building in the Democratic Republic of Vietnam', *Asian Survey*, vol. XVIII, no. 5, May, 1977.
15.   T. Skocpol, *States and social revolutions* (Cambridge University Press, 1979).
16.   B. S. Odeh, *Lebanon, dynamics of conflict* (London: Zed, 1985).
17.   R. Gilmour, *Dispossessed* (London: Sphere, 1982).
18.   G. Chaliand (ed.) *The Kurds and Kurdistan: a people without a country* (London: Zed, 1981).
19.   F. Halliday, 'The other Irans', *Times Literary Supplement*, **20** (June, 1986).
20.   F. Halliday, *Iran: dictatorship and development* (Harmondsworth: Penguin, 1979).
21.   J. Kirkpatrick, *Dictatorship and double standards: rationality and reason in politics* (New York: American Enterprise Institute/Simon and Shuster, 1982).
22.   See B. Moore, *Social origins of dictatorship and democracy* (Harmondsworth: Penguin, 1967). Also E. Gellner, *Thought and change* (London: Weidenfeld & Nicolson, 1964); and 'Democracy and industrialisation', *European Journal of Sociology* (1967). Also J. A. Hall, *op. cit.* (1985) ch. 8.
23.   B. Buzan, *op cit.*, p. 16.
24.   B. Buzan, *op cit.*, p. 16.
25.   See M. Mann, *op. cit.*, J. A. Hall, *op. cit.* (1985); and D. Sears, *The political economy of nationalism* (Oxford University Press, 1983). Also J. A. Hall, 'Capstones and organisms: political forms and the triumph of capitalism', *Sociology*, **19**, 2 (May, 1985).
26.   M. Mann, 'The autonomous power of the state: its origins, mechanisms and results', *Archives Europeennes de Sociologie*, XXV (1984). It is noteworthy that many of the articles in J. A. Hall (ed.), *op. cit.* (1986); see Mann's formulation as a starting point. The contributors are drawn from a wide spectrum of social scientists.
27.   B. Buzan, *op cit.*, p. 18.
28.   White and Wade, *op cit.*; and A. Amsden, 'The state and Taiwan's economic development' in P. Evans, D. Rueschemeyer and T. Skocpol (eds) *Bringing the state back in* (Cambridge University Press, 1985).
29.   For the example of China see White and Wade, *op. cit.*
30.   cf. Mann's concept of military Keynesianism in *Sources of Social Power*, *op. cit.*
31.   See *World Development Reports*.
32.   B. Buzan, *op cit.*, p. 19.
33.   This brings to mind Gellner's argument cited above that Third World states cannot be judged by the standard of Western liberties; liberalism in those states must mean something different, for example, the generation

or distribution of wealth.

34.   See A. H. Somjee, *The democratic process in developing societies* (London: Macmillan, 1979).
35.   See M. Manley, *Jamaica: struggle in the periphery* (London: Third World in association with Writers and Readers Publishing Cooperative Society, 1982).
36.   T. Shanin, *Russia as a 'developing society'* (London: Macmillan, 1985).
37.   J. Donnelly, 'Human rights and development: complementary or competing concerns?', *World Politics*, **36**, 2 (January, 1984).
38.   For some thoughts on this, see E. Gellner, *Muslim Society* (Cambridge University Press, 1981); G. H. Jansen, *Militant Islam* (London: Pan, 1979) and Halliday, *op. cit.* (1986).

Index